MARGARET THATCHER

For Seamus

By the same author

A Concise History of Irish Art
Orpen: Mirror to an Age
What Kind of Country
Modern Irish Politics, 1968-1983

Fiction

A Singer at the Wedding
The Song of the Nightingale
The Muted Swan
Running to Paradise

MARGARET THATCHER

A Study in Power

by

BRUCE ARNOLD

HAMISH HAMILTON
London

First published in Great Britain 1984
by Hamish Hamilton Ltd
Garden House 57–59 Long Acre London WC2E 9JZ

Copyright ' 1984 by Bruce Arnold

British Library Cataloguing in Publication Data
Arnold Bruce,
   Margaret Thatcher.
   1. Thatcher, Margaret   2. Prime ministers
   —Great Britain—Biography
   I. Title
   941.085 7 0924   DA591.T47

   ISBN 0–241–11160–9

Filmset by Ann Buchan (Typesetters)
Printed and bound in Great Britain by
Biddles Ltd, Guildford

CONTENTS

Prologue	9
Part One: General Election, 1983	
1 'The Field of Battle'	21
2 'There is no Hope'	32
3 'A High-Risk Enterprise'	42
4 Manifesto	47
5 'Some Way Still to Go'	56
6 'The Headmistress'	60
7 The Raising of the *Belgrano*	71
8 'Shooting a Dead Horse'	84
Part Two: Winning	
9 'Disdain and Scorn Ride Sparkling in her Eyes'	100
10 'Pride will not let me fail.'	113
11 'A Voice like Tinkling Glass'	126
12 'The Next Name on the List'	134
13 Defeating Callaghan	149
Part Three: Power	
14 Promises, Promises	164
15 Cabinet Management	173
16 The Grassroots	181
17 'Authority from Britain'	188
18 European Power Games	195
19 'The Unique Relationship'	202
20 Falklands	209

21 'A Nation of Shopkeepers'	220
22 Cadenza	232

Part Four: 'The New, Happy Life'

23 'A Source of Great Strength'	242
24 Murdering Prime Ministers	251
25 Pavlov's Dogs	258
26 The Consistency of Rhetoric	268
Appendix	275
Index	281

ILLUSTRATIONS

Between pages 144 and 145

1   The Mask of Ambition, October 1970 (BBC Hulton Picture Library)
2   Summoned to Office, June 1970 (Popperfoto)
3   Pre-election Cabinet, January 1974 (BBC Hulton Picture Library)
4   Leadership Candidate, October 1974 (BBC Hulton Picture Library)
5   Wins first ballot, February 1975 (Popperfoto)
6   Becomes Leader, February 1975 (Popperfoto)
7   After US Tour, September 1975 (Popperfoto)
8   Opposing, 1976 (Popperfoto)
9   Workload, 1977 (BBC Hulton Picture Library)
10 Crucial Vote, 28 March 1979 (Popperfoto)
11 Election Victory, May 1979 (BBC Hulton Picture Library)
12 Conservative Conference, October 1980 (Popperfoto)
13 Rethinking the Economy, April 1980 (BBC Hulton Picture Library)
14 Conservative Conference, October 1981 (Popperfoto)
15 Falklands Stress, April 1982 (Popperfoto)
16 Falklands Spirit, October 1982 (Popperfoto)
17 Launching Manifesto, May 1983 (Popperfoto)
18 Eve of Victory, June 1983 (Popperfoto)
19 'Round and About', Summer 1983 (*The Director*)
20 The Face of Power, Summer 1983 (Times Newspapers Ltd)

She is wedded to convictions – in default of grosser ties;
Her contentions are her children, Heaven help him who denies! –
He will meet no suave discussion, but the instant, white-hot, wild,
Wakened female of the species warring as for spouse and child.

Unprovoked and awful charges – even so the she-bear fights,
Speech that drips, corrodes, and poisons – even so the cobra bites,
Scientific vivisection of one nerve till it is raw
And the victim writhes in anguish – like the Jesuit with the squaw!

So it comes that Man, the coward, when he gathers to confer
With his fellow-braves in council, dare not leave a place for her
Where, at war with Life and Conscience, he uplifts his erring hands
To some God of Abstract Justice – which no woman understands.

And Man knows It! Knows, moreover, that the Woman that God gave him
Must command but may not govern – shall enthral but not enslave him.
And *She* knows, because She warns him, and Her instincts never fail,
That the Female of Her Species is more deadly than the Male.

From *The Female of the Species*
By Rudyard Kipling

PROLOGUE

It seems she has been consistent; this is the over-riding quality around which Margaret Thatcher's political character is built. What she stood for when she became leader of the Conservative Party, in 1975, is what she stands for now; what she stood for then was consistent with her convictions and their expression through her speeches during the previous fifteen years; and arguably that was what she had always stood for, long before party politics intruded into her life.

Basic principles and beliefs seem always to have been there as part of her character; we are invited to go back to a bedrock, a birthright, of certain standards and attitudes. They are simple, homespun, familiar, at times based upon cliché, at times derived from remembered homilies, from family sayings, from domestic proverbs, from the advice of a grandmother who not only believed and said that cleanliness was next to godliness, but is remembered by Margaret Thatcher for that wisdom. Remembered, too, is her father's diligence, his independence of mind, his religious faith encompassed in a reported belief that 'Methodist means method', and that it 'taught what was right and wrong in very considerable detail'.* We go back for the roots of that consistency to an eager, solemn child in a grocer's shop on the corner of a street in Grantham. We go back there for the beliefs which have now become central to Conservative Party thinking, a political philosophy born among bags of bicarbonate of soda, granulated sugar, wholemeal flour and porridge oats. Is this appropriate? Is it fitting? That a nation of shopkeepers, a nation whose historical wealth has been based on trade as well as

---

* Patricia Murray: *Margaret Thatcher: A Profile* (London, 1980) p. 13

manufacture, should be led by a woman who has built her political philosophy so deliberately out of first-hand experience of the fundamental rules that prevail across the counter of a shop where all is paid for, and no credit given?

It is accepted. That is what democracy ordained in her remarkable personal triumph in the 1983 general election. It is of profound significance for the Conservative Party that this is so, and for the British people, as a whole, that her philosophy has become central to British beliefs and British Government policies; that it is adumbrated by the press, and by the public at large. Such is the degree of her impact, such is the failure of what went before, that a precise and narrow logic that has brought down inflation, created two million or more unemployed, wrought havoc in certain areas of industry, spent the resource of North Sea oil with lavish prodigality, is revered as the basis for power to a degree that seems unassailable.

Margaret Thatcher has not adapted herself to the Conservative Party as she found it when first she joined it. She has adapted the Conservative Party to herself. She was the living embodiment of what she believed it should have been; and when the time was right, and the power was there, she began to change it.

The change has been variously presented. On the one hand, as a simplification, a turning back, a restoration of Victorian values or those of some historically admirable period of British greatness, a restatement of fundamental beliefs consistent with diligence and just rewards. This is the benign view of what Margaret Thatcher has tried to do.

The alternative version is rather different: that she has used the obvious appeal of strict, old-fashioned values to take possession, first of a party which was floundering in the wake of a double defeat, and seemed to have lost its way, and then of a country ill-served by mediocre politicians, by divided and temporarily demoralised political parties, particularly the Labour Party, and by out-dated policies. This is the malign view, that she is where she is by default, and by fear; that what has triumphed is a takeover, engineered by advertising men using the shallow language of slogan and simplification, but directed in what they did by a shrewd woman who understood the nature of power.

She has given clear expression to certain essential characteristics of those who pursue power for its own sake, one of which is that their beliefs become the basis for all beliefs; they are the centre of the world over which power gives them control. In their mind's eye this constitutes a universe, in which their beliefs are envisioned without limit. In reality, in Margaret Thatcher's own terms, this begins by being the United Kingdom of Great Britain and Northern Ireland over which she has precise, popular, elective authority. Such power also extends outwards and beyond the shores of the direct territory over which she has control. By virtue of foreign policy, defence strategy, alliance, war, trade, money, Margaret Thatcher has extended the range and influence of that same set of fundamental beliefs. Or she has appeared so to do. Because they seem real, and because she is real in her determination to be their controlling practitioner, and spread them, the extent of her impact internationally had grown into an accepted and respected world force. Even one that is feared. To achieve this it is necessary to appear consistent and reliable, and to have beliefs which are simple, direct, easily understood, logical; they may also be painful, unworkable, devasting in their effect, cruel, dangerous and divisive. But the fervour and dedication are what matter.

Margaret Thatcher has such beliefs. She would have us know that she has always had them, and in order that we should remember them they are frequently paraded. This emphasises their consistency, or the semblance of it. Consequently, we are encouraged to go back. Her values, and her father's, and her grandmother's, and those of Victorian England and Rudyard Kipling, and Wellington, and John Wesley are all offered. It is the parade of a standard set of authorities. There are others more esoteric in reserve, like Solzhenitsyn and T. S. Eliot, ready to be drawn forth for hero-worship, or for more profound accenting – 'History is now and England' – ultimately as the central literary, cultural, atavistic and human embodiment in Margaret Thatcher.

*

The Conservative Party, as she came to know it, was a broadly satisfactory vessel in which to deposit herself and her beliefs. It was the best available; to choose anything else would have been eccentric. To choose the Conservative Party was to acquire an approximation of her own belief. Nevertheless, an approximation which was in need of tightening up and strengthening.

Her membership of the party did not derive from active family allegiance. It came, at Oxford, as the natural as well as formal clothing for all the things she had been taught; comfortable, loose-fitting, there was no real friction. Neither the party, as she then experienced it, nor herself, were in the business of rethinking purpose or direction; consistency prevailed. Hers was the simple approach, and this became increasingly important as a way of presenting herself. She expressed her ideas in simplified form, occasionally to the point of banality. It was a determining principle behind her style, one which does not necessarily interfere with the much more complex grasp she has of the economic and social issues which she seeks to make plain and comprehensible.

She has made both a virtue and a handicap out of her taste for simplifying issues and then making them matters of principle. She does not necessarily get them right, and the handicap lies in the voicing of principles and precepts in support of essentially pragmatic actions. But in the wake of a period during which many fundamental beliefs had gone awry, Margaret Thatcher's approach when she came to power seemed refreshingly clear and direct. It was particularly the case over the economy. What had increasingly happened was that a common government obligation to provide employment, shared by Labour and Conservative administrations, had become a maverick factor within both the economic and social equation. Whatever the reason, by the early 1960s she was giving expression to an alternative view. Not new, perhaps, but on her lips it seemed original. In the eyes of certain thinking men within the Conservative Party at that time, most notably Sir Keith Joseph, she must have represented that rarity at any time in political, religious, or indeed creative life: a true primitive, the basic and at first partly inarticulate embodiment of a whole set of fundamental Conservative truths. Most obvious on the management of money, it stretched into areas such as the defence of Western democracy, the stubborn opposition to totalitarianism, her general belief in British greatness, and in moral, military and emotional integrity. It was a construction of fervent belief which made her of enormous potential value.

How many recognised this, and how deeply, is a matter for conjecture. Her critics disremember her economic views in the sixties, or relegate her impact to almost nothing at all. Her supporters are often at pains to relate her impact to their own, not quite showing that they led the way and she followed, but hinting at such a view. Most of those who have knowledge decline to say; those who do speak must be treated with caution, if not outright scepticism. But the record is convincing, from her maiden speech on February 5, 1960, onwards. In any analysis of British Conservatism between 1960 and the 1975-1979 period when she was in control, at least of that much of the country's future destiny, she turned the Conservative Party along lines which reflected her fundamental beliefs. Those sharing those beliefs are convinced she saved the party; those opposing them from within the Conservative Party believe that she is destructive of much they have stood for; those outside, that she has simply made the party her own.

She has undoubtedly made the party her own for the time being. Doing so was central to her approach to power. She possesses it, and uses it, completely. Has she made the country her own as well, or has she divided it, to make such parts of it her own as she could? If the latter, has she merely carried on a process which was set in motion by the failures of her predecessors? Or is it the inevitable outcome of that consistency which is the first fundamental aspect of Margaret Thatcher's character?

The second is that kind of simplicity which carries to relentless proportions the simplification of objectives into pocket-size nuggets of homely wisdom. As characteristics these two limitations prevailed during the twelve years in which Margaret Thatcher worked towards her first major objective: membership of the House of Commons. In what she did then, and in order to make possible this first objective, she allowed herself to become the creature of the party. Her words, thoughts and actions were the unmemorable expression of a political way of life which embraced, better than any other, those principles and beliefs which made up her character as child, girl and woman. She did not deviate from them; at the same time she did not make them scintillating, combative or memorable. It was a period of hard slogging. Narrow and unimaginative, perhaps boring even, her views were essentially at home within the easy framework of a conservatism which was far from precise or easy to define. Nothing that has so far been published about her suggests anything that contradicts a mundane set of political ideas. They were matched by a period in Conservative Party history of consensus politics, particularly under Harold Macmillan.

Since 1945, the party had been in a state of transition and adjustment. The primary objective had been to come to terms with the welfare state. Between 1947 and 1959, when she entered Westminister as the Conservative MP for Finchley, the party had gone through three relatively short periods under different Prime Ministers – Churchill (1951-55), Anthony Eden (1955-57), and Harold Macmillan (1957-63). There had been the profoundly emotional upheaval of Suez. By the time she achieved her first critical ambition, in the summer of 1959, the general state of the Conservative Party was that of an organisation amenable to varied expressions of leadership, policy and directions. Under Harold Macmillan's skilful management the party had recovered its post-Suez equilibrium, and was embarking on a consensus approach to both national and international affairs. This was Macmillan's great strength. It was essentially at odds with what Margaret Thatcher believed. But she was of no account then, and simply worked within the changes which took place.

The Parliament from 1959-1964 saw a fourth post-war change of leadership of the Conservative Party, to Sir Alec Douglas Home, as he then was, who became leader and Prime Minister in October 1963, and led the party into defeat in the general election of October 1964. Margaret Thatcher served as a junior minister – she was Joint Parliamentary Secretary at the Ministry of Pensions and National Insurance – under both Harold Macmillan and Alec Douglas Home, then had various spokemanship responsibilities up to the time of Edward Heath becoming prime minister in 1970. It was only then, in the period of Conservative Government between 1970 and 1974, that her political consistency became an adversary force, and very slowly an increasingly public one. It was defective, however. Although her preferred perception of herself during this period is of a member of Edward Heath's Cabinet who stood out, along with Sir Keith Joseph, for rectitude over public spending and against the U-turn of 1972-73, the reality, in terms of her responsibilities as Secretary of State for Education, was that she spent generously and was constantly demanding increases in expenditure. Behind the much publicised cutting of school milk lies a plenitude of extravagance not consistent with a remembered attitude. Moreover, she seems to have adopted a different attitude within the Cabinet from the one she had outside it, among backbenchers and junior ministers opposed to the U-turn. Former colleagues who served in that Cabinet remember her as going along without demur; monetarists outside the Cabinet remember her verbal opposition expressed in their company, and her stated belief that it was better not to resign, but to attempt to influence from within. This ambivalence was resolved swiftly enough into a stern monetarist rectitude which led her into the leadership battle which followed Edward Heath losing two general elections in a row, in one year, February and October of 1974.

Consistency was a chosen image. So was belief. So were values. They became generalised but essential principles, governing her performance as Conservative leader in Opposition. She worked towards, and then constructed her 1979 general election manifesto around, a belief that Britain had lost its way, and that there were certain 'values we used to share' which were recoverable. The first of these was consistent money which kept its value year by year. The second was consistent reward to create incentive. The third was consistent obedience to authority, particularly by the unions whose undermining of that authority had been central to Britain's loss of both direction and values. The route she offered was accepted. Having been taken, it proved difficult, and became more so. It was politically dangerous, and increasing numbers of people recognised this, including growing numbers on her side. And here lay part of the danger, the greater part. But then the goddess Fortuna, potent for the fruits of the earth and the life of women, smiled on her, adding to her consistency the luck or good fortune of a necessary, just and successful war. That, for a political leader in the 1980s, was luck indeed. The consistency, like a thin thread of base ore through rock, was turned miraculously to gold, and became the basis for an election.

She is, one needs to remind oneself, a woman. She brings different values and different rules to the game of politics. At a time when men, who had refereed and performed in the game for centuries, seemed peculiarly at sea with economic and social problems, with recession, with inflation, with trade union militancy and lawlessness, with youthful unrest and with racial tension, a new leader offered herself with what appeared to be a new set of principles and beliefs. They were not very clear; they were not very precise; but they *seemed* to be. They *seemed* simple, and determined, and different.

And they persuaded many people. She is a Christian, says Paul Johnson, 'the first proper Christian as a political leader that we've had for a very long time.' True? The first *proper* Christian? When asked to define her beliefs, her vision in religious terms, she is evasive, imprecise and rather silly.

She is sincere, says Brian Walden, 'and the sincerity shows.' (*'Unhappy that I am, I cannot heave my heart into my mouth'*). He dismisses emphatically the idea that she 'determines quite coldly what the majority think and then chooses to pretend to believe it or perhaps in time actually comes to believe it. Margaret isn't like that at all.' Yet her beliefs, moral, social, economic, ideological, have been the enemy of her acts, a set of handicaps to mock both the precision and the flexibility needed in the day-to-day affairs of Government.

More than any other leader, she has expatiated on beliefs and then turned them inward upon herself, implying that she is their fountainhead and their practical embodiment. This compounding of belief with action can be very dangerous indeed, giving a false and inflexible motive to practical and essentially pragmatic actions. The Falklands was a case in point. She oversold it as a vindication of her beliefs, her courage and determination, her unflinching defence of liberty and opposition to aggression. Useful as a prelude to a general election, such structures can prove a heavy handicap thereafter. A re-examination of these and many other perceptions about her, which have been central to her rise to power, is overdue.

*

She has slipped, and is slipping, away from the pristine faultless image of her first phase in power. She nevertheless occupies more firmly than ever the centre or throne-room of that realm. And, in the realm of power, time is always present. Biography, history, gossip, habit, appearance, are the servants of the moment. The chronology of power always begins now, and its study must follow that rule. But 'now' is perpetually slipping away and becoming 'then', so that artifice is necessary to counterwork the nature of time. Margaret Thatcher used artifice for this purpose herself. Her world is always in the present. The perspective of time is lifted for the benefit of current advantage. It is for this reason one used the words 'It seems' as a prelude to 'she has been consistent'. It is not a denial. It is not an affirmation. It is an observation related to the fact that the study of power is *always* in the present, the response of those in power *always* of the present.

The 'present', for the purpose of this book, is the general election of 1983. Already in the past, it has a shape, a pattern, a finite measure in the result. Called in circumstances of the artificial drama of expectation, fought on a favourable battleground against a weak and divided enemy, its conslusion was precisely what everyone had predicted. Loaded with artifice, pumped up with consistency, supported by ministers in a fashion not seen since the days of Queen Elizabeth I, conducting her press conferences like an audience at Hampton Court, Margaret Thatcher was more fully herself thus than in any other guise. There is no woman more real behind the woman we see. There is no mask.

It is part of the prodigality with which her 'person' is brought into contact with the people by means of a communications industry which is instant, diverse, massively comprehensive. The texture of her skin, her hair, the timbre of her voice, what she is wearing, the 'flash' in her eyes, the deliberate modulation of a set of responses between concialiation and scolding, all of this and much more comes to us, *at* us, in a relentless ourpouring which is given purpose, reason, compulsion by virtue of the grasp on power which lies behind it, and justifies it. If it were not there – and it demands a huge suspension of belief – she would fluctuate between being boring and being ridiculous. Because it is there she is fascinating.

Her political career is made up of watersheds, the greatest of which was becoming leader of the Conservative Party. By comparison with that, winning her first election in 1979 was in a substantially more modest category. It could almost be described as inevitable. Essential to her that it be inevitable, otherwise she would have been as swiftly stripped of the leadership which she had so swiftly acquired. The 1983 general election, again a watershed, was something quite different: won more by a combination of default and good luck than anything else. Only her consistency stood out as a positive, shining virtue, in electoral terms. For the rest she relied on being surrounded by a massive and collective failure of British politics. It was this which created the foregone conclusion. And she handled it with consummate skill. She handled her own consistency in the same way. She spread it over the thin material of her four-year administration. It embraced a successful minor war, a modest cutback in inflation, and very little else beyond the frequent and determined articulation of principle and objective, the creation in the collective, reluctant, but ultimately believing mind of the people, that the rectitude preached by Wilkins Micawber could be made to work, in the future, by her.

As Williams Deedes was to put it, on the Friday of her first press conference during the general election campaign, writing in the *Daily Telegraph*: 'Mrs Thatcher's basic philosophy, which is roughly that we reap as we have sown, clicks with a phenomenally strong current running through this country, in one of its rare moods of critical self-examination.'

He is right about it 'clicking'; but it is a process which derives from a number of different emotional and ideological responses, not all of them, by any means, deriving from 'critical self-examination'. That 'phenomenally strong current' is a necessary purgative for the British psyche, a required dose of realism which just may get the books balanced and the accounts in order once more, though even this seems doubtful and the price too high. It will not make Britain great again; rather more is required for that miracle. But it will have the effect of changing one set of illusions, if only for another. And if democracy is still able to contain the upheaval then that is the survival which matters. In the end, power is in conflict with the very structures on which it depends. Throughout history it has been so, and most catastrophes have derived from conflict between people and the systems which should contain them. Margaret Thatcher's approach to power has made one conscious of this in a manner that was not the case with her predecessors certainly back to the second world war. The passion with which she seeks it, and the reasons for which she wants it, together with the ways in which she uses it, raise questions about the nature and health of the democracy within which she operates. That is a necessary and overdue examination, embarrassing to the Left as well as the Right, but potentially of greatest value to the centre in restoring an understanding of the truth that freedom is preferable to greatness, and that the choices which democracy continues to offer will be exercised against her when the time comes.

PART ONE

General Election, 1983

CHAPTER ONE

'The Field of Battle'

The announcement of the 1983 general election came in a Downing Street statement at 2.15 on the afternoon of Monday, May 9. The dissolution was to be on the following Friday, May 13, just four years and nine days after the previous election. The poll was fixed for June 9. The new Parliament would assemble on June 15.

The odds for a Conservative victory were 5-1 on from Ladbrokes, 4-1 on from William Hill. The odds against Labour were 7-2; against the SDP-Liberal alliance, 50-1. The only bet worth having was on the 28-1 odds against a Conservative majority of more than 97. That other and more serious indicator, the Stock Exchange, received the proposed dissolution calmly; the *Financial Times* Share Index dropped 4.2 points to 690.2. Sterling lost 1.1 cents against the dollar.

The most dominant of all the indicators, the opinion polls, which would rule the election as they had ruled the months leading up to it, governing decision and charting opinion, were thick on the ground: two on Sunday, one on Monday, one on Tuesday, one on Wednesday, and all of them unanimous in their findings. The Conservative lead, which had been consistent since the beginning of 1983, was overwhelmingly so now. Mori, Marplan and Gallup, over the first four months, had given the Conservatives, on average, 43.8 against 30.8 for Labour and 22.1 for the Liberal/Social Democrat Alliance. It would spell danger, if not doom, for the Conservatives under proportional representation. Under the 'first past the post system' it offered a clear and commanding lead. Wiseacres nodded their heads, and referred one to Harold Wilson's commanding lead of 49.5% over the Conservatives at 42% in May of 1970, which turned into a 46%-44% victory for the Conservatives under Edward Heath. It was a form of psephological prophylactic; but it lacked heart and soul. If Heath had been good during the 1970 election, Margaret Thatcher looked as if she would be better; if Wilson had been deficient, Foot promised to be hopeless.

Opinion polls are the new opiate of the people. They have both narcotic and compelling qualities. They appear to answer questions to a certain precise point; beyond it, they abdicate responsibility. Claiming detailed assessment, they nevertheless plead that they are no more than a time-clock, recording a common-denominator view at one precise period of time. By summarising thought they substitute themselves for it, demoralising the function of challenge and criticism. Instead of deliberating over the number of bad eggs or rotten tomatoes thrown at politicians, the arguments that earned them, and whether they were deserved, interest centres instead on shifts of a percentage point or two in the fortunes of political parties and individuals.

Collectively, the opinion polls suggested a Tory majority of well above 100. In a more comprehensive way than ever before, they set a highly predictable seal on the outcome, an elaborate statistical scene within which the protagonists would present themselves.

Margaret Thatcher did so, initially, by giving an undertaking which would underline her image of consistency: there would be no personal attacks on Michael Foot, simply because she did not believe in personal attacks. 'I have never, as you know, in my life, had personal attacks. I have always tried to stick to issues; always, always, always. We always put, very much, our positive case. Certainly, I will try to show up the shortcomings of Labour Party policy.'*

Generous? Or dismissive? It was both. Whatever else the general election was about, it was not about Michael Foot. Swiftly enough it would prove not to be about Labour Party policy, with shortcomings or without. It was about Margaret Thatcher. And no one was more delighted with this fact than she was. As *The Guardian* put it in its editorial on the morning of May 10, 'The Conservatives do not chart their intentions in endless documents emerging from committees. They do not need to do so. Mrs Thatcher is their statement of intent. If she wins, it will be a triumph for her instincts, an electoral vindication for her

---

*BBC Radio interview, May 9 1983.

belief in her own judgments rather than the caution of senior colleagues. The banner of Victorian values will be run up over Downing Street like the red flag over Islington Town Hall. The welfare state, though not, strictly speaking, destroyed, will be eroded to a point at which large parts of the community will be left with only the most basic provision. And whatever Mrs Thatcher and her colleagues may tell us during their election campaign about the better days now ahead, thanks to their sober and diligent stewardship, the weapons of economic management will be the same crude weapons on which she and they have relied on (sic) over these past four years. Unemployment and the fear of unemployment are their one sure remedy for industrial discipline and the control of incomes – or at least, of some people's incomes. Having resorted to that course, there will be no way in which she will be able to relax it without threatening those achievements, most especially the reduction of inflation, for which she now claims credit.'

It was a just and balanced summary of the arguments upon which millions of words had already been expended in anticipation of the previous day's announcement. One of only two national dailies – if one excepts the *Morning Star*, a special case – to be and to remain opposed to Mrs Thatcher's re-election, the *Guardian*, in well under a thousand words, summarised the arguments and ideas, and did so with a sharpness of expectation, even of hope, which Opposition politicians could not live up to. Labour and the Alliance had thirty days in which to reverse 'the now forbidding portents of the polls'. Otherwise, the anticipated and predicted outcome would create, 'quite simply, Mrs Thatcher's Britain. That defines it better than a thousand scholarly words. And the predominant issue of this election, in a way that has not been true of any election in recent memory, will be the Prime Minister herself: her hopes and fears, for herself, her party and the people: and the lengths to which she is ready to go to see that her will prevails.'

The portrait offered by the *Daily Telegraph* was of a leader who had agonised over the timing, a political discretion she found unattractive, and had 'allowed her practical good sense to triumph over her natural inclination to see the thing through to the end'. She was facing the test of her political maturity; she would not rest on her laurels.

Though perhaps a trifle sanctimonious, about it, the *Daily*

Telegraph, on that first morning, addressed itself to the political considerations in a manner which concerned itself more specifically with Margaret Thatcher's personal understanding of, and grasp on, the elements of decision-making which bore directly on her retention of power. And in this, of course, she had, as the paper's leader-writer claimed, 'agonised'. Tactics were an essential part of political success, and the timing of battle crucial. The timing also was at her absolute discretion, one of those lonely decisions where the upward curve of expectation had to be judged in conjunction with the fluctuating curve of approbation and judgment of her performance. She knew it as fickle; she had known it as adverse; and she knew it now as unprecedently in her favour.

Except in wartime, the only parliaments since 1900 which had lasted longer under the same prime minister were those of 1924-29, under Stanley Baldwin, Clement Attlee's post-war government of 1945-50, and Harold Wilson's of 1966-70. There was a legitimacy, a logic, and a sense of natural order, in part created by the lady herself, in the timing. The *Daily Telegraph*, in its defence of her, glossed over the arguments: 'The Government has reached the point in its work where an election comes naturally; and the country seems to be prepared for one.' A more robust political and personal case could be made on timing, and with the help of those who were seeking to make an election issue out of it: the Opposition.

The very point of their argument, that the Conservatives were going to the country in haste, at a favourable time, before the further clouds of recession descended again, was a perception which, while not actively canvassed, was implicitly welcomed by Margaret Thatcher and her supporters in order to intensify the combative atmosphere in which the opening of the general election campaign would be seen. If she was acting in haste, they were acting in fear. Again, the *Daily Telegraph*: 'This is not one of those elections, like February 1974, when the decision to go to the country is central to the political argument. The campaign will develop its own momentum, and no one but politicians will be interested whether October would have been better, or next spring more dignified. Having decided, Mrs Thatcher is right to go quickly. Her party is much better organised and financed than its rivals, and will adapt well to the rigours of a quick campaign. More important perhaps, a lack of delay suits Mrs

Thatcher's temperament well. With a clear aim now in view, she will throw herself with great zest into the fight. She is a skilled populist, an energetic campaigner, and a great raiser of her own supporters' morale. She can set the pace, and will be proud to do so.'

She did the opposite. Remembering the experiences of 1979 gave her an acute sense of judgment about seeing the campaign from the enemy point of view. She, in Opposition then, had watched Jim Callaghan, following his parliamentary defeat on March 28, lead off a campaign which she could not and would not follow because of the murder of Airey Neave which took place two days after the Commons defeat sustained by Callaghan. But she turned this very definitely to her own advantage. That defeat, in itself, had been historic; the first time a British government had been voted out of office in fifty-five years.* And it was followed by the opening week of campaigning in which almost all the focus of attention was on the defeated prime minister defending himself and his record.

Putting herself into a position in 1983 in which she deliberately handed the initiative for starting the campaign to the other side was more difficult since she had not been defeated and forced out of power; quite the reverse.

Also, precedent is a treacherous master. But in so far as there were tactical and strategic lessons to be learnt from the past and absorbed into the present, the most important and most immediate concerned the using of the first phase of the general election as a means of assessing the strength and determination of the enemy; and this meant that she had to give that first phase, or appear to give it, to the Opposition parties. Meanwhile, she would continue to govern the country; more importantly, be seen so to do.

From Monday May 9, in spite of having the overall planning of the general election and its timing entirely under her own control, Margaret Thatcher allowed ten days to elapse before the publication of the Conservative manifesto, on Wednesday May 19, and a further two days before she held her first press conference of the campaign, on Friday May 21. For well over a third of the time between calling the election and the poll itself she

---

* In 1924 Ramsay MacDonald had been defeated in a vote in the House of Commons and had requested a dissolution. In the ensuing general election he had lost power to the Conservatives, and Baldwin came back as Prime Minister.

therefore held herself and her party's formal presentation of its programme in check.

It was cool, deliberate and intelligent. It had tactical and strategic characteristics, military in kind. Margaret Thatcher took a calculated risk about timing which appeared to hand to the Opposition parties ten clear days of direct campaigning, while she 'dictated' that, as far as the Conservatives were concerned, the general election would begin on May 18. In reality it began straight away in all constituencies, particularly the marginals, and preparations which had gone on for months were wheeled smoothly out in the form of documentation, posters, advertisements, recordings for radio, films for television, a positive arsenal of prepared weaponry. A marketing campaign, designed to sell a relatively boring, limited and inflexible product, was being mounted with huge attention to detail, massive expenditure and that aggressive, narrow imagination which is the hallmark of advertising executives. It took an act of will, an exercise in intellectual determination, to put upon the events which were being unpackaged and set in motion the true reality of politics; this was how Britain would choose to be governed, and by whom; this was how an electorate of 40-odd million people would determine the laws which would shape their lives and their country for the foreseeable future.

*

The emphasis at the outset was on trivia, deliberately so; and the principal feelings were of relief, that the suspense was over. And it was not without a measure of excited expectation that one waited for Carol Thatcher's *Diary of an Election** to discover something at least of the human background to this. The strain of holding back, for a woman of Margaret Thatcher's temperament, must have been enormous.

Yet, according to her daughter, Margaret Thatcher spent the first weekend, after calling the election, planning her Finchley campaign, dealing with the official red boxes, and reading 'The Campaign Guide', the 550-page Conservative Party document covering every aspect of the election and designed as an election

---

* Carol Thatcher: *Diary of an Election: With Margaret Thatcher on the Campaign Trail. A Personal Account* (London, 1983).

weapon, so that party workers would know their stuff. Carol Thatcher was confused that weekend. 'Recovering from jet lag', as she says herself, she spent the weekend 'generally trying to acclimatize myself to the new atmosphere of the political campaign trail'. She got days, facts and places wrong, and the only quotable comment she elicited from her mother was to the effect that 'the one thing you're not short of during a campaign is food, everyone presses it on you'.

'We didn't talk much about politics,' Carol Thatcher wrote under the heading 'Friday, 13 May', 'there was (sic) going to be endless amounts of that to come. And anyway, campaigns seem always to have the same ingredients – smears, scares and banana skins.' In fact, on that Friday Carol Thatcher was travelling back from Australia and her mother was in Perth, Scotland, so that exchanges between mother and daughter were confined to the Saturday evening and the Sunday. Nevertheless, the diary revelations are thin to the point of absurdity. Margaret Thatcher, that weekend, faced with the central question of whether she had got all her political judgments right in choosing May 9 to June 9 for the campaign, was depicted as confident about getting enough food!

Whether the campaign would remain under Margaret Thatcher's control – and this was a key objective, if not *the* objective – would depend on the personal impact of Michael Foot, David Steel, Roy Jenkins, the additional impact of their parties' policies, and the choice, by them and the public, through press, television and radio, of the issues which would become dominant. While Margaret Thatcher had no intention of letting control of any of these pass out of her hands, she wisely realised that, as part of her strategy, the opposition to her should be given the first opportunities to present their cases and their champions.

She had been decisively in control of the British political scene for four years. She had gone through a dramatic pre-election period, during which her ultimate discretion over the dissolution of Parliament and the calling of the election had been used to maximum advantage. She was aware, above all else, that error by herself was the biggest possible danger. She enjoyed an unprecedented lead in the opinion polls. She had the main body of Fleet Street behind her.

Though she could guess at it, she did not know how good her

opponents would prove to be, nor what impact they would have. She could not forecast, and be sure about, Michael Foot's electoral, as opposed to his parliamentary, appeal. She did not know how the country would take the joint, middle-ground programme of the Alliance, or the massive manifesto of the Labour Party. The very fact that she had dominated political action, and had therefore been a decisive force in deciding what issues were important in the period before the election was called, made it absolutely imperative to allow these judgments to be tested out. And this meant waiting.

*

She put this obligation of waiting to the best advantage, not just domestically, by pursuing a measured conclusion to the final days of Parliament before dissolution, but also on the international front, by the equally considered handling of two imminent summits. It gave the initial impression of a leader to whom the general election was incidental to the business of running the country, an interruption the outcome of which would be inevitable. No immediate decisions were made about the two important international meetings, the Williamsburg world economic summit, scheduled for May 29-30, and involving the United Kingdom, United States, Germany, France, Japan, Canada and Italy, and the European Council meetings at Stuttgart, planned for June 6-7. In its opening editorial, May 10, the *Daily Telegraph* counselled Margaret Thatcher not to go to Williamsburg; furthermore, that the idea that this would enhance her authority 'would be a mistake', implying disrespect for the humble British voter. 'A general election is the one time in politics when the opinion of ordinary people is systemetically sought and is cumulatively decisive. The politicians asking for this support should do so with humility, not expecting it as of right. Between now and June 9, the Conservatives must devote all their energies to offering their services to the British people.'

Margaret Thatcher had no perceptions about the necessary recipes for victory. Quite the reverse. She told President Reagan that she would not be able to pay the planned private visit which was to precede the Williamsburg summit. This decision was made at the beginning of the general election campaign, and announced the day after the calling of the election. But she appeared to be keeping her options open on the world summit meeting, and did not finally decide until a week later.

On the question of Europe, the situation was more delicate. The Stuttgart summit was planned for June 6, only two days before the end of the general election campaign. It was about specifics, unlike Williamsburg, and central to those 'specifics' was the question of the size of Britain's EEC Budget rebate for 1983. While 'winning' or 'losing' were not issues at Williamsburg, which could be turned to the British leader's advantage without too much trouble, a different prospect attached to the planned encounter of the ten leaders of European governments. Judging from past experience, as well as from the issues themselves, there was the distinct possibility of a stalemate, or worse.

For the first week after calling the election, the position on Europe was also kept open. Then the confirmation of the decision to fly to Williamsburg, and by Concorde, coincided with Francis Pym taking over the main burden of argument at the foreign ministers' conference at Gymnich, near Cologne, during the weekend of May 14-15. He made clear that firm commitment on a precise rebate figure for Britain was a necessary pre-requisite for Margaret Thatcher's presence at Stuttgart. In addition, it was made clear that the rebate expected by Britain was to be of about the same order as in previous years. It was an impossible combination. For the Nine to give her the agreement on a figure in the region of £800m (she eventually came away from Stuttgart, after the election, with just over half that figure) would have represented an unacceptable climbdown, in advance of a conference regarded by many as the most important European summit since Britain, Ireland and Denmark had joined the EEC ten years earlier. Indeed, it would have looked alarmingly as if Britain's partners in the EEC were entering the election campaign itself, and endeavouring to ensure the return to power of the staunchly pro-EEC Conservative administration in decided preference, either to a Labour Government, or to a non-Conservative coalition in which an anti-EEC element would be sizeable enough to provoke instability at a time of potential crisis within the Community.

Francis Pym played delicately on this theme, during the weekend, his main and most formidable opponent being Claude Cheysson, the French foreign minister, who was determined to block the British rebate if Britain's agreement on a farm price increase could not be gained at the same time.

It was a tough stance to adopt, containing considerable risk of an immediate pre-election rebuff, and suggesting bad timing in the choice of June 9 for the poll. It was therefore welcome to Margaret Thatcher when Dr Helmut Kohl, the West German Chancellor, postponed the Stuttgart meeting until after the election. He announced this on Tuesday May 17 after a telephone conversation the previous day with Margaret Thatcher. Before the Kohl announcement, but after the telephone conversation, she had already told political journalists that she would not be going. She was still then in the first phase of the campaign, as far as her language and imagery were concerned: 'A general does not leave the field of battle when coming up to the climax' was how she put it.

Denis Healey was more down to earth. He anticipated the decision to postpone, claimed that Margaret Thatcher was 'committing every professional foul in the book', and correctly predicted no chance of the demanded rebate being got.

Quite clearly, if the alternative of prior agreement had been achieved, Margaret Thatcher would have been only too glad to follow the 'responsible' course, on Britain's behalf, and go to Stuttgart in order to bring home, in that vulgar but appropriate phrase, the bacon.

This particular piece of stage-setting, involving international events, was completed within the ten-day span of the first phase, and well in advance of the launching of the Conservative Party manifesto. It had been nicely judged. A 'responsible' world summit which would not deal with specifics; a postponement of the harder horse-trading of Stuttgart.

*

An equally 'responsible' domestic approach was adopted, beginning with the carefully measured running down of parliamentary business. From the Conservative point of view it was more desirable to gain agreement on the substantial parcel of measures which remained before the House, gaining at the same time a sober and dignified end to the Parliament. This was of particular importance since the Speaker, George Thomas, was retiring. A much-loved man, elected first in the Labour interest in 1945 for Central Cardiff – Michael Foot referred to the 'appeasing lilt of Tonypandy' – he had been Speaker since 1976. This meant that he had presided over the formal introduction of sound broadcasting of Westminister in 1978, the point to which Margaret Thatcher referred when she called him 'a legend in his own lifetime'.

The day of the tributes was also the last Prime Minister's Question Time before the dissolution. 'You gain jobs by gaining customers,' she said. 'There is no other way. . . . Failure to deliver on time loses a lot of orders and therefore jobs which we would otherwise get. It also gives Britain a bad reputation. We need greater industrial efficiency and goods delivered on time.' She was prompted by a Midlands MP of her own party, John Stokes, with the sobering observation that the predicted landslide in the opinion polls should not be taken for granted, and there should be 'no complacency whatever'. 'We have to work to win,' she agreed.

She was much more trenchant in what she had to say to 'her own people'. Addressing a packed meeting of the 1922 Committee, on Thursday night, May 12, she presented a more confined set of election priorities: defence, public expenditure and trade unions.

These were the combative issues, the ones that could be expected to provoke maximum confrontation, and to delineate the lines of battle in a campaign the character of which had yet to emerge. Margaret Thatcher nevertheless needed to bide her time until the fuller picture emerged of what her opponents had in store, and how it would be received by the British electorate. This meant careful observation, not just of the launching of the Alliance manifesto, on the same day as her final session at the despatch boxes in the House of Commons, and the launching four days later of Labour's manifesto, but also of their treatment by the press, and their impact in the opinion polls. All of this was allowed for in Margaret Thatcher's timetable. An exception to her restraint was the well-judged outburst on ITN's *News At Ten* programme on Monday night, May 16, when she described the Labour Party manifesto as 'the most extreme that has ever been put before an electorate'.

CHAPTER TWO

'There is no hope'

The SDP/Liberal Alliance came first with their manifesto, almost precipitately so. Strategically, the main Conservative plans had been made against Labour. But the possibility that, by sheer force of personality and brilliance of policy presentation, the Alliance would force a change in strategy, was not to be dismissed too lightly.

Initially, the Alliance seemed to invite such dismissal. Its election manifesto was launched in the absence of both leaders. David Steel was in Scotland; and, although Roy Jenkins was in London, he kept away from the press launching of 'Working Together for Britain' at the National Liberal Club, for the sake of 'fairness'. Instead of either of them, Shirley Williams, the Alliance President, presided, epitomising – as she does all too often – the plight of compromise.

For a vital document in a vital campaign, the hastily-convened, ill-attended launching was inauspicious. Those present, and those absent, emphasised equally the multiplicity of vying talents and alternative points of view. The Conservative Party Chairman, Cecil Parkinson, was dismissive, commenting that the Alliance programme was the watered-down, Wilson socialism of the sixties, in which the very people who now led the Alliance had been involved. It was, he said, a mixture of 'irresponsible election promises and bribes'. It had failed.

Compromise was apparent also in the approach to defence by the Liberal-Social Democrat Alliance. The manifesto was imprecise or muddled about Cruise missiles, the timetable for the phasing out of Polaris, and the direction that should be taken on NATO priorities and on disarmament. Judged on the basis of both the launching of the manifesto, and its content, as well as the important press, radio and television reaction, the Alliance did not represent any serious threat. They were the nice, agreeable team they had always been. And as is the fate, generally, with nice teams, they could, at their initial showing, be relied on to finish last.

The Labour Party, from the outset, however, seemed determined to compete with the Alliance for this unappealing position. From the moment of launching its manifesto, those personalities within the Labour Party – from the leader down – who should have been responsible for a clear and descisive explanation of the issues were drawn almost immediately into unedifying arguments and conflicting attitudes about what it meant or did not mean. The fumblings of Michael Foot, the benign and then rasping joviality of Denis Healey, the capacity for argument of Peter Shore, the ill-concealed indications that others within the Labour Party, like Roy Hattersley and Neil Kinnock, were already conscious of an impending leadership struggle after the general election had ended in defeat, suggested an approach that was unprofessional and inadequate.

The distinct possibility that even within the Labour Party leadership there were men who felt they could 'grin and bear it', in the knowledge that the manifesto they were presenting to the British people at the beginning of the second week in the general election could not, and would not, be implemented, even in the unlikely event of an overall majority, was warmly suggested by *The Times* in its editorial of Tuesday, May 17, in a sustained and relentless attack on the whole message of the Labour Party's document, 'The New Hope for Britain'. Promising more detailed examination in the days ahead, *The Times* contented itself on the day after the launching with broad principles, and with 'tone': 'There would be an unpleasant atmosphere created by an incoming Labour Government determined to introduce economic and social policies far to the left of any programme in West Europe, including that of the Italian Communist Party. The atmosphere would be xenophobic, illiberal, syndicalist and confiscatory. This Party promises the moon; but it would have to borrow the moon. Somebody else, as always, would have to pay. There is no "New Hope for Britain" in this document. There is no hope.'

This was dismissal of a high order, and it might be argued that

Margaret Thatcher could confidently end the period of waiting and go on the offensive. On all sides she was witnessing widespread newspaper, and indeed television and radio reaction against the Labour Party, its manifesto, its leader, those who seemed to be more preoccupied with his job than with winning the election, and all the ideas for running the country which had brought the supposed 'Left' into such disfavour. Yet this was exactly the point of maximum danger for a leader in power seeking a repeat mandate in circumstances of unprecedented depression. The job that Margaret Thatcher and the Conservative Party might have to do was being done for them with an efficiency and zeal that was spread almost universally through the media. Honourable exceptions were to be found. But the great body of opinion-formers, which had been lined up in any case on the side of Margaret Thatcher, was reinforced in its dedication by the Labour Party's own set of policies. In such circumstances even the words of dismissal she added to the general debate seemed superfluous.

Better by far, if one maintains the language and metaphor of war which seemed to dominate Margaret Thatcher's vocabulary in the early stages of the election, to allow the natural forces in war – weather, terrain, disease, disagreement between allies – to undermine and debilitate the enemy before the actual clash of battle. Her limited commentary, in the first ten days, if superfluous, was not really damaging. It simply helped to nudge public opinion in a direction towards which it had been moving steadily since the summer of 1982, and the Falklands War.

*

In addition to being right in principle, as well as being militarily successful, the Falklands War had shown the seriousness with which Margaret Thatcher applied herself to the business of leadership. Detached from war, and treated simply as an indicator of the quality and strength of her leadership, her handling, of the war, had been impressive. And reminding people of this was subtly done.

She had not compromised, not even in the face of the greatest challenge of all, that of armed conflict. Reapplied to the economy, this quality of iron determination gave a wholly new credibility to her will to succeed. It made her words more credible. It restored faith in the integrity of politicians. For the British public, many of whom did not understand fully whether or not she had 'turned' as far as economic policy was concerned and who in any case judged her economic skills in a very circumscribed and subjective way, the fact that she had been resolute in the face of war gave her undoubted bonus marks. It is part of the weakness of the general system of political opinion polls that they tend to break down issues into relative importance, and then measure the degree of success or failure of the politician in handling a certain number of given problems. This removes a crucial, if subliminal extra dimension, that *performance* in an area of minor significance can affect *judgment* about performance in an area of substantial importance.

Margaret Thatcher had to believe that, between 1979 and 1983, she had brought about a major transition in British political thinking, particularly about the economy. She could hardly go into a general election with well over three million unemployed and an election programme of continuing rectitude if she did not believe it. It was not necessary, given the existence of the SDP-Liberal Alliance, to believe in a total conversion to Conservative ideology; that would have been an impossibility. It was necessary only to sustain a belief within her own party while at the same time spreading and encouraging disbelief in the alternative. Their failure, even if only partial, was an essential part of her success. In electoral terms it was the first stage. If no dents were made in Conservative Party popularity by the launching of all the alternative manifestos, then this would obviate the need for any change in her election programme. Tactically, the most counter-productive approach by Margaret Thatcher would have been to attempt to dictate the course of events during this period.

She did not. Relatively speaking, she sat quiet. It was a repeat of 1979. Deliberately chosen now, rather than being forced on her by any event, she needed to see just how secure was the position which the opinion polls suggested she was in. If the full blast of the Opposition manifestos failed to shift her popularity, then she needed, above all else, to be careful. More than that would be a form of prodigality.

*

On the day following the launch of the Alliance manifesto,

Margaret Thatcher flew to Scotland for the Scottish Conservative Party Conference in Perth, where she delivered a fighting political speech which could be regarded either as her first of the campaign or, more correctly, as a tactical exercise. She invited the 'Falklands test' as a litmus paper to election programmes and policies, and initially to policies on defence. The relationship of 'the swift and sure response of our young men in the South Atlantic just a year ago' to those broader domestic objectives which represented the prizes for which the Conservative Party was fighting was central to her speech. In other words, the country's economic problems would be solved by the 'Falklands spirit'. How, remained vague.

The Perth speech was a preliminary skirmish. She was in the delicate process, at this early stage in the general election, before the launching of her party's manifesto, of testing the mood in which the election would be held, and of preparing a stylistic approach for it which would create the right character and atmosphere.

In this experimental phase, she touched on most of the issues. In Margaret Thatcher's case she was combining consistency of purpose with simplicity of approach. As far as the detailed presentation of performance was concerned the Conservative Party was campaigning on its record, and this was already presented, in the Conservative Party Campaign Guide, under nine headings. And she was simplifying and hammering home that message at every available opportunity. The Perth speech was a trial run for the presentation of the package to the country.

It was based on the Campaign Guide objectives. Briefly summarised, these fall into three main areas, the economy, foreign policy, and domestic administration involving social commitments and law and order.

The four sections which dealt with the economy were in the form of claims about what had been done combined with promises about further endeavour along the same lines. For example, strict monetary and fiscal controls had reduced inflation and brought Government expenditure under control. There would be more of the same. The second claim, combined with a promise, was that a programme of reformed and reduced taxation had been started and would continue. This was aligned, in the third area of economic endeavour, with the encouragement of business enterprise. And the fourth and final part of the economic package concerned trade union reform; a recovery programme could not be completed without discipline and control, part achieved, part yet to come.

Foreign policy had economic and defence dimensions, both linked with the idea of making Britain 'Great' again. If the economy could be got right, this would represent one half of the equation; but it was backed up by the other half, involving NATO and European commitments, the firm defence of Western democracies against the threats of totalitarianism, and the special relationship with the United States. Emotive and general expression was given by the Falklands sacrifice and the Falklands spirit.

The third area was the domestic one of social commitment balanced against law-and-order policies; strengthening the police and sustaining the war on crime went hand-in-hand with the 'caring' elements in the Conservative Party's listing of benefits, the preservation of the welfare state; yet offered as a set of benefits which could only be sustained by a healthy economy.

To these three campaign objectives must be added a different and more general target, designed to act as a catalyst by which an overall style would be imposed: conveyed by the emotive and euphemistic phrase, 'rolling back the frontiers of the state', it indicated the nature and character of Margaret Thatcher's conservatism far better than any of the more precise but more limited objectives.

'Rolling back the frontiers of the state' (it is actually the title of paragraph five of the section in the Campaign Guide dealing with 'The Record, 1979-83') is a vague concept. In some respects it is illusory, totally so in the context of law and order, where the State's encroachment on the individual's rights and privacy was likely to increase significantly under proposed Conservative legislation, in particular the Police and Criminal Evidence Bill before its pre-election emasculation. Nor could trade union reforms, however desirable, be seen other than as the opposite of 'rolling back'. And where it was likely to be effective and determined, within the framework of the welfare state, it had an inevitably malign side to its character. For every council house sold, if the money yielded to the State is not re-deployed in providing more housing for future candidates among the underprivileged, then the sale, however attractive to one generation of council house owners, must represent the wasting of a finite and circumscribed asset. Indubitably , the frontiers of the state were being rolled back, but to what ultimate end? Encouraging private medicine may, in theory, 'reduce the strain on the National Health Service'; but if reducing the strain becomes synonymous with reducing the expenditure, then does not a sinister side to a basic service emerge?

Nevertheless, this ninth objective, against which the Conservative Party invited the public to measure more generally its record of achievement after four years, was different in kind from the others, and offered a broad basis on which the style and character of the Conservative Party could be judged. 'Rolling back the frontiers of the state' was a Conservative cornerstone, amounting to little more than a cliché, in the presentation of that more general message which had been the main political thrust in Margaret Thatcher's more electorally-minded activities since the beginning of 1983. While a more detailed analysis of this appears elsewhere, it is sufficient to point out at this stage that, from her Falklands Islands visit of January 9 1983, she agreed to a succession of interviews designed to present her version of Conservative philosophy. This is to put rather a high premium on what emerged. The all too obvious agony of one political pundit after another, striving to exact something special, distinctive, real, and 'exclusive', from the limited resources of philosophic thought over which Margaret Thatcher had command, is apparent in the splendidly presented page-long 'scoops' in newspapers, or segments of airspace during which she submitted to interrogations the fruits of which were meagre. Deliberately so on her part, for she was determined on using such encounters for a debate on her own homespun political wisdom, a debate always conducted on her terms.

A typical example was the Kenneth Harris interview in the *Observer*, run for two consecutive Sundays, the second of which, headed 'My vision for the future', appeared on May 8, the eve of her announcement of the general election.

It could be said that public sector cuts were an important impending issue and, in fairness, Kenneth Harris saw this, and raised them in the context of Ronald Reagan both admiring what she was doing, and at the same time criticising her because it was not enough. In the course of a voluble and trenchant reply, Margaret Thatcher claimed to have 'got it about right', to have cut 'quite a lot of controls', to have 'cut out the bureaucracy', to have spent 'more' on National Insurance, to have 'increased' spending on the NHS, and ended up, 'at all levels we have controlled public expenditure'. The questions raised by this comprehensive, yet at the same time vague, answer are numerous, and absolutely vital to her past performance and the forthcoming general election. Kenneth Harris tackles them by asking in what seems to be unquestioning admiration: *'Why are you able to control expenditures if previous governments couldn't?'* So openly invited to use him as a platform, who can blame the Prime Minister for a lengthy exposition on 'real' and 'volume' term expenditure planning, and how it has been 'got right'? Wonderingly, Kenneth Harris asked: *'Why didn't departments behave like that in the past?'* And, unsurprisingly, another little homily on Britain's recent economic evolution emerged.

On this as on other occasions, one has to admire her ability to run virtually all her interviewers firmly into the ground at the outset, and then proceed to rescue them just sufficiently to permit the continuation of her self-exposition on questions of general, personalised political philosophy. This reached its high point in her handling of Sir Robin Day, to which more detailed attention will be given in due course. It belongs to a slightly different phase from the pre-election one, where the emphasis in the long sequence of carefully planned interviews was on economic and social achievement. Once the election was called, this changed, and Margaret Thatcher's judgment moved aggressively in favour of combat and confrontation. With the opinion polls very substantially in her favour, even overwhelmingly so, she was actively looking for a fight, this time not face to face with Kenneth Harris or some other worthy protagonist of the people, but on a public platform speaking to party workers and candidates: 'Tonight we go forth from Perth to battle. Great things are expected of us.'

Top of her list of priorities among those 'great things' was defence. Yet it was carefully balanced against other, less militant targets. Her combative style had not led her into the mistake often made by such leaders in electoral contests: that of attempting to dictate what the election issues are. The danger of this approach being analogous to a general leading a large army towards an enemy which has moved away in the night. At the end of a working week between calling the election and having what was really a trial launch of the campaign for the Scottish

Conservative Party, no clear picture had emerged of what, or who, apart from herself, would dominate. Consequently, in a speech which was very definitely her own, in its main substance and in its fine tuning, she covered virtually everything else as well.

*

The reasons for her hawkish opening stance, with its use of battle imagery and divisive tones, disdainful of Labour, dismissive of Alliance, but essentially cautious and in no sense underestimating the task ahead, are complicated. She did not really know which direction the campaign would take. Her popularity, reflected in her own and the Conservative Party's standing in the opinion polls, should have derived from her handling of the ecomomy, and indeed this *appeared* to be the case, since economic issues, as they always do, dominated. Yet she knew, instinctively, that her political popularity derived substantially from her handling of the Falklands War, and the resilience and fortitude revealed by this. Without it, her position would have been entirely different.

Nor is that by any means all. If the central element in her political character, and therefore in her self-asserted right to power, is the semblance of consistency, then the Falklands war, and the way in which she handled it, whether its precipitation was accidental of contrived, justified or not, becomes in itself an added dimension in demonstrating tough, single-minded devotion to the ultimate interests of the British people in a context infinitely more simple to grasp, as far as the vast majority of the population were concerned, than consistency in the economic field.

Furthermore, in absolute terms, the consistency in war had been far more clear-cut, and far more swiftly rewarded by success, than was the case with the economic policies proffered since before 1975, actively pursued since 1979, but still very restricted in what could be described as 'success'.

The policies had not worked out in practice. They had been changed and adapted. They had reduced their architect's political standing to the lowest level of any British Prime Minister since such things were measurable, and they had left her fighting an election with more people unemployed in the country than there had been in half a century.

This was the paradox facing Margaret Thatcher during that first weekend. Against all the odds, she seemed set to win.

CHAPTER THREE

'A High-Risk Enterprise'

The all-important judgment of public opinion, guided and represented by the press, radio and television, measured and confirmed by the endless series of polls, could be readily predicted from the start. It was. An unnervingly solid support for a slim set of options for the future, and an indifferent record in the past, presented itself.

The frailty of her case was underlined by the 'Trog' cartoon in the *Observer* on Sunday May 15, 1983: it showed her in a toy aeroplane named 'Inflation Beater' heading towards a flag which displayed the sign 'Air Fair 9 June 1983', and printed on the side of the aeroplane was the additional message: *'Built by the unemployed'*. It was a ponderous, if truthful statement of her case, and of the country's predicament. But, if the frailty of her case was so stated, the strength of it was to be found in an article underneath the cartoon by Anthony Howard, and entitled 'Why Foot has doomed Labour'. Howard, who was honest enough to confess his delight and excitement in November 1980 at Michael Foot's election to the leadership of the Labour Party, seemed to be suggesting that Denis Healey would have proved better. It was authoritative stuff, but hardly germane to the reality that Foot happened to be leading Labour.

Howard could have found better use for his time by applying his not inconsiderable energies to the issues, rather than to the personalities. He might then have fulfilled the injunction about his profession which appeared on the same page, immediately beside his own article and beneath the *Observer* editorial for that day: 'Serious journalism is a high-risk enterprise.' The quotation, pointedly chosen for the 'Sayings of the Week' column in the context of quite another story, that of the Hitler diaries, had been culled from the pages of the *Sunday Times* of the previous weekend. Intended as a legitimate piece of point-scoring between two rival papers, one the victim of forgery, the other partly responsible for its exposure, it could be taken at a deeper level as a sombre warning about the realities of the campaign.

At the foot of that particular page in the paper was an article by Charles Wintour under the heading 'No Worries for the Tories in Fleet Street', the first in a series by the former editor of the *Evening Standard* on the newspaper coverage of the general election. Illustrated with photographs of 'The Prime Minister's three trusty Knights' (the editors of the *Daily Express*, the *Daily Mail* and the *Sunday Express* – Sir Larry Lamb, Sir David English, and Sir John Junor respectively) the message of the article was to the effect that Fleet Street was already predominantly behind the Conservatives and could become overwhelmingly so. And though he could not pronounce, either on the *Observer*'s position, or that of the other Sunday 'qualities', all appearing that day for the first time since the calling of the election, Wintour's prediction for several of them, that 'it would be surprising indeed if they did not support the Conservatives in the last resort', was borne out by the tone of the main editorial on that page which talked of Foot's 'lumbering carthorse' and Roy Jenkins's 'precarious craft' falling to earth 'with either a bang or a whimper'. While the writer talked also of applying certain criteria to the parties in the election in the weeks ahead, those criteria, in the main, reflected Conservative Party policy.

It was, in summary form, not a bad approximation to the introduction Margaret Thatcher had written for the Conservative Party manifesto, which was to be launched four days later. Even so, the *Observer* editorial writer was cautious: 'It would be a mistake to write off the election as already a foregone conclusion: if the winner seems obvious, even before the off, the race has still to be run.' This was the first sentence. The last was even more perceptive: 'One of the great things about elections is that they make us all think.' The only really thought-provoking sentence on the whole page has already been quoted: 'Serious journalism is a high risk enterprise.'

The *Sunday Times*, one of its rivals in the search for truth, was to come down later on Margaret Thatcher's side in its advice to voters, not as a result of judgment or analysis, or indeed on foot of any 'Insight' inquiry or examination, but simply 'in the absence of any realistic alternative'. On this basis, that first Sunday, it declared: 'A Tory win is therefore the best thing for the country. But two other results are also desirable. The first is that there should be no Tory landslide, which could unleash the forces of illiberalism lying not far beneath the surface of modern Conservatism. The second is that the Alliance, in recognition of its commonsense and constructive thought, should get a sizeable share of the popular vote and a respectable holding of parliamentary seats. It would be a great pity, for example, if the SDP leaders – the so-called Gang of Four – failed to be returned to the House of Commons, to which they have so much to contribute.'*

Have they, or had they? If so, what? The *Sunday Times* never told us. Nor did it examine at all closely that 'commonsense and constructive thought' which so clearly failed to catch and sustain sufficient of the imagination and support of the electorate. Perhaps much more important, the paper signally failed to delve into those 'forces of illiberalism' not far beneath the surface of modern Conservatism. They were an issue, of concern and direct relevance, and part of the overall presentation of itself by the Conservative Party which it was the duty of the press to turn inside out and then judge. The *Sunday Times* claimed as its criterion, to examine 'how closely each party programme accords with our own publicly stated views on the major items of foreign and domestic policy'.* Yet in fact the *Sunday Times*, on the second Sunday following the publication of the Conservative Party manifesto, provided no more than a general essay on the overall drift of the document's main points, suggesting that 'quite a lot that is good' had been achieved. There were no hard, well-reasoned judgments, however. A pattern of media acceptance, clearly to be perceived at the outset, prevailed throughout the election.

*

The first phase had achieved the major objectives for the Conservatives of bringing out onto the field of battle the electoral enemies, and of assessing their separate strengths and their potential cohesion into a fighting force capable of defeating the Conservatives. With the exception of the Perth 'skirmish', a

---

* *Sunday Times* editorial, May 15 1983.

testing ground of considerable value, Margaret Thatcher had expended no shot.

How was this all measured? The Alliance Manifesto was launched on May 12. 'The New Hope for Britain' was launched on May 16. Four opinion polls were conducted between the calling of the general election on May 9 and the 'Alliance Manifesto on May 12. They were by Marplan, Mori, Harris and Mori again, and were respectively for the *Guardian*, *Daily Star* , Thames Television and the *Daily Express*. Published on May 13, 11, 12, 13, they showed Conservative support standing at 46, 46, 52 and 49 percent. And they showed the Alliance support at 19, 21, 17, and 15 percent.

Following the Alliance Manifesto's launch on May 12, and between then and the launching of the Labour Party Manifesto on May 16, a further four opinion polls were conducted (Audience Selection, Mori, N.O.P. and Gallup) and they showed no appreciable shift in the relative standing of the parties: Conservatives: 46, 44, 49, 46 percent; Labour: 31, 37, 31, 33 percent; and Liberal/SDP Alliance: 21, 17, 18, 19 percent.

A similar stability prevailed in the period between the launching of the Labour Party Manifesto, on May 16, and that of the Conservative Party Manifesto, on May 18. Three polls were held (Mori, Harris, Mori) on May 17-18, 18-19, and 19, for the *Sunday Times*, Thames Television, and the *Daily Express*, and they revealed no serious change: Conservatives: 47, 45, 46 percent; Labour: 30, 35, 37 percent; and Liberal/SDP Alliance: 21, 17, 16 percent.

Opinion polls followed at the average rate of one a day for the week between the Conservative Party Manifesto and Tuesday, May 24, which was to prove a critical day for Margaret Thatcher in the context of her *Nationwide* appearance. If the Opposition manifesto made no appreciable impact on public opinion, the Conservative Party Manifesto was equally sterile. At the end of two weeks, the average figures for all polls conducted by then were: Conservatives 47 percent, Labour 34 percent, and Alliance 18 percent. This compared with 46, 34, and 19 percent in the Marplan poll for the *Guardian* of May 9-11, and published on May 13. Having deliberated on that the paper published a Gibberd cartoon on its front page the following Monday, showing a running track with a succession of tapes held by Mori, Marplan, Gallup, Harris and ORC opinion pollsters. A triumphant

Margaret Thatcher, in running gear and spiked shoes, is breasting tape after tape. Behind her, handicapped by having their feet bound together for a three-legged race, are Roy Jenkins and David Steel. At the back, his feet stuck firmly to starting blocks labelled 'Popularity' and 'Unity', is Michael Foot, struggling to get into the race.

It was hardly surprising that the *Economist*, in its 'Poll of Polls' summary, an article on the background and overall interpretation of the unending succession of opinion polls, should have concluded: 'Mrs Thatcher's 13 percent lead is large enough to defy any statistical error. And its inertia looks awesome.'

These two facts, the lead which Margaret Thatcher and the Conservatives enjoyed over their rivals, and the stable nature of their lead, had become election issues in themselves. The first had been there from the start, a phenomenon of almost a year's standing, but nevertheless the main seedcorn for political comment. The second, being new, overtook the first in importance, and became an even greater phenomenon. It was a daily, factual reflection of her consistency, and therefore of a major aspect of her political character. By contrast, the only consistency displayed by her opponents was in their failure to make any inroads on her lead; daily they displayed, through the opinion polls which relentlessly informed the world of her strength, their own weakness. It begged the essential question: if her political nature was in essence the abstract characteristic of consistency, how then was it to be clothed? Notwithstanding the fact that she had been in power for four years, and had governed according to certain principles and objectives, there was a natural and legitimate requirement, fed by expectation, fuelled by delay, and by the willingness with which the field had been given over to the Opposition during the first ten days, to explain the issues one was consistent about; to produce a manifesto and answer questions. Phase Two of the general election was about to start.

CHAPTER FOUR

Manifesto

The Conservative Party's advertising campaign began in the national newspapers on the morning of Wednesday May 18, on the same day as the launching of their manifesto. The first advertisement, massively displayed – in the case of *The Times* across two full pages – was in the form of a last will and testament, listing fifteen simple declarations which would be made by anyone who voted Labour: 'I do not mind paying higher rates', 'I sign away the right to buy my own house', 'I empower the Government to borrow as much money as they wish from other countries and I agree to let my children pay the debt', were just three of them.

Couched in simple, blunt terms, the list of individual declarations summarised the whole election campaign in less than 350 words. Three of the declarations were about the right to choose – on schooling, on medicine and health, and on trade union membership – and what it would imply under Labour.

Five of them were about substantial policy differences on major national and international issues: continued membership of the EEC, defence and the nuclear deterrent, nationalisation, borrowing, and devaluation. All but one of them were so worded as to make direct and personal the impact of Labour's intentions. Going out of Europe would put at risk two million jobs, and 'my job may be one of the 2 million'; on foreign borrowing 'I agree to let my children pay the debt'; and nationalisation would be 'whatever the cost to me in higher taxation'. Loss of money was implicit in seven of the paragraphs; loss of jobs, freedom, the right to choose, and perhaps life itself, in a further seven. It left only the last: 'I understand that if I sign this now I will not be able to change my mind for at least five years.'

Following this aggressive prelude came the Wednesday morning launch of the manifesto. Flanked by key members of the Cabinet* Cecil Parkinson, William Whitelaw, Francis Pym, Geoffrey Howe, Norman Tebbit and Michael Heseltine, Margaret Thatcher presented the document to a packed press room at Conservative Central Office. She did not exactly do so to the strains of 'Land of Hope and Glory', yet Elgar's martial, nostalgic music was quietly played in the background as journalists assembled, along with 'Onward Christian Soldiers', both presumably to encourage tough objectivity among the hardened and ruthless cohorts of the world press.

Margaret Thatcher was understandably tense throughout; she bridled at questions, indulged in sarcasm, and set a general tone of brusqueness which was to characterise her handling of the press from then on. She presented the arguments of the manifesto with emphasis on their robustness and the vigour of the party's approach. She was picked up on the omission of any mention of Trident by Sir Robin Day, but instead of giving a straight answer, to the effect that it was an error, she made some remark about consulting with him over future drafts. It was sarcasm to conceal her defensiveness over a blunder of not inconsiderable proportion. Not mentioning Trident was compounded by not noticing the omission. She also dismissed, bluntly enough, the question of Northern Ireland on the grounds that none of the parties wanted it as an issue.

Curiously enough, the first question from the 200 or so journalists crammed into the rather stuffily re-furbished ground floor press conference room was absolutely central to the whole compaign. Margaret Thatcher herself failed to see it as such, a view shared by many others. It came from Peter Kellner, of the *New Statesman*. He asked if the people and the places in the Saatchi and Saatchi advertisements during the campaign would be 'real'; or would the doctors and teachers, hospitals, nurses, schools be other than what they seemed, like the dole queue in the 1979 Conservative advertisement, made up of employed members of Hendon Young Conservatives Association? Margaret Thatcher said she was 'very interested' that this was Kellner's top priority.

Well she might have been, since he had identified the

---

*Details of Margaret Thatcher's Cabinets, with changes, are given in the Appendix.

essentially orchestrated nature of the Conservative Party's approach. She wanted 'straight' questions, not real ones. She wanted questions on what Conservatives stood for, and not on how they were handling their campaign. She wanted the election to be about certain selected issues, not about the fundamental issue, which was how to stay in power. This was what Peter Kellner was curious about, the whole carefully constructed fabric of calculation, planning and presentation. He wanted to get behind the scenes and expose the illusion. He wanted to discover what no actor willingly reveals, how disbelief is suspended.

Margaret Thatcher was a consummate actress in all of this. She had studied her part, resolved character problems, learnt her lines, rehearsed her timing, gone laboriously over her script, considered carefully every detail of her wardrobe, and was on stage delivering her opening speech in undoubtedly the most important production in which she had ever starred. Yet here was an irreverent critic asking if the actors in the drama were 'real'. In her terms it was not only a meaningless question, since nothing was 'real' in the sense of being unplanned or unorchestrated; it was a damaging question as well, since it hit at the very heart of the production. Too much of that kind of challenge, and the intended melodrama of confrontation, the combative language of war and freedom, the subliminal messages about where the main body of British support would lie, could be swiftly turned into a farce.

To some extent it was, by Frank Johnson, in his column in *The Times*. But he did it benignly, within the strict and careful comic discipline of the traditional lobby correspondent. The jokes he made about Margaret Thatcher's torrential twenty-minute opening speech, which 'took in all topics at present known in British politics' and was followed by 'whoops' in the direction of Sir Robin Day, did not puncture the basic and well-established conventions of such encounters between political journalists and politicians.

The overriding impression given at that first encounter was of the Party leader's complete dominance over her colleagues and the press. She gave a clear demonstration that she was running the show, from beginning to end. She contradicted Francis Pym, virtually silenced William Whitelaw, took over one question from Sir Geoffrey Howe, and looked with indulgence only upon

Norman Tebbit and Cecil Parkinson. It was *her* election, *her* Party, *her* manifesto. And it was going to stay that way.

*

What, then, is to be said of this document, on which she and her strategists had spent months of preparation, honing and refining its language, rewriting over and over again its many carefully balanced messages? What weight and solemnity do we attach to it? The *Sunday Times* took the unusual step of giving a half-page in the review section of the paper to the literary critic John Carey, to review all three political manifestos from the point of view of 'style'; and there can have been little surprise, and considerable self-satisfaction among Conservatives, when its own sloganless document was judged as 'easily the best written', and 'the only manifesto that shows any overt concern for language'. Carey confused language with style in his review; and the result was that he rendered the concept of style shallow. Better to have gone for that far deeper meaning, as Schopenhauer recognised: 'Style is the physiognomy of the mind, and a safer index to character than the face.'* And if this is true of literature it is at least as true also of politics. Margaret Thatcher's mental physiognomy, her political character, are contained in the ultimately trivial if determined phrases of this manifesto booklet, part of which is concerned with concealment. As with her alternative 'performance', before television cameras, in the streets, making speeches, answering press conference questions, being interviewed, both the negative and the positive elements of expression are part of the style, and may be assessed for what they tell us of the nature of her mind. It is not necessary to know all she has done; 'it will be enough, in the main, to know how she has thought. This, which means the essential temper or general quality of her mind, may be precisely determined by her style. A woman's style shows the formal nature of all her thoughts.'*

Only a small portion of the Conservative Party manifesto is directly attributable to Margaret Thatcher herself. In less than 500 words she presents a signed message about 'The Challenge of Our Times'. She manages to employ the following vocabulary

---

* Schopenhauer; Essay on *Style*, with gender changed.

of words and phrases: confidence, self-respect, regard, admiration, integrity, steadfast progress, recovery, traditional liberties, distinctive way of life, peace, security, freedom, justice, strength, incentives, protect, heritage, our history, free people, great claim, greatness, enduring courage, honesty, flair, ability. It could express both the illusion and the reality of consistency, and of the personal qualities implicit in many of the words.

It sets the stylistic tone for the remaining forty pages, and comes up through the document, like the large and well-spaced bubbles in cheap champagne, giving a periodic verbal lift to a document basically constructed by many minds, but approved and finalised by one mind, and therefore reflective of that particular physiognomy and character. Its fundamentals include curious cornerstones, the earliest of which is the dismissal of the past, and the strong emphasis on the present. While earlier she may have used words like 'heritage', 'our history' and 'great chain of people stretching back', in reality, life, political life, for Margaret Thatcher began in 1979. There is no focus whatever in the document on Conservative traditions. In the swift summary with which its first chapter opens, the fact that Britain is 'once more a force to be reckoned with' and that 'national recovery has begun' is related specifically and exclusively to actions since May, 1979. And the whole corpus of intent for the economy, expressed in two sentences near the beginning, is framed within a repeat, more or less, of the five objectives which were at the beginning of the 1979 Conservative Party Election manifesto. The sentences: 'The truth is that unemployment, in Britain as in other countries, can be checked and then reduced only by steadily and patiently rebuilding the economy so that it produces the goods and services which people want to buy, at prices they can afford. This is the task to which we have steadfastly applied ourselves with gradually increasing success.' And the framework, the 'five great tasks for the future' which in 1979 were presented as 'our five tasks': the stabilised economy, the responsible society, the rule of law, the quality of life, the defence of freedom.

How is this to be done, in view of the fact that the years of recession are '*now* coming to an end' (my italics); it is to be done by firmness towards the trade unions. These, because they relate to legislation, are the most precise set of paragraphs in the document; they represent a challenge to political opponents which was never really taken up, and which the Conservatives held in reserve until the final week in the campaign, when the Black Knight, Norman Tebbit, was brought into the lists as Margaret Thatcher's ultimate champion.

The benign tenor of the third chapter on 'Encouraging Free Enterprise' was enormously selective, emphasising, above all, three areas crucial to Margaret Thatcher's carefully planned campaign: tax reforms, small firm encouragement schemes, and help for the new technologies. Here her voice comes through, and with it the physiognomy of her mind: selectively positive, narrowly vibrant.

'Responsibility and the Family' expresses the moral balance between responsibility and freedom. It is *almost* a genuflection towards traditional conservatism; but the contemporary nature of *her* achievement – that is, since 1979 – is underlined by the essentially Thatcherite: 'Under this Government, the property-owning democracy *is growing fast*. And the basic foundation of it is the family home.' It was not Conservatives, but the Conservatives under Margaret Thatcher who had given 'every Council and New Town tenant the right to buy his or her home', and no one was to forget it. Equally, part of the utilitarian 'character' of Margaret Thatcher's mind is deliberately embraced in the idea that money required for education, described as 'the pursuit of excellence', must be spent in the most effective way.

Law and Order produce emotive alliteration: 'The rule of law matters to every one of us. Any concession to the thief, the thug or the terrorist undermines that principle which is the foundation of all our liberties. That is why we have remained firm in the face of the threats of hijacker and hunger-striker alike.' It is a good, precise, determined and detailed presentation of the 'crime-fighter' image.

Dullness pervades the chapter on 'Improving our Environment'. The portmanteau term is rejected as 'a clumsy word for many of the things that make life worth living', a phrase which for its banality and bathos destroys the effect. But this is the superficial linguistic hair-splitting of John Carey's review.

A far stronger use of words in the manifesto's last chapter, 'Britain and the World', restores faith in the seriousness of style as an expression of the fundamental shaping of character. On defence and on Europe, two of the five sections, Margaret

Thatcher herself speaks, and speaks in order to push an intentionally divisive wedge between her own views and the quite different ones of the Labour Party. 'We have stood up for Britain's interests' is the theme, and it is applied with pithy brevity to world trade, Europe, maintaining peace, resisting aggression, and winning the Falklands War. It is a rousing final chapter which in style betrays a more substantial Thatcher input than the previous ones.

Whether this is the reality has been difficult to ascertain. But it is, or would be, an entirely logical and legitimate development. It was an area of policies about which Margaret Thatcher could be positive after four years in power. Much as she would like to have been positive about the economy, the scope there, with reduced inflation her main achievement, was extremely limited. She is a political leader who hates admitting wrong or accepting reversals in fortune, no matter how small or limited. Even after the final youth rally of the campaign she would not accept that Kenny Everett's remark about kicking Michael Foot's stick away was in bad taste, excusing it as 'comedy'. And on much bigger issues, such as prescription charges put to her by Sir Robin Day in the *Panorama* programme, she fought with remarkable resolution to defeat his perceptions and protect herself from an admission of wrong. And she did the same with all his other clumsy efforts at criticism. The relevance of this kind of political mind to the formal presentation of a programme by means of a party manifesto will be readily apparent.

After four years in power, the best achievements, judged in emotive terms, but basically for their *positive* qualities, lay in the realm of foreign rather than domestic policy, thus reversing the promise in her political character which had been dominant in 1979. Her grasp then, on the range of world affairs outside the shores of England, had been limited. She had needed Carrington and others to put her right on Rhodesia, Northern Ireland and the Republic of Ireland, on America, Europe and the Third World.

And in any case her strong suit was economic. A fundamental shift had taken place, diamonds giving way to spades to maintain the metaphor. War, Williamsburg, world defence and nuclear deterrence all presented her with opportunities for adopting an aggressive stance. It was expressed in phrases about standing up for Britain's interests, those interests being the stability of the existing world order, and the mutual support of allies and friendly nations.

In this, too, there is the nature of Margaret Thatcher's sense of loyalty. It is of a simplistic and primitive kind: Kenny Everett had stood up publicly for her and the Conservative Party she had forged, therefore defending him was more important than objective truth about the actual basis for his comic spirit. Ronald Reagan and the American people had basically stood by Britain and the Falklands, and Britain would do the same in return, *no matter what the price*. That was a test of loyalty that remained in the future.

In summary, the Conservative manifesto, which was a short-term political document, was weighed and measured precisely towards maximum gain and minimum loss: high profile on foreign policy, strong and confident profile on law and order, persuasively independent profile on personal freedoms and responsibilities, tough and detailed profile on trade unions, broadly hopeful profile on jobs and the economy, a self-congratulatory profile on the encouragement of free enterprise.

As a revelation of the 'physiognomy of the mind', in the sphere of the real and determined search for power, the final short paragraphs of the eighth chapter, 'the Resolute Approach', were very serious indeed. 'This Government's approach is straightforward and resolute. We mean what we say. We face the truth, even when it is painful. And we stick to our purpose. Most decisions worth taking are difficult. . . . the rewards are beginning to appear. If we continue on our present course with courage and commonsense, those rewards should multiply in the next five years. We shall never lose sight of the British traditions of fairness and tolerance . . . confidence is brushing aside pessimism at home . . . Britain is regarded for the first time in years as a country with a great future as well as a great past. We mean to make that future a reality.'

It was a truly remarkable message, with the highest level of unemployment ever seen, a puny, suspect, high-risk and immensely expensive foreign 'war' to her 'credit', a shaken and unstable industrial economy over-dependent on high technology and small business enterprises, a prodigal use of Britains's biggest natural resource, oil, a potential widening of social division, and a set of moral values which were elusive and illusory. But there was no alternative. And this was the great strength in the package she offered. It could not be challenged by Margaret Thatcher's political opponents; it was to be ineffectively challenged by her critics in press, radio and television, in part because they all saw no alternative. Orchestrated with a musician's care, it was a pomp and circumstance march with which, given the British electoral system, a majority would undoubtedly identify.

CHAPTER FIVE

'Some Way Still to Go'

It was, of course, intended that the response should be directed elsewhere, notably towards the Conservative Party advertising campaign, which did indeed provoke hostile reaction. That campaign certainly had more political teeth than the manifesto, but who takes issue with clever copy-writers and poster designers? Much of the impact is subliminal; the will-and-testament format, suggesting the signing away of one's life, was basically more effective as an attack on Labour than anything else offered by the Conservative Party during the election. Everything else possible had already been done, including repeated parliamentary defeat and humiliation, Government performance and policies which were consistently and convincingly more popular, and a party more united behind its leader than either of the Opposition groupings, notwithstanding Francis Pym's almost solitary defiance about the size of potential victory.

Nevertheless, there was a logic in the transfer of aggression into the realm of advertising while at the same time neutralising the more serious arena in which conflict might develop over policy intentions. The anodyne manifesto was no accident.

The degree of advertising outspokenness was finely judged. And while the basic standards required by British advertising, that it should be 'legal, decent, honest, truthful', were breached in letter and spirit, and admitted to have been so by advertising practitioners, notably on the *Today* programme on BBC on Monday May 23, it was also readily admitted that nothing could be done about it, as it could in the cases of breaches over margarine or make-up, and in any case wasn't it all something of a joke? There was ribaldry about the need for a health warning on political advertisements, but the 'robust tradition' in political campaigning was invoked to excuse any blatant assault on delicate sensibilities.

It failed as an excuse in one area. The Conservative Party had budgeted £16,000 for an advertisement which was to be placed in fifteen ethnic weeklies. The advertisement consisted of a photograph of a young West Indian or Asian, the main caption being 'Labour says he's black; Tories say he's British'. Arif Ali, the editor of the most radical of the ethnic newspapers, the *Caribbean Times*, refused to carry the advertisements, and described it as 'insulting, obnoxious and immoral'. The Conservative Party Chairman, Cecil Parkinson, said this was 'censorship', and that people should be allowed to make up their own minds. The majority of the newspapers did accept, however, and were divided as to the impact on voters. It was *finely judged*; in the country as a whole the likely impact of this particular piece of campaign material, as with the more general run of posters and newspaper display advertisements, was admiration for its overall cleverness.

It was left to Stephen Cook in the *Guardian*, as he did on other issues, to present a reasonably detailed analysis of all party policies, all of which contained 'more radical proposals' than in any previous election. The Conservatives, he found, were the 'most confined': opposed to discrimination, in favour of real equality; the party would be pushing 'its sensible, useful track record'.

*

The catchy, stinging, highly effective and occasionally borderline advertising campaign contrasted sharply, as it was meant to do, with the manifesto, seen as calm and restrained; 'unnecessarily cautious,' the *Daily Telegraph* said, in its leader, headed 'Mid-term Manifesto'; while both it and *The Times* emphasised the self-confidence being restored in the midst of a battle against major and widespread social and economic difficulties.

The former paper was uncompromising in the conclusions it came to: 'The prevailing quality of the manifesto is its reasonableness. Its picture of Britain as a nation of growing self-confidence, but still battling with industrial and social difficulties on a large scale, is one that most people would accept. Its emphasis on economic reality and on the limits of what government can do, is honest; and its attention to the internal and external security of the nation is in strong contrast to the attitude of Labour. Like Mrs Thatcher at yesterday's press conference to launch it, the manifesto shows no failure of nerve and no failure of energy. It is not a programme for Utopia, but something much more sensible – the basis for a sound government acceptable to the people.'

The judgment by *The Times* was similar. The accepted wisdom, political, social and economic, that unemployment was unavoidable was 'realistic', it said, and 'once realism has crept in, can optimism be far behind?' it added sententiously. Then, going beyond 'these priorities', it offered 'other policies which will receive more detailed examination on these pages'. Yet, from that day, three weeks before the general election poll, until the outcome was secure, the basic burden of such examination was handed out by the paper to partisan contributors who tended on the whole to cancel each other out. The staff of *The Times* reported press conferences, published regular constituency profiles, produced, in Frank Johnson's daily 'campaign trail', the funniest writing of the general election, and in editorials continued to camouflage instinctive partisanship with the 'high sentence' of judgment. But the paper left much of the hard work of criticism to outside contributors.

*

The Conservative manifesto was a skilful and subtle document, firmly and precisely linked to the campaign's progress, the opinion polls, and the reception afforded to the manifestos of the Alliance and the Labour Party. The two-page will-and-testament advertisement was an excellent summary of overall strategy. Its links with the manifesto were direct and close.

There seemed to be a press determination to play down the Conservative manifesto as a safe, cautious and undramatic document. It was anything but. In his 'Comment' column, in *The Times*, Geoffrey Smith began with the sentence: 'The Conservative task in this campaign is not to win votes; it is to make sure that they do not lose those they have already got.' There must have been laughter in Downing Street about that, but also a measure of satisfaction. The overall burden of a message which was considerably more emotive, dramatic and confrontational than the arguably more crucial manifesto approach in 1979, was being got across subliminally.

CHAPTER SIX

'The Headmistress'

Just as Margaret Thatcher had decided to follow a strategy for her overall campaign based on the principle of delayed action, to allow her opponents to lead off into the field, revealing their not altogether convincing armoury, so now the principle was invoked a second time, in the further gap between the presentation of the manifesto on the Wednesday morning and the first formal Conservative Party press conference on the Friday morning. The 48-hour gap brought the first sharp exchanges between the parties and leading individuals, with Denis Healey accusing Margaret Thatcher of lying, and basing this accusation on a leaked 1981 report from the Central Policy Review Staff, which had warned that unemployment would rise above three million.

Healey's point was that, knowing about this and other forecasts and recommendations in the report, Margaret Thatcher had said the opposite. It immediately became a tangled issue; contradictions flowed in from Norman Tebbit and Sir Geoffrey Howe, and correctly the first substantial engagement of the campaign developed around unemployment.

Yet it did so without any appreciable advantage to the Opposition proposals for the solution of what was seen by a majority of the electorate as the country's most pressing problem. True, a slight dent in the Conservative Party's lead in the opinion polls was recorded for Friday morning. But not enough to be significant, and not perceptibly related to any new wisdom about the responsibility for those out of work, or the relative merits of the various prescriptions, all of which were not available for comparison. There was no evidence of widespread belief that responsibility could be laid at Margaret Thatcher's door. What Denis Healey was accusing her of was the relatively minor, and politically more than justified decision not to forecast, in 1981, the doom-filled and awesome reality of 1983. What he was signally failing to do, with his leaked document – always a dangerous weapon in an election campaign – was to change in any way the remarkable achievement by Margaret Thatcher in diverting blame or responsibility for the country's foremost problem. Her opponents might cry from the rooftops her blemished performance in producing work for the unemployed. She was worried only at the impact of such noise on the voters.

And this made her confident and aggressive when the point was put to her, at a quarter to ten on the morning of Friday May 20, mid-way through her first press conference. She was accused of a 'level of cynicism towards unemployment' in her Government. It was not exactly a 'question' with which she was faced; and what she replied to it was not exactly an 'answer'. It came at the end of a series of exchanges lasting five minutes, and related to the issue which had become dominant in the previous twenty-four hours as a result of the publication in *Time Out* of the leaked confidential report.

Since the document and its leaking had been the lead story, or at the very least front-page material, that morning in a number of newspapers, it was obviously going to feature substantially in the first press conference. Initially, it did so rather weakly, with an oblique reference to the capacity of her advisers, in 1981, to predict the current (1983) level of unemployment, and a question about whether this meant that forecasts forward into 1985 were possible, and, if so, what they were. 'I think,' said Margaret Thatcher, with an obvious and careful feigning of perceptions and predictions worthy of Miss Marple, 'I think you are referring to the CPRS Report. Um, you will *know* that the CPRS Report *itself* made *no forecast whatsoever*. It recorded a collection of forecasts by other forecasters *which had all been published.*' And she went on to engage a number of journalists in a series of exchanges which revealed a very detailed and comprehensive briefing, and a compelling command of the overall set of issues which was substantially greater than that of any of her questioners, probably of all of them added together. 'I'm very grateful to you for giving me the chance to clear up that point', a point which she had not cleared up particularly well, and which in any case was not the point she had originally been asked to clear up.

Much of what she said was marginal to the central issue raised by Denis Healey, if not altogether irrelevant. While this did not detract from the compelling quality of what she had to say, the authority and range of her delivery, and the combative stance she adopted to a series of journalists who wanted to pursue the main story of the morning, it did lead to the challenge about a motive, or a note of cynicism.

'No, er, no. No one is this Government is cynical about unemployment *in any way*. All of us are pursuing policies to reduce it, and may I refer you to the speech I made last night – it was fully press-released – and what I said about unemployment, and there one pointed out the best you can do, or one of the best things you can do to help unemployment is to get *inflation* down and to pursue policies which get *interest rates* down to get rid of the concealed unemployment in the overmanning, to *in fact stimulate* the growth of *new products* and *research* in new technology, that is the response of the Alvey Report, and *also* to *stimulate* the growth of new businesses for which this Government has the *best set* of policies and measures I think the world over. The *immediate* response to the report to which you are talking about was, of course, the, er, the, er, the *enormous one year youth training* scheme. It has taken some time to get ready because we had to go out to industry and commerce to get some 460,000 places, and the *whole idea* behind that, and I've mentioned it many times in the House of Commons, was that young school leavers, or at the age of 16 or 17, have a choice. They can either go on with education into *further* education, or they can, many of them get jobs, as you know, or they can go into a year's training, but the whole point and the whole response is that it's *terrible* for young people to be doing nothing, and therefore we started up that *immense* new training scheme so that *when leaving* school *unemployment* is *not an option. That I think is, I hope*, what one might try to call the silver lining in the dark clouds of the world recession. And no one's worked *harder* at it than this Government because we believe that one of the worst things that can happen to young people is to have time on their hands – we've also as you know got *job-splitting schemes* which help some of them to be working at any rate part of the week so they really have a fair percent of interest. But the *youth training scheme* I think is the most *go ahead* and exciting scheme we've *ever* introduced in this country. There are other things as well, but I won't go on. Perhaps I'll save them for an answer to another question.'

Her long statement had not been an answer, as such. It had not addressed the disparity between public and private documents on unemployment projections, and it had not dispelled the suggestions of cynicism. It had, however, eliminated all her questioners, and silenced those who might have wanted to pursue her about that cynicism. In fact, there was a momentary, stunned pause before someone raised the question of a landslide victory and led the press conference off again, this time in a more light-hearted, Francis Pym-baiting direction. The echoes of that sentence, of an unbroken, Proustian dimension, lingered on. It was a skilful diatribe, cleverly directed against both Labour and the radical Left, as represented by *Time Out*, though without mentioning either. It swooped, eagle-like, from prey to prey, haunt to political haunt, picking up, to begin with, the strong arguments of inflation tackled and interest rates brought down, then taking in the true road to recovery, through stimulation of growth, and the best industrial route to that recovery, through new technology; only then was youth employment, itself a small part of the overall employment problem covered in the paper, embraced, and this was done in positive terms, with the Government, indeed Margaret Thatcher herself, being cast in a vibrant and vital role, going out and getting half a million places for young people in industry and commerce. References to 'hope' and to 'the silver lining in the dark clouds of world recession' were delivered more slowly, in a softer, and suddenly more emotional voice. Only marginally so, but just enough to alter the tempo of the diatribe, turning it into nation-saving rhetoric.

It was followed, in reply to the question involving Francis Pym's remarks about not wanting a landslide, by a biting attack on the Labour Party's policies; 'I want as many Conservative candidates to win as we can possibly get. I believe that we are fighting the most extreme manifesto that's ever been placed before the electorate in Britain. It is State socialism rampant. I believe it will set out to change the whole of our society. I believe people do not want that change, and I believe the best way to indicate that is to vote Conservative for every Conservative candidate. Um, I think I could, er, handle a landslide majority.'

It was easy going from then on. It had, in fact, been easy until then. But the central challenge, coming in the middle of the carefully controlled half-hour series of exchanges, had provoked the most characteristic style of all, swooping, elliptical, selective, with the hammer-blows of emphasis giving an incomparable force and appeal to mundane sentiments and incomplete information. It had also been entirely positive. That miraculous capacity which Margaret Thatcher sustained throughout the general election of avoiding any negative admissions whatsoever was central to that first press conference and remained central from then on. Failures there had been; but they were the regrettable failures of sections of the British people, of vested interests like the trade unions, less frequently of management, but never of herself and of those virtues and actions for which directly she was standing, and on which she adopted an admirably resilient stance each morning.

*

Margaret Thatcher had escaped the real issues, of which there were several. Cynicism? 'We must show that we have some political imagination: that we are willing to salvage something, albeit second best, from the sheer waste involved. . . . This scheme needs to be aggressively marketed . . . if we are to sell this scheme effectively and get some credit for it. . . . It needs to be branded with a snappy title. . . .' (All from the memorandum by John Hoskyns on the CPRS Report.)

Lying? Denis Healey had been basically right on all his charges with the exception of his suggested CPRS forecast of over three million unemployed. The figure was implicit rather than explicit. But it was a complicated and 'political' form of lying, and it would need Jonathan Swift and the pages of *The Examiner* in order to study it fully enough. This, in turn, would have missed the point. She had more than survived the lame and feeble cross-questioning during her first press conference.

She had in fact completely dominated it. Briefly, at the beginning, Sir Geoffrey Howe had been given a total of three minutes in which to present a report on the economy which included a polite challenge to the Labour Party to come clean about the cost of their programme, reminding Michael Foot of his own words, that it would be 'a cruel deceit' for any party to campaign on an uncosted programme. They would have to have the figures. Howe suggested 'by Monday'. 'If he doesn't do it by that time then we're prepared to do it for him.'

Thereafter, Sir Geoffrey sat silent until, towards the end of the half-hour, the Williamsburg summit brought him in with further comment on world recovery. Patrick Jenkin contributed about the same amount of time, something over three minutes, in which the Industry Secretary offered his personal impressions of Industry's view of the Conservative Government. He was heard at the beginning, and on three further occasion, each of them for less than a minute.

This was to continue to be the pattern for the rest of the campaign. On that first day the only other person present on the low platform was the Conservative Party chairman, Cecil Parkinson, looking polished and very severe. He said nothing throughout, on that first day, just sat there, the cool, clean hero.

Even when Geoffrey Howe and Patrick Jenkin did come in with answers, Margaret Thatcher tended to add her own subsidiary reply or comment. There was a curious sense of *distancing* between her and them, as though her briefing had been separate from theirs (as it had), and therefore as though she represented a more fully armed threat to *them* as well as to everyone else. She followed on one issue dear to her heart, the Falklands. It came up by way of a question from a journalist from a Scottish newspaper which had received letters from families of dead Scots Guardsmen who had been buried, but over whose graves no memorial stones had yet been erected. She was clearly unaware of the background to the question, the relevance of which was unclear. But it certainly found a mark, and drew from her a touchy reference to the fact that 'normally all these complaints do come straight to me. I have received none.'

Had it been any other issue than the Falklands, the abstruse nature of the query would have earned the kind of disdainful dismissal on grounds of tedious irrelevance at which she is so good. Because it was the Falklands, and in spite of having no answer to the question, she declared that if anything was causing distress it would have to be put right.

As a half-hour expression of political style, the first press conference had presented the most important facets of character, and clothed them with issues, attitudes or prejudices. Her central quality of consistency was demonstrably present over all the main economic challenges 'for which this Government has the best set of policies and measures I think the world over'. International affairs, the Williamsburg summit, the Falklands, however glancingly, had been embraced, And her handling of Howe and Jenkin, together with her remarks about Francis Pym, had shown emphatically just how firmly she was in control.

*

Why, then, for those who were not partisan, was the occasion so *depressing*? Primarily because she was, at one and the same time so good and yet so lacking in relevance to the agonies of life being lived outside by millions of Britons. She was so good as a performer; with cracking conviction she had learnt her lines in a pageant of truly huge proportions, on the details of which immense and extravagant care had been expended. Nothing had been spared in terms of organisation, materials, lighting, music, a panoply of different acts to suit all tastes and ages. New and diverse extravaganzas were in reserve; changes in tempo had been thought out; and rank upon rank of clone-like chorus-lines imbued with a single message were available with an endlessly repeating 'routine'. But it was not about life. Some of the questions had been about life; they had actually recognised the magnitude of reality and the illusory quality of the answers. But the occasion itself had been artificial. Such occasions generally are. Across the road, in Transport House, a fairly knockabout routine had been running for several days; yet, as with theatre, differences of a deeper kind were manifest in the artificiality of everything about her: style, words, thought, tones, that swooping, emphatic, sincere evasion; that selective stress on positive achievement, most of it yet to be reached. She did not answer questions. Like a bad teacher, she came back with a voluble response, but on a different trajectory, even on a different subject at times. And the heavy emphasis, a conversational tone permanently in italics, was a form of camouflaged didacticism. She invited paper darts, morsels of chalks, practical jokes of the rubber cushion variety, objects precariously suspended above the half-open door. She did not get them of course, not even in the low level questioning; but the urge towards mischief produced the image and the expectation.

Senior Conservatives were reported as being upset at her 'headmistress' approach, following the interruption of Francis

Pym during the Wednesday launch of her party's manifesto. She had corrected him then about the level of discussions, if any, with Argentina, should formal hostilities come to an end. In his absence she corrected him again on Friday, at her press conference. He had said on television the previous night, 'landslides, on the whole, don't produce successful governments.' It had been a very silly comment for a senior government minister to make mid-way into an election campaign, whatever its truthfulness. And she had corrected this view very firmly, adding a remark about ex-chief Whips being 'very unusual people'. It was lost on few people that, as well as Francis Pym, Edward Heath belonged to the exclusive 'club'.

But, if anything, the exchanges indicated a determination to maintain the basically aggressive style which, while it may have been a matter of concern to unidentified 'senior Conservatives', was so central to her overall political character and public style as to be immutable. While examination of this did not arise at the press conference, it was raised later on Friday during the course of a BBC interview when Margaret Thatcher stoutly defended headmistresses, and their capacity to launch talented pupils upon successful careers. 'I had one myself. I was very, very grateful.' She had no intention of changing her campaign style. It would mean changing her character and outlook. Whatever the reservations within her own party, and among its senior but anonymous members critical of her, there was little evidence that her personal abrasiveness or dictatorial approach was necessarily causing doubt. She was the party's biggest asset, whatever the flaws, supposed or real. 'I am what I am,' she told her radio audience. 'And I'm too old to change now. . . . Yes, my style is one of vigorous leadership. Yes, I do believe in trying to persuade people that the things I believe in are the things they ought to follow.'

*

It could be said, indeed it was said, that both she and the Conservative Party managers of her campaign were reluctant to allow Margaret Thatcher to try persuading people about her beliefs in places other than those which gave her a high degree of protection; the following week's *Economist*, for example: 'Mrs Thatcher is confining her campaigning to gentle tours of the provinces, including safe Tory rural areas. Her strategists have decided that, with such a lead in the polls, there is no point in risking sorties to many of the potentially hostile industrial heartlands of the country. Some have been declared no-go areas by Tory managers. Wednesday found her in remote Norfolk villages and Thursday in the spa town of Harrogate.'

A comparable degree of caution was exercised about public meetings which she addressed. They were almost exclusively 'ticket-only' affairs, with careful audience-vetting, thus avoiding the kind of heckling which had once been a central characteristic of electioneering, but which, with the advent of television, had been adjudged embarrassing, at least with certain candidates. Margaret Thatcher fell clearly into a category of politician not brought up in the traditions of public meetings, open to all, or street corner heckling. Her abilities lay elsewhere. She could cope with a limited amount of spontaneous or unrehearsed attack; but her annoyance threshold was relatively low, and the response of her campaign managers was to programme her round, rather than through, such potential embarrassment.

The same applied to her campaign tours. Whether sloshing through mud in Cornwall, simulating an intense interest in micro-chips in Wiltshire, or tasting different flavours of marzipan in Mitcham, the essential atmosphere was false. Nor was this any different from her performance at press conferences, in the House of Commons at Prime Minister's Question Time, making a speech at a political meeting or a Conservative Party conference, answering Sir Robin Day, or telling the crowds outside Downing Street about the sacrifices made by 'our boys' in the South Atlantic. 'She's an actress. She has an image which she wants to project, something of queenliness. She is very conscious of the impression she is making.'*

There is an absurdity inherent in this form of campaigning, and it is treated correctly by journalists like Michael White of the *Guardian* and Frank Johnson of *The Time*, when they deal with it in comic terms. But there is a seriousness about it, as well, as serious as the make-believe of theatre. The local requirement, which is most often the winning of a marginal seat, is satisfied by the presence of the party leader, more or less irrespective of

---

*Nicholas Wapshott and George Brock: *Thatcher* London, 1983, p. 95. The words are attributed to a 'mandarin'.

what she says, so long as she treats the people seriously (whether employed or unemployed) and shows a grasp of local issues and the political terrain.

Nationally, however, it is a different matter. Since it is quite irrelevant where the Prime Minister is, because she will inevitably become the focus of media attention, the quayside in the Cornish fishing village of Padstow is as much part of the moving stage on which this consummate actress plays her part, as is the press conference room at Conservative Central Office. While there is an apparent absurdity in the British Prime Minister haranguing an 18-year-old unemployed Padstow youth called Peter Warne about the policy measures for youth employment which had occupied so much of the morning's press conference in London, the encounter was essentially more vivid, vital and relevant than the involved and elusive ellipsis of her earlier statement under pressure. The same ambivalence between absurdity and direct relevance applied also to details about the benefits of EEC membership to Britain's agriculture being spelt out to a Devonshire farmer among his friesian cattle, or the intricacies of the fishing policy to the men displaying lobster and dogfish for her inspection.

The conscious response, by journalists, was more to the absurd than the serious. Frank Johnson had the Prime Minister wearing 'green wellies', Julia Langdon, in the *Guardian*, had her in 'new black-with-white-soled wellies' and put Denis into the green ones. Ian Gow had no wellingtons at all, and remained in the farmyard. Much later it was revealed that Margaret Thatcher's wellingtons were in fact at Chequers, and that she was wearing her daughter's, which had been tried on for size on the train to Gatwick. Carol herself had striped bootees, 'clearly not designed for wearing outside SW1'.

It was a visit which emphasised the strictures made about her tour by the *Economist*. While Labour, with its extreme election manifesto, was the main enemy, the constituency for this first tour was one in which the Labour Party invariably lost its deposit, and had in 1979 secured only 3.2 percent of the vote, its worst performance in the whole of Britain. Perhaps it was an intended irony to choose it for the first campaign visit in an election in which the first target, indeed as it eventually transpired, the only target, was the Labour Party.

By the weekend of May 21-22, with the manifesto launched,

the first press conference negotiated, and the first campaign forays completed successfully, the Conservative Party had been launched by its leader with minimum damage sustained. Everything was 'on the table' as it were, more or less fully revealed; all manifestos, most documents, candidates, challenges, arguments and differences. And the overall effect was one of predictable victory for the Conservative Party. So much was this so, that the weekend saw rising speculation about Cabinet changes for the next five years. It must have been comforting, after one day in the fields of Cornwall, a single half-hour press conference, a well-publicised trip around her local supermarket in Finchley, where Carol paid the £11.94 bill, and the usual run of interviews and replies to questions from reporters, for the Prime Minister to be faced with such encouraging evidence of her potential success. She had convincingly dealt with 'everything known to British politics'. Everything is so busy here in Government, she seemed to be saying; all of us, in Stevie Smith's words, are galloping about, doing good.

CHAPTER SEVEN

The Raising of the Belgrano

Mrs Diana Gould of Bristol was not part of the rehearsed script. She had not been orchestrated as part of the Prime Minister's programme. She could not be avoided, or etched out. She was there, real and threatening, asking about lives and judgment and truth; and she was interested in these things rather than in performance or in winning. When, later in the campaign, the prime ministerial entourage came face to face with a related form of reality, a former sergeant of the Scots Guards, Steven Sherrett, who had fought through the Falklands Campaign taking part in the battle of Tumbledown Mountain, and had left the army but failed to get a job; when he presented himself outside the Elgin weaving mill, in the Grampians, in Moray, a marginal constituency, bearing a banner with the message on it 'Unemployed Falklands Hero', the word 'hero' crossed out, Margaret Thatcher avoided him. Her aides consulted together in tense concern, but advised against an encounter. There was something about the awful conjunction of the two problems that decided them; and, coming out of the press conference which had been held in the factory (always time for 'our boys' in the media), she waved to the crowd standing round him and said, 'We are very late.' She could not do the same with Mrs Gould of Bristol. And Mrs Gould of Bristol would not go away.

She was there, palpable and politically threatening, a member of the public recruited for BBC *'Nationwide'* programme, in which a public figure is directly confronted with both question and questioner, who has the right to follow up his or her interrogation. This Mrs Gould did.

'I think it could *only* be in Britain,' said Mrs Thatcher, 'that a Prime Minister was *accused* of *sinking* an *enemy ship* which was a danger to our navy. *My main motive* was to protect the *boys* in our *navy*. That was my main motive and I'm very proud of it.'

'Let me ask you this, Mrs Gould,' said Sue Lawley. 'What motive are you seeking to attach to Mrs Thatcher and her Government? Is it inefficiency, lack of communication? Or is it a desire for action, a desire for war?'

'It is a desire for action, and a lack of communication,' said Mrs Gould. 'Because giving those orders to sink the *Belgrano* when it was sailing *away* from our fleet, and *away* from the Falklands, was in effect sabotaging any possibility of any peace plan succeeding.'

Truth wrestled with fact, in that '*Nationwide*' exchange on May 24, and truth triumphed. Margaret Thatcher told a lie. Just one. But a lie, nonetheless, visible, inescapable, related to an issue which should have been part of the campaign, but had been hardly mentioned. And all one's judgments shifted, or should have shifted momentarily, just then.

Mrs Gould: 'Mrs Thatcher, why, when the *Belgrano*, the Argentinian battleship, was outside of the exclusion zone and actually sailing away from the Falklands, why did you give the orders to sink it?'

Margaret Thatcher: 'It was not sailing away from the Falklands. It was *in an area* which was a *danger to our ships*, and to *our people* on them.'

Then followed all the arguments, the changing of the rules, the questions of danger and threat, the course set for the vessel on 280 degrees, 'just north of west' from a position to the south-west of the Falkland Islands. She knew her stuff, Mrs Gould, and was not afraid of saying it. The blank relentless failure to connect, when two people are having a conversation with each other, but each looking at the other's face framed in a television screen, was made more startling by the urbane handling of it all by Sue Lawley. It was performance against reality, political skill against truth, fact against instinct. And it shook the edifice. Something deeper than the *Nationwide* hair-do, put in hot curlers at four o'clock that afternoon, was being demolished. And though the great architect of her image, Gordon Reece, flown back from his work for Armand Hammer, the man who had made vast fortunes from selling grain to Russia since the days of Lenin, was with her in the studio, it did not help. 'An example of the most crass nastiness and discourtesy shown to a Prime Minister on a television programme' was how Carol described Mum's ordeal, going on to quote at length from an old age pensioner's remarks, and not mentioning the *Belgrano* at all!

Politically, it did not matter. Her performance remained resolute, coming up to match the challenge offered by Mrs Gould. The facts were fired off like torpedoes, the face and eyes became more penetrative like radar equipment, and the ghosts and skeletons of 368 South American sailors were justified. 'We had *warned* at the end of April, we had *given warnings* that all ships in those areas, if they represented a *danger* to our *ships*, were vulnerable. When it was sunk, that ship which we had found, that ship was a *danger* to our *ships*. My duty was to look after *our* troops, *our* ships, *our* navy. And, my goodness me, I lived with many, many anxious days and nights.'

Mrs Gould remained unsatisfied. 'Mrs Thatcher, you started your answer by saying it was not sailing away from the Falklands. It was on a bearing of 280 and it was already west of the Falklands, so I'm sorry, but I can't see how you can say it was not sailing away from the Falklands—'

'When it was sunk—' said Mrs Thatcher.

'When it was sunk—' interrupted Mrs Gould.

'When it was *sunk*,' said Mrs Thatcher, with growing determination, 'it was a *danger* to *our* ships.'

'No, but you've just said at the beginning of your answer that it was *not* sailing away from the Falklands. And I'm asking you to correct that statement.'

She could not. Margaret Thatcher could not possibly correct that statement. She could not say that the *Belgrano* was sailing away from the Falklands, *and* she ordered *'our men'* to sink it. Even though it was the truth; even though it was on record already, from the commander of *Conqueror*, the nuclear submarine which had been tailing the *Belgrano* for some thirty hours before the rules were changed, the torpedoes fired, and the ship sunk.

Was the confusion itself deliberate? Mrs Thatcher replied to Mrs Gould: 'Yes, but it was *in* an area *outside* the exclusion zone, which I think is what you're saying is sailing away—'

'No, I'm not, Mrs Thatcher—'

'—Which was a danger to our ships—'

'Mrs Thatcher, I'm saying it was on a bearing of 280, which is just north of west. It was already west of the Falklands, and therefore nobody with any imagination could put it sailing other than away from the Falklands.'

'Mrs— I'm sorry, I forgot your name.'

'Mrs Gould,' said Sue Lawley.

'Mrs Gould,' said Mrs Gould.

But Margaret Thatcher went on without mentioning the name. She did not want Mrs Gould's name. She wanted time to think. She had not spent the mid-fifties as a lawyer at King's Bench Walk for nothing. 'When orders were given to sink it, and when it was sunk, *it was in an area which was a danger to our ships.* You accept that, do you?'

'No, I don't—'

'Well, I'm *sorry*, but you must accept—'

'No, Mrs Thatcher—'

'Well, you must accept that. When we gave the order, when we changed the rules which enabled them to sink Belgrano, the change of rules had been notified at the *end* of April. It was all *published*. That *any* ships which were a *danger* to ours within a *certain* zone wider than the *Falklands* were likely to be *sunk*. And *again* I do *say* to you, *my duty*, and I'm very proud we put it this way and adhered to it, was to *protect* the *lives* of the *people* in *our* ships and the enormous numbers of troops we had down there *waiting* for landings. I put that duty first. (Mrs Gould unsuccessfully tried to interrupt.) And when *Belgrano* was sunk, when *Belgrano* was sunk, and I ask you to accept this, she was in a position where she was a *danger to our navy*.'

Mrs Thatcher offered all the facts, but 'in about thirty years' time'. It was not good enough for Mrs Gould, but the Prime Minister insisted on telling her again, 'I lived with the responsibility for a very long time. I *answered* the *question, giving the facts. Not anyone's opinions.* But the *facts.* Those Peruvian peace proposals, which were only in *outline*, did *not reach London* until *after* the *attack* on the *Belgrano.* That is *fact* – I'm sorry, that is *fact*, and I'm going to *finish* – did not reach London until *after* the *attack* on the *Belgrano. Moreover*, we went on negotiating for *another* fortnight after that attack.'

The points put to Margaret Thatcher by Diana Gould were cold and deliberate; the answers she got were evasive. *Fact* comes only at the end, and is confined to one issue: the peace proposals. The only motive acknowledged by Margaret Thatcher was 'to protect the *boys* in our *navy.* That was my main motive, and I'm very proud of it.' The real motive for sinking the *Belgrano* and the facts surrounding that sinking, which were the central issues raised by the redoubtable Mrs Gould, are both deliberately and consistently ignored by Margaret Thatcher. And when *fact* is asserted strongly, as it is *solely* in connection with the Peruvian peace proposals, the crucial question of the whole exchange once again is ignored.

Motive and fact were invoked by Diana Gould; opinion trailed in afterwards. Motive and fact were belatedly taken up by Margaret Thatcher and distorted. The only acknowledged fact concerned the arrival of the outline report. Other facts follow 'in about thirty years'. Other motives are in the realm of the unthinkable.

*

Questions flood into the mind, like the pressure forcing the bulkheads in that ancient, decrepit vessel with its doomed cargo of life struggling with an engagement which made little sense. The newspapers, the day following the *Nationwide* programme, had the whole thing under control. Eight inches on page one of the *Daily Telegraph* headed '*Belgrano* decision defended'; the story in the *Daily Star* led with Mrs Thatcher's support for hanging, bringing in a reference to the *Belgrano* at the end, and suggesting that she 'rounded angrily on one viewer' (another case of forgetfulness about Mrs Gould's name?). Others came firmly to her defence, and then the matter dropped.

More than a week passed until, for the wrong reasons, and setting up the wrong priorities, the Labour Party turned its mind to the matter of the Falklands. Not until Wednesday June 1 did the war which had restored Margaret Thatcher's electoral fortunes become central to an election campaign in which it should have occupied an important position for several reasons. And even when it was raised first by Denis Healey, then by Neil Kinnock, what a disastrous mess they made of it. Clumsy, inept, choosing marginal points rather than the central question, trampling over susceptibilities and emotions which should not have been disturbed – the other ghosts of conflict from another hemisphere – they threw away a prize the weight of which had made Mrs Gould's arms ache as she held it out and was ignored.

Why was the Falklands War important? How had it become

taboo? Was not this an election on which, from the start, focus had been invited on issues? It was like an Irish general election; the unity of the country, and therefore the issue of Northern Ireland, is central, yet no one debates it. The same sensitivities surrounded the Falklands War.

Most puzzling of all, where was Michael Foot on the issue? It was one peculiarly appropriate to him, coming close, in the moral questions it raised, to the heart of his political character. The best book he ever wrote, because truest to his nature, human and political, was *The Pen and the Sword*. In it he dealt with the deepest and most permanent instincts in his being, not just as a politician, for he is no great shakes at that, but as a man of intellect and feeling and conviction. And it was a book about war whose theme is by no means far distant from the issue of the *Belgrano* raised by Mrs Gould. Yet more than a week later, more than three weeks after the calling of the general election, in spite of the fumbling and ill-judged intervention of the deputy Labour leader and of Neil Kinnock, nothing whatsoever had been said by the leader of the Labour Party. It was his job to address himself to this huge and awesome question, containing within it the certain seeds from which Margaret Thatcher was reaping, before his eyes and to his ultimate and total political annihilation, a victory which arguably she did not deserve. Worse still, if Mrs Gould had truth on her side, Margaret Thatcher was obtaining her victory as the result of a catastrophe, deliberate or accidental, which had precluded the kind of peace to which Michael Foot had dedicated his life.

Mrs Gould, the Falklands, the nature of war, defence, the sinking of the *Belgrano*, the expenditure of British taxpayers' money on the campaign and its subsequent defence burden for the islands, as well as its deployment in loans to Argentina, and its continued use of war materials, *some of which were finding their way to that country* — all of these things found wanting the man who had apostrophised Jonathan Swift, 'the prince of journalists', for his destruction of the Duke of Marlborough, Britain's greatest general, for the same sort of wastage, irrelevance and contradiction. The battle of Blenheim may have been a glorious victory; but whose interests did it serve?

Robin Oakley, in the *Daily Mail*, saw the 'coldly calculated attack' as indicative of Labour's growing desperation; the *Daily Express* political editor, John Warden, quoted 'election strategists' as seeing the twin onslaughts of Kinnock and Healey 'as a major blunder, and a measure of Labour's despair'.

If it had been a 'coldly calculated attack', a real issue might have found its way onto the general election stage. In the event, the reverse happened. Political party headquarters faced a storm of protest about the remark on glorying in slaughter; Margaret Thatcher refused any *Belgrano* inquiry; Denis Healey half-withdrew his attack; and the Alliance sat silent and smiling, as they contemplated their six-point gain in the opinion polls.

The press took up sharply opposed views. Two examples will suffice. Paul Johnson was a marked case of pro-Thatcher bias. Quite incorrectly, he claimed that Margaret Thatcher took more questions on the sinking of the *Belgrano* 'than on any other topic, and banged them back across the court with ferocious top-spin'.* He sat through a majority of the Smith Square press conferences. The only occasion on which the sinking of the *Belgrano* came in for consistent and sustained questioning was at the morning press conference following the remarks by Denis Healey and Neil Kinnock. The questions began just after 9.45, widening out to cover the sale of arms to Argentina, and ended by 9.58 when an American journalist suggested that everyone had heard enough, which provoked cries of 'Hear! Hear!', one of them from Paul Johnson himself. In his view Margaret Thatcher 'knows quite well that the overwhelming majority of British people (including most journalists) welcomed the sinking of the cruiser because it persuaded the rest of the Argentine fleet to stay in harbour for the duration and thus saved many lives'.

This is a correct, if somewhat bloodthirsty interpretation of the basic fact that the sinking of the *Belgrano* was militarily necessary, *even if the ship was returning to harbour*, in order to rescue a difficult task force operation from the decidedly uneven odds loaded against its success otherwise. And this view is supported by the concluding remarks in Simon Jenkins's article, 'The Truth about the *Belgrano*' which appeared in the same issue of the *Spectator*: 'The *Belgrano* was attacked because the British War Cabinet was coming near to running scared. It had no impact on the likelihood of peace, except possibly to enhance it. But the sinking had a dramatic impact on the course of the war. Had it not occurred and the enemy fleet not been terrified back to port,

---

* *Spectator*, June 11 1983.

the unmentionable might have happened. Mrs Thatcher's Falklands gamble might have failed. It was the turning point of the war.'

While all of this is true it neither proves nor disproves the 'extraordinary mythology' which Paul Johnson suggests had been constructed around the Falklands War by the Left. 'According to this, Thatcher, who desperately wanted a war in the Falklands, partly because she likes war anyway but chiefly because she needed one to boost her desperately sagging political popularity and keep herself in office, was terrified that the "Peruvian Peace Plan" would lead to a negotiated settlement. So she broke her own rules of engagement and ordered the *Belgrano* to be sunk, though at the time it was returning to harbour intending to take no further part in the affair. Thus, at a stroke, she torpedoed not only the cruiser but the peace talks too and so got her war – and her political dividends.' With the exception of the word 'broke', which should be 'changed', this brief outline is either true or unprovable. Yet Paul Johnson's judgment is that 'every single element in this fantasy is false, and has been shown to be false over and over again'.

The logical comparison is the *New Statesman*, which addressed itself to the *Belgrano* issue in its main editorial on May 20, and published further short detailed articles on May 27, June 3 and June 10. They were factual, in as far as facts were ascertainable, and after that the speculation was logical enough. The official story had been constantly changing, the paper said, 'usually a sign that an account of events is being manufactured after the event in order to meet political requirements'.

What the paper stressed, in the mixed area of available fact, was that the talks between Haig and the Peruvian president, Bellande, *began* on May 1, and that the purpose of the two men was to act as brokers between Argentina and the United Kingdom by endeavouring to find a peaceful solution to the crisis. Between May 1 and May 2 sufficient progress was made to lead to a seven-point draft for an agreement. At this stage the Foreign Minister, Francis Pym, who flew to Washington on May 1 and gave a press conference there, said that current hostilities, which meant the air attacks, mainly on Port Stanley, were intended to concentrate the collective mind of the junta on a peaceful settlement: 'No further military action is envisaged at the moment, except to keep the exclusion zone secure.' Yet the order to sink the *Belgrano*, without the involvement of Francis Pym, was given from Chequers on May 2, and the torpedoes were fired later that day. Margaret Thatcher's spirited but highly selective presentation of the facts about the *Belgrano* being sunk before the peace proposals reached London is completely irrelevant. Talks begun one day are not deliberately pre-empted the next, and in so crude a fashion, unless the motive is equally deliberate *against* settlement.

In the three subsequent issues of the *New Statesman*, Commander Wreford-Brown's reported claim that he detected the *Belgrano* 24 hours before the Government said he did is reported, along with an outline of exchanges and contradictions which support the theory of a set of rigged replies; Diana Gould's questioning provoked a simple enough heading to the story on June 3: 'PM lies about *Belgrano*', with the emphasis on the illogical sequence of international exchanges on May 1 and 2; and then in the issue of June 10 the *New Statesman* reminded its readers of a significant fact: Francis Pym's assertion on *Newsnight* that 'he was not consulted over the sinking of the *Belgrano* and that he did not report the Peruvian peace proposals to London until after the sinking'.

Nothing in Sir Nicholas Henderson's lengthy essay in the *Economist* (12 November 1983), the latest and fullest account of the diplomatic background, resolves any of the essential political points. If anything, it serves to emphasize the truly amazing lack of consultation between the Prime Minister and the Foreign Secretary at a time when negotiations were potentially active and when naval action could well have been postponed; certainly, until the *Belgrano* changed course back towards the British targets. Such statements in that essay as 'I do not believe that anybody in the Government ever preferred the military route', simply beg questions; they do not answer them. What is clear is that the War Cabinet did *not* consider the Peruvian seven points, and did not consult with Pym, a member of it, Haig, Bellande or Henderson before ordering the sinking of the *Belgrano*.

Margaret Thatcher 'won' the *Belgrano* confrontation, and turned the wider issue of the Falklands War to her advantage. She did so because she was better than any of the opposition, either political or non-political. She was well-rehearsed in the real facts, and knew more of them than did anyone else. She did not reveal them, and there was a legitimacy and precedent for this which was also a substantial political advantage. She deployed emotion aggressively, and in place of logic and of truth. She declared that her heart was in the right place, and she was believed. It was a political triumph the true nature of which will never be known.

Something was wrong here, and it was not just with politics. Winston Churchill had said, of Marlborough's times, 'these were not days when public men could afford to disdain the Press.' Yet here, in the cold, wet, early summer of 1983, with Mrs Gould asking her flat, logical questions, *where* was Grub Street? *Where* was Michael Foot? What one ponders upon is not the same judgment which Swift made of Marlborough; nor is it the judgment one might wish to make about the wisdom, justice or set of principles at stake in the Falklands war; nor is it about the political sense, or the party gain, which might have guided poor Michael Foot, 'not waving', as he seemed to have been at the beginning of the campaign, but almost certainly drowning now; it was about truth.*

Confronted with Britain engaged in war, that activity which he reviled most of all, and on which, like Margaret Thatcher, he had his own kind of consistency, a consistency which had coloured strongly his political and his intellectual life, he abandoned his principle in favour of a negative form of opportunism. Would it have been counterproductive politically to make the Falklands an election issue? When everything one does is counterproductive, the freedom of choice becomes unlimited, surely?

*

The *Nationwide* programme came mid-way through the general election, on Tuesday May 24. It exposed a lie. It exposed also certain fundamental weaknesses in the case made for the war, at the time, and in the subsequent pursuit of the war. It suggested the possibility of a variety of conspiracies, within the Government, between the Government and the armed forces, between the Governments of Britain and the United States. It partly unfolded the following sinister interpretation of events, involv-

---

* *Private Eye* depicted Michael Foot on its cover, with his dog on Hampstead Heath, waving his walking stick; the caption: 'NOT WAVING, BUT DROWNING.'

The Raising of the Belgrano

ing, first, motive; then action; then events; then the manipulations, concealment and false presentation of facts:

First, motive: in early 1982 Margaret Thatcher's standing as premier was at an all-time personal low, and she enjoyed the unenviable reputation of being the most unpopular British Prime Minister of the century. She was incontrovertibly in danger of electoral defeat, no matter when she went to the country, if her own party did not remove her from leadership first. In such circumstances one goes to war. Domestic trouble is always eased by uniting the country against a common enemy.

If this motivation was clear enough as far as Britain was concerned, it was also clearly apparent that it aligned itself with American motives internationally. The United States were concerned about Europe, and specifically about Britain, in defence terms. The greatest potential ally Washington could have was Margaret Thatcher in control of a clear majority, and therefore with a five-year mandate to implement favourable defence and nuclear strategy policies which were already, from 1979 onward, closer than any alternatives within Britain to the interests and objectives of the Reagan administration, and closer than any other European major power. There was, therefore, as strong a United States motivation for the recovery of Margaret Thatcher's electoral fortunes as there was within the British administration.

This, in turn, raises what is referred to in Whitehall and elsewhere as 'the conspiracy theory'. Put simply, it suggests the the *Belgrano* was sunk to pre-empt the Peruvian or any further peace initiatives, to deprive the negotiations of that reality which derives from a deliberate holding-back to the limited level of hostilities represented by the bombing of Port Stanley, and to turn these minor hostilities into irreversible bloodshed on a major scale. As it was, the *Belgrano* went down slowly, and *only* 368 died. It could have been a casualty list close to the total of deaths for the whole war. While the sinking of the *Belgrano* becomes, therefore, a crucial link in the chain of events, identified, relentlessly questioned, and then written about as such by Tam Dalyell MP, an equal if diffuse attention had to be paid to the lengthy period of time covered by the Franks Committee of Privy Counsellors in their 'Falklands Islands Review', published in January 1983.

A more detailed account of this, raising also a number of other issues, among them the question of Anglo-Irish relations which played a small but crucial part, is the subject of a later chapter. What is important in the context of the general election is how it was handled as an issue.

Margaret Thatcher had said, from the very beginning, that she wanted the general election to be based on issues. Faced with a major issue, if not *the* major issue of her political career, related to 'the resolute approach', 'making Britain great again', and incidentally recovering her reputation, she was severely embarrassed, out of the blue, by a persistent and completely unknown interrogator from Bristol. And her response was to avoid the issue, resort to emotionalism, tell a lie, and express amazement at the exercise of that right to free speech which she was there to protect.

Much later, we were to learn of the quite extraordinary admission made by Michael Foot privately to Robin Day that he did not regard the Falklands as an election issue, perhaps the most telling revelation of all of Foot's political innocence. He failed to distinguish that he was the deciding factor in this because he failed also to distinguish between the Falklands as a legitimate and a just war and the Falklands as an issue about which Margaret Thatcher had, and still has, a number of very important questions that she will not answer.

There is no doubt that the Cabinet was derelict in its responses to events leading up to the Argentinian invasion, precipitate in its subsequent responses to that invasion, and at best questionable in the degree of consultation and reticence with which it handled the war itself. To be ruling it out, as an election issue, a year later was an irresponsible approach, and indicative of a failure to recognise the degree to which political issues can and should be separate from a national one when the question of power is paramount.

In the precise electoral context which was concerned with retaining power, and therefore with surviving such embarrassing encounters, Margaret Thatcher emerged relatively unscathed, if bruised and angry, from the *Nationwide* studio. What mattered more than that, and more than any 'palpable hit' by Mrs Diana Gould herself, was the subsequent reaction. By any standards the balance of advantage was finely weighed. The Prime Minister had given considerable expression to sentiments of sacrifice and dedication – her own and those of 'our boys' –

and it was likely that as many of her viewers felt outrage as they did uneasiness. But the critical issue was media and Labour Party reaction. The former, as we have in part seen, was limited and not very objective. The latter bordered on the crass. Having delayed until the final week of the campaign, Neil Kinnock, on Wednesday June 1, called for a *Belgrano* inquiry. Denis Healey accused Margaret Thatcher of 'glorying in slaughter', and of 'wrapping herself in the Union Jack'.

The decision to raise the Falklands issue was correct and overdue. The Conservatives were rattled by it. It coincided with the moderate growth in support for Alliance, and the prospect, still at that stage fairly remote, of a combination of factors depriving the Government of an overall majority. At Margaret Thatcher's press conference the following morning, Thursday June 2, concern was expressed by more than one of her aides at the impact Denis Healey in particular might have had. They need not have worried. Kinnock had chosen the wrong issue, and Healey was using the wrong words. It was all right for Diana Gould to single out and persist on a single absolutely crucial event. It looked like a form of panic to be returning to it more than a week later, having let it and all the related detail of the issue of the Falklands lie fallow for the previous three weeks. In such circumstances the only possible approach was a broad and concerted analysis and questioning of the massively escalating costs and the even more massive risks of the whole episode, in the context, not just of the *Belgrano*, but of the fairly lamentable story outlined in the Franks Report. And all of this should have been presented with an icy deliberation and in entirely unemotional language, as a genuine and serious counter-attack, related to an overall electoral strategy, or at least appearing to be so related.

What happened instead was that the ostensibly unco-ordinated outbursts from the two leading Labour Party spokesmen cancelled each other out.

CHAPTER EIGHT

'Shooting a Dead Horse'

Margaret Thatcher began the final week of the campaign more sure of victory than she had been at any time during it, or indeed at any time since 1979, when, in her first conference speech as Prime Minister, she directed Conservatives to think differently: 'It is not the first hundred days that count. . . . It is the first five years, and the next five years after that. We have to think in terms of several Parliaments.' By the final weekend before the poll she was already being advised to think in terms of the next Parliament, and more specifically in terms of her Cabinet. Speculation about who might be dropped, who promoted, and who brought in, was combined with the dismissal of Michael Foot. The *Sunday Telegraph*'s page-one lead on June 5 was 'Labour has "hell of a job," says Foot', with the strap-line above, 'Polls show Alliance is creeping up.' The paper could afford to delegate to the body of the story (written by its Political Correspondent, George Jones) the fact that all the main opinion polls were showing a Conservative lead of between 14 and 19 percent, and that this translated into a predicted Conservative majority over all other parties in the next Parliament of between 150 and 200 seats.

Only a catastrophe could change that. The Conservative Party's campaign had worked supremely well. The middle period had been disturbed by the awkward issue of the *Belgrano*, and had also produced the initial embarrassment of leaked documents which revealed for a time the somewhat cynical way in which employment schemes were viewed. In both instances the two-way impact of the controversies had a cancelling-out effect. The underlying difficulty of raising the Falklands at all was augmented by the inept handling by the Labour Party, and the real issues were not discussed. On unemployment, the basic belief that such solutions as there were lay more firmly within the framework of Conservative strategy outweighed the impact of an ill-sustained suggestion of cynicism and concealment.

The success for Margaret Thatcher of the final week began with the *Panorama* interview with Sir Robin Day, and ended with the important decision to change the emphasis in the final phase of the Saatchi and Saatchi advertising campaign. Both were 'successes' in the negative sense. The switch in advertising reflected the failure of the Alliance to achieve its promised breakthrough; and it was Day's failure, as much as Margaret Thatcher's success, which turned the *Panorama* encounter, about which she was 'apprehensive', into something 'positive'.

Day's confession, following the *Panorama* interview, that he had 'failed', could be taken as an epitaph for the fourth estate as a whole, and in particular for its performance during the fourteen national press conferences which Margaret Thatcher had chaired in so dominant a fashion. 'I thought I handled it badly,' Day said. 'I failed to ask a number of important questions to which the viewers were entitled to have answers.'*

After the *Panorama* programme, many people commented on how good it had been. Christopher Chataway rang Robin Day to congratulate him. Ludovic Kennedy said it was quite brilliant. Others did the same. But the stress was laid on the performance, not the content; Margaret Thatcher calling him 'Mr Day' underlined the real failure, which was one of combat. Freedom of speech combined with the real privilege of exercising it against the most powerful person in the country, had produced no new set of perceptions about her. She had not been made uncomfortable, or effectively revealed as evasive, defective, dishonest, weak, uncertain, inadequate, shallow, superficial. Quite the reverse; it was she who had shown up extensive defects in Robin Day. And he was, in the view of the *Sunday Times*, 'the key media figure in the television election'. The paper went so far as to assign another not inconsiderable journalist, Simon Winchester, to do a lengthy piece entitled 'A Week in the life of a Day' which was published in the June 5 issue of the paper, the last before polling day.

In his public 'confession' of having let down the British people, he was effectively countering the kind of questioning

---

* The *Times*, June 2 1983.

about his performance which truth requires. His was not just failure to ask important questions; it was a failure on the assembly of the facts, some of which he got lamentably wrong, the framing of the interrogation, the adequate studying of her personality and technique and, most important of all, the psychological failure of simply underestimating her. His gruff, avuncular 'let's not split hairs about statistics' approach simply fell down in the face of her single-minded determination to defeat him by splitting all the hairs she could. He put to her the principles of middle-of-the-road moderation, balance between 'wets' and 'dries' within the Conservative Party, the idea of consensus inherent in a modest rather than a landslide majority, and the possibility that the Conservative manifesto concealed harsher intentions. She rejected him on each count. She did not even toy with the idea of meeting him midway on that common ground into which television interviewers endeavour to invite their guests. By the time he reached the contentious issue of prescription charges, only four minutes into the encounter, he was fumbling with the almost amateur phrase, 'I know what you're going to say', while she was calmly advising him, 'Let me give you the quotation . . .'.

He repeatedly failed to control or direct the interview. He was unable to make her answer questions, mainly because he appeared not to have studied her answering technique, which is evasive in the extreme. When precision suits her, she deploys it well, with quotations, particularly of details. But when vagueness suits, or outright evasion, then they are deployed. Day accused her of having 'a policy of high unemployment'. He had no grounds for such accusation, and should not have made it. 'There is no such policy', said Margaret Thatcher, and she *may* have been right.

He suggested that her Government had responsibility for the unemployed. It was put to her interrogatively. Just as she had picked up the parallel question at her first press conference, and used it so impressively then, she did the same with Day, and entered on a long and sustained plea on behalf of her performance, punctuated by brief interjections by him, most of them unsuccessful in either interrupting or redirecting her flow of words.

At the end of fifteen minutes, in what was beginning to look very much like professional panic, Sir Robin Day raised the detailed substance of the Government document on employment. He got his facts wrong, identified a paragraph in it incorrectly, claimed that it said one thing and was corrected by Margaret Thatcher reading out what it did say, and was left re-directing the exchanges between them with a pathetic 'Anyway?' It gave her the opportunity to deliver her 'Good News' list, which she did, followed by a similarly positive response to his challenge that she had achieved nothing at Williamsburg on world unemployment. She brought down his cost of the unemployed to the exchequer, a figure of £15, £16, £17 billion, he was far from sure, to a precise £5 billion, the different ingredients of which she gave, and added, 'I can't stand false, phoney, distorted figures' in a fireside kind of voice, as though deploring dust on the piano or rubbish dropped in the streets. And she made it seem, not as if Sir Robin was purveying such figures, but more as if the two of them were in it together as innocent victims of a statistical conspiracy conducted somewhere else.

He did not accept that offer of conciliation but claimed, first, that he was quoting widely accepted figures, and then added, 'We can't have an argument about statistics.' Gently, she pointed out that it was he who was responsible for the wildly erroneous facts. Defence, NATO, nuclear disarmament, capital punishment, on each she convincingly held her own. In a rag-bag at the end came the fate of the 'wets'. She hardly deigned to answer; she was not prepared even to accept that they existed.

It was a sad moment. Robin Day was indeed a 'key media figure' in the election, and both on television and radio had been effective in other circumstances. He simply underestimated Margaret Thatcher, imagining that she would play according to the 'soft' rules of such encounters which he had worked to such advantage in morning radio programmes, on *The World at One*, and in the evenings. Such an approach would have been inconsistent with the public character she was selling to the British people and would have meant answering questions, some at least of which were embarrassing. She wasn't there for that. As in everything else, she was there to win.

The decision to change advertising strategy came four days after the Robin Day interview, and marked that point when there must have been fairly overwhelming conviction that victory was assured. On the Tuesday of that week, May 30, the Conservative

Party's advertising agents, Saatchi and Saatchi, had placed a £75,000 order for three pages of advertising in the *Sunday Times*, with similar commitments in other papers. The advertisements were separate, one each covering the Labour Party, the Alliance, and the Conservative Party, all of course placed at the Conservative Party's expense, and all designed to encourage Conservative support. The page devoted to the Alliance, for example, contained two sentences only: 'Vote Alliance if . . . 1. You can guess what their policies are. 2. You don't mind Labour getting in by accident.' The rest of the page was left blank.

On Friday June 3, the order was cancelled. An order made two weeks previously, for a two-page advertisement listing the 15-points 'will-and-testament' critique on the Labour Party, was reinstated, and appeared on pages 22-23 in the main news section of the paper on June 5. No reference was made to the Alliance. Public opinion polls, and the private ones done for the Conservative Party, were registering a clear and emphatic message, that the SDP/Liberal Alliance had failed to make the necessary breakthrough. As opponents, they were irrelevant. The *Sunday Times* put that breakthrough at 30 percent. Even Labour were failing, more often than not, to reach that magic figure. But Labour, in its own heartlands, could still command substantial support and seats. What would have been serious – a genuine, substantial and sustained climb by the SDP and Liberal parties – had not happened. And while David Steel was reported to be jubilant in the morning papers of Friday, June 3, the facts provided insufficient evidence for more than modest and temporary pleasure at a statistical gain of some six points, mainly at the expense of Labour. The details, published that morning, were: Gallup (for the *Daily Telegraph*) Conservative 47.5 percent, Labour 28 percent and Alliance 23 percent; Marplan (for the *Guardian*) Conservatives 47 percent, Labour 30 percent, Alliance 22 percent; Harris (for *TV Eye*) Conservatives 46 percent, Labour 28 percent, Alliance 24 percent.

By lunchtime on Friday the decision that the Alliance challenge had failed was transmuted into the cancellation and reordering of advertisements. The Labour Party was enemy number one. It was the target. In such circumstances, the eventual £50,000 spent with the *Sunday Times* for two full pages, and the similarly vast sums spent elsewhere, looked a bit like overkill.

It is a measure, not of her confidence, but of her lack of confidence, that Margaret Thatcher maintained throughout the election campaign a self-protecting remoteness. It was done positively, and with skill. But it was done from an apprehensive standpoint. She also did it while at the same time being readily available, professionally. She answered questions, was interviewed, met the people, made speeches, and was mildly heckled, yet she managed to immunise herself more or less completely from serious challenge to her views.

The essence of what Margaret Thatcher was offering can be readily summarised. Her presentation of herself, her government, her party and her performance in power during exactly four years depended upon claiming the following achievements: she had stabilised the British economy, and brought it under control – 'restored to an even keel' was her phrase; she had improved Britain's defences and asserted that the exercise of them was real; she had demonstrated international leadership; she had raised the maintenance level of law and order; she had rolled back the frontiers of the state, removing Government controls and expanding the private sector's self-expression; she had reduced tax; she had encouraged enterprise, in microtechnology particularly, and also in small industries; she had maintained the social service structures on which the people universally depend; she had initiated trade union reforms.

This, in brief summary, was the basic record of four years. It was offered, with (strategic and tactical) good sense, as an unfinished job. 'We have to think in terms of several parliaments.' It was consistent with what had been promised four years earlier. It therefore answered the primary requirement in Margaret Thatcher's political character, that the essential consistency in her personality should be reflected in the 'good works' for which she claimed overall responsibility.

But it had also to lie as much in the future as in the past. There are dangers in being consistent, particularly if one completes a programme. Clement Attlee did that, and undermined his own relevance for the future. Churchill had done the same immediately before. Both had offered success in two sharply differing situations, and had delivered what they promised. But they had neglected to pay sufficient attention to a dominant human expectation, which is concerned with what lies ahead, thinking instead that past performance is rewarded. It is not. Gratitude had little place in politics, and none in the pursuit of power.

A job completed in politics – and it rarely happens – carries with it certain dangers; success can prejudice the hold on power almost as much as failure, whereas being midway between the two can offer the foundation for a convincing electoral platform. And this had been successfully attempted in Margaret Thatcher's case.

She had offered the public a four-year record in power, under nine broad headings, on which her campaign had been constructed. And, if the opinion polls were right, the public was more than ready to buy the package. Because of this the questions had ceased to be 'Was it real?', 'Was it right?, 'Would it work?' or even, 'Was it truthful?' They had become academic, for the time being anyway.

*

The biggest confrontation of philosophies within the economy, the point where key election documents may be said to have clashed, and where the very fundamentals of Britain's industrial society seemed under examination and threat, was covered by the Conservative Party emphasis on enterprise, and the expression of this in terms of micro-technology, together with the encouragement of, and special provisions for, small businesses and new businesses. Any detailed analysis of the kinds of places in which Margaret Thatcher deployed her intensely serious and exhaustive interest in how things are made and sold, would present a fairly bizarre picture of where the industrial giant which once was Britain had arrived in the early 1980s. Knitwear factories, manufacturers of dump trucks, makers of breakfast cereals and of marzipan, all received determined and positive scrutiny. But numerically they were equalled, if not surpassed, by the Prime Minister's pet form of industrial enterprise, euphemistically grouped under the collective title: high technology. 'Today was a "high tech" day for the Prime Minister,' writes Carol Thatcher in her *Diary of an Election* for Friday May 27, and briefly details the fact of no less than five visits to 'micro-electronic, digital, quantisied television and computer colour-matching factories'.

One of the factories was Racal Research in Reading, a top manufacturer of walkie-talkie radios, part of a group with a £644 million turnover. It suited Margaret Thatcher's purpose in outlining a policy option: 'I think that the fact that we're going into science-based industries gives countries like ours a new phase in opportunity. We're good at this, not merely good, we're brilliant at fundamental research, we're brilliant at invention. We hope that by being here today we're advertising you to the rest of the world.' It was, of course, a very nice thing to be doing.

It was a piece of truly accidental irony that Denis Healey should have chosen the same day on which to emphasise the opposite side of the industrial coin when he spoke of the Prime Minister's 'dictatorship by dole': 'Margaret Thatcher has imposed a dictatorship on the British people, dictatorship by dole and fear and poverty. Poverty is now tied, very much like law and order, to the growing number of unemployed.'

He was speaking of the great gulf that existed between the clean, smooth progress of high technology enterprises in places like Newbury and Reading, and the old industrial cities like Newcastle or Hull with high unemployment, where Britain's dirty, scruffy, old industry, on which wealth had once depended, struggled to survive.

The application of the market economy, together with 'the rolling back of the frontiers of the state', had both Healey's dark side to it as well as Thatcher's light one. The unarguable logic is cruel as well.

*

Another Conservative Party press conference ends and journalists make their way out. It is towards the end of the campaign. The crush is orderly, the pace slow. It is quiet, too, in an almost embarrassed way, made worse by the talkative exceptions, one of whom, day after day, has relentlessly buttonholed complete strangers – if there are ever 'complete strangers' in the media – in order to explain, with noisy and intense passion, how closely what was happening in Britain in 1983 compared with events in Europe in the thirties. It adds to the embarrassment, emphasises the prevailing restraint on opinion. Then a girl working for a broadcasting team says to one of her colleagues: 'It's bloody terrifying!' The colleague nods, but his agreement is at heart noncommittal. At best he wants to discourage further observation about the nature of this terror which has so clearly failed to seize upon the phlegmatic men and women stalking forth.

It is difficult to work out. 'Terrifying' seems too grand a word. Working it out is not necessary, of course. This is a chance remark by a girl who looks young enough to be a first-time voter, and angry enough about her job or her family or her home town to forget momentarily that it is democracy she is labelling as terrifying. Yet the urgency sticks. It is a blind expression of frustration and rage, aimed indiscriminately, not at Margaret Thatcher and her ministers, not at the journalists, but at the event: *'It's* bloody terrifying!'

As is always the case the journalists, busy men and women with urgent jobs to do, and for fear of being either wrong or banal, keep silent; and such comments, all too audible, awkward for those expected to reply as well as those who overhear, jar on that muffled silence.

That same atmosphere which prevails at the end of class, or as one emerges from a lecture, is dominant; some impertinence or witticism seems in order, is even provoked by the awkward, deeper embarrassment of not being able or willing to make judgments. There is a sharper, more apt comparison: the packed throng, moving slowly in a crush towards the door is not unlike the guilty audience leaving a Soho cinema after watching blue movies, concerned that they might meet someone they know, draw attention to themselves, have to answer some ribald or inapt comment. The embarrassment of collective will and purpose, all knowing that we were there for the same purpose, all ashamed that it had somehow been a failure, a dreadful mistake, an aberration, a slightly shameful exercise in self-gratification which in the end had been unsatisfying, was repeatedly the feeling immediately in those minutes after ten each morning which it took to get back to the fresh air of Smith Square, and was particularly so on that particular morning.

Was it the sense of failure that was terrifying? Either we had failed, or she was perfect; and as well as being perfect, invincible. Yet where was the success? The press had even failed to gain any kind of consent to the idea that the Conservative Party Youth Rally on the Sunday, with Kenny Everett joking about 'kicking Michael Foot's stick away', and 'bombing

Russia', had somehow overstepped some increasingly ill-defined and vanishing set of standards or restraints. Was she completely impregnable?

*

The final week had been one of failure and embarrassment. It had been a long and continuous 'blue' movie, the colour political rather than moral. And the blueness was everywhere during that final week, pervasive, triumphant, already victorious.

It induced a shifting of gear. Margaret Thatcher changed her make-up. the tone was more muted, the texture softened. She altered her vocabulary. The language of war was replaced by the images of peaceful conquest. Without too much humiliation a defeat was being inflicted. Deep within her own past experience, part of the reality that nothing in her political career had ever been easy still provoked an aggressive desire to win as convincingly as possible; and this in turn made her cautious of any suggestion that her supremacy was assured. It was this that Robin Day had underestimated. Nevertheless it *was* assured, and an altered strategy that looked forward a little into the future, and offered a more positive set of objectives was allowed, now that the end was in sight.

Her gladiatorial nature still required combat, but in the last week it had been narrowed down to an enemy more fearsome in a way than the Labour Party, but at the same time a post-electoral enemy: the trade union movement. And it was trade union reform which became the issue the Conservative Party sought to pursue, particularly in the closing stages. Pursue it they did. While Margaret Thatcher was not directly the protagonist, it was clear to everyone how much she favoured Norman Tebbit as her chosen champion in this area.

Tebbit had already been dominant in press conferences, notably on Wednesday June 1, when he had roundly attacked Labour's policy for keeping young people on in full-time education, and promoted as an alternative the Youth Training Scheme. But on Friday, June 3, he was brought in by her for more fundamental work. She seemed to do so with a degree of confidence in his ability not displayed up to then in the campaign, and not shown so overtly in respect of any other person. Norman, good for the chop-logic of such debate, had prepared effective material for his brief talk. Hanging up on an easel to the right-hand side of the press conference platform were guideline quotations: 'We make it as difficult as we possibly can for people to contract out of paying the political levy' was from Gavin Laird of the AUEW, taken from the *Financial Times* of March 28 1983. Norman was nothing if not thorough. The choice quotations were brought up with a fuller list of plum items: 'Get rid of the crazy Left before they get rid of you,' Sid Weighell had said, on January 4 1983, quoted from the *Daily Mail*; and Frank Chappell, reported in the same newspaper of September 13, 1982: 'I believe that the single reform which would give the greatest benefit to the trade union movement is the provision of secret ballots for the election of its leaders.'

Norman was going to go further than that, however. Though in his list of quotations under the heading 'strike ballots' he could not present a reputable trade unionist proposing secrecy for the decision in favour of industrial action on the payment of the political levy, he had that and more in mind on the morning in question.

Margaret Thatcher was in ripping form. To the surprise of everyone, a question was directed at the Conservative Party Chairman, Cecil Parkinson. His jaw, pink and clean-shaven, which had been angled at the press more or less immovably for the previous ten or so press conferences, began to move in answer to a question about accepting a secret ballot for his own election as Chairman of the Conservative Party. He replied swiftly and with commendable certitude that he was selected by the Prime Minister and appointed by her, and that she got her authority from the members of the party.

'That's a super answer!' said Margaret Thatcher, and there was much laughter. Opening gambit. It was time to strip for action. Cameras were rolling. Norman started in on the liability of the trade unions in law for damages. His leader listened and watched him, approvingly. When he came to a stop, she said: 'Are you convinced? Would you like him to go on for two minutes?'

It was faintly threatening, a trifle embarrassing. As always, the press are profoundly put out when asked questions.

Norman went on for a good deal longer than two minutes, ranging coldly through a number of different political positions which the Government might adopt. He was proposing, he said, a series of step-by-step changes. And that gaunt face which conceals a most able and logical mind, unexpressive, perhaps deliberately, of its flexibility and range, continued to stare out balefully at the packed audience.

He moved from positions to Acts. He knew them well. He was a convinced performer. The '71 Act, and the '72 Act, and the '80 Act were displayed for their virtuous necessity, and the fact that they had led to a marked decline in violent, massed and unlawful secondary picketing. We don't want legal confrontation, he told us; we want fair play and good relations. He had an audience convinced of the need for fair play and good industrial relations, and a lot more of it. And its relevance to unemployment? 'Enormous,' said Norman. And he explained how a militant approach to industrial relations, with an emphasis on the strike threat, undermined jobs. He tapped his list of quotations, reminding us of Terry Duffy: 'I do believe tragically that in the British car industry we seem to be arguing while stopping work, while other nations seem to be working while arguing.'* Norman was going to change that, because it was putting off investors and reducing the kind of job creation we all needed. It was damaging our competitiveness.

He launched into another long, flat disquisition into the implications of the 1913 Act, and the effect of proposed changes on the Labour Party, the trade union movement and the people. The effect on his own party was implicit, and he was more than ready to consult with the TUC. Already it was after a quarter to ten; half of the press conference had been given over to Norman's demonstration of positions and Acts. Yet it was conducted under the admiring gaze of Margaret Thatcher who, on most mornings, preferred to look through her notes while ministers spoke, and the relentless clatter of camera shutters went on in front of her.

'I wouldn't want to be accused of shooting a dead horse,' said Norman, referring to the whole trade union movement without enthusiasm, and grimly surveying his audience. It provoked the next question, about the *Belgrano*.

His performance prompted a repeat on the Monday. But his role was passive the second time. He was there as a symbol rather than as a performer. The emphasis was on Geoffrey Howe, and how 'the cyclical indicators were all pointing upwards'. It

---

* Quoted from the *Daily Mail*, March 30 1983.

made Norman look less gaunt. He and the Chancellor and Margaret Thatcher had 'no intentions that are not disclosed in the manifesto'. There were no broader plans, no hidden costs, no reckless promises; all would operate in response to market forces; they would dictate mortgages, interest rates, growth. Would it be up to the Government to cut expenditure, or raise taxes, or both, at any time? Yes, said the Chancellor, but we will operate within our declared policies. It was at that moment that Margaret Thatcher seemed to be offering Norman an encouraging word: 'Your turn will come, Norman,' perhaps? It did not. Instead, Cecil Parkinson's jaw came into action again as he talked about Labour's heartlands, and the Conservative Party's ethnic policies.

This was at Margaret Thatcher's penultimate press conference. She spent Tuesday morning in the BBC *Morning Call* studio with Robin Day, and then, on Wednesday, June 8, she led the same seven-man team that had launched the manifesto three weeks before back onto the blue-draped stage for the concluding series of exchanges. Norman couldn't express warmly enough how much he had enjoyed the election. It had been particularly interesting because of the reluctance of trade unionists to take part.

*

That was the calm beginning to a strange final day. Carol Thatcher called it 'a kind of bonus day', in which 'the sun and the sea featured, and there was the added excitement of rides in helicopters, a trendy new observation aircraft (me only), and a hovercraft.' The first of these 'excitements' brought Margaret Thatcher to Wiltshire and into Salisbury, where she faced the biggest protest of the whole election, as far as she personally was concerned. Some 300 Labour Party demonstrators carrying banners in Salisbury market-place where she was addressing a crowd of about a thousand, heckled her repeatedly until she turned on them: 'You stand there shouting because you have no arguments. How pathetic is the party you support. How pathetic you are. Just standing there shouting and with banners because you have not got any arguments left.'

The 'high camp' climax to the day's campaigning came with Margaret Thatcher's Isle of Wight landing. She arrived, standing on the foredeck, moulded like Britannia, into 'the shape of the prow of the Hovercraft'. Her daughter imagined it in terms of an Andrew Lloyd-Webber production, or a film in cinerama. Frank Johnson's column in *The Times* implied that the press corps had over-indulged heavily the previous night. The photographers had managed to equip themselves with navy blue T-shirts labelled 'Hilda's Personel Photographer'. 'A worthy journalistic feat,' according to the Prime Minister's daughter, whose amazement at a journalist's ability to open a book and look something up is only equalled by her disdain for 'the reptiles'; 'the research to find Mum's middle name had been done in *Who's Who*'. It is also on page 9 of Patricia Murray's life, page 10 of Alan J. Mayer's book, page 25 of Nicholas Wapshott and George Brock, and in most directories. But this level of research was normal for the campaign generally. It seemed sadly in keeping with the superficial progress now coming to a mildly hysterical end, as photographers lined themselves and her up against the backdrop of 'the largest Union Jack in the World' which covered the hangar doors of the British Hovercraft Corporation in Cowes. The 'invasion' of the Isle of Wight, wittily transmuted by Frank Johnson into a Falklands-type island assault – the journalists' regiment being 'Too Paralytic' rather than 2 Para – brought campaigning to a close.

*

Polling booths opened at eight o'clock on the morning of Thursday, June 9. The turnout was 72.7 percent, almost the same as in October 1974, but 3.3 percent down on 1979. The Tory vote, at 12,991,377 was only marginally down from the 13.6 million in 1979, and in percentage terms, at 43.5, only 0.4 percent down. The party gained 46 seats and lost 10. Its total number of seats was 397, giving it an overall majority of 144. The swing to the Conservatives had been 3.8 percent. It was a triumph for Margaret Thatcher.

The Labour Party, with 8,437,120 votes had dropped its share from 36.9 percent in 1979 to 28.3 percent. The Alliance had almost doubled its percentage, from 13.8 to 26, and its total, 7,775,048, was less than a million short of Labour. Yet the Labour total was 209 seats, Alliance 23. The election result represented a convincing case for proportional representation; also, arguably, for legal compulsion to vote. Margaret Thatcher's power rested on support from only 31.6 percent of the total electorate. Labour commanded 20.6 and Alliance 18.9.

The main Government changes were made straight away, and the new Cabinet announced on Saturday. Francis Pym was dropped. Sir Geoffrey Howe, Chancellor of the Exchequer and Margaret Thatcher's main economic spokesman since 1975, became Foreign Secretary, with Nigel Lawson taking his place. Leon Brittan, appointed to the Home Office, was the youngest member of the Cabinet. Norman Tebbit remained as Employment Secretary, in charge of the as yet unfinished trade union reform. A third promotion (in addition to Lawson and Brittan) was that of Cecil Parkinson to Trade and Industry, a new merging of two departments. William Whitelaw, who was given a viscountcy, became leader of the House of Lords. David Howell was dropped from Transport.*

Michael Foot's replacement became inevitable and was set for the autumn, a decision preceded by the start of campaigning for the post, with Neil Kinnock as favourite. Roy Jenkins resigned straight away as SDP leader, and was replaced by David Owen. David Steel remained Liberal leader but, fatigued and unwell, took an extended break from politics.

Parliament met on Wednesday, June 22, for the Queen's Speech, which indicated a firm continuation of Margaret Thatcher's programme of legislation for Britain; familiar Bills were restored; others which had been foreshadowed were promised with greater clarity. Margaret Thatcher then went to Stuttgart to solve the EEC crisis, which she did by accepting a greatly reduced refund for Britain of £450m. Business, and reality, were restored to normal.

Was she happy? She was triumphant. More important, she was *satisfied*. And, in Graham Greene's words, 'she had reached an age when the satisfied woman is at her most beautiful'. Relevant to the pursuit of power? In woman, yes.

---

* See Appendix for full details.

PART TWO

Winning

CHAPTER NINE

'Disdain and Scorn Ride Sparkling in her Eyes.'

One might well apply to the leadership struggle which ended with Margaret Thatcher taking over from Edward Heath in February, 1975, those same words which she addressed on another occasion towards another party: 'How pathetic the party you support. How pathetic you are.' The scorn which she directed towards Labour Party hecklers in 1983 was not dissimilar from the dismissiveness towards failure which was a necessary prerequisite to any challenge by her for the leadership of the Conservative Party. She needed to be less blunt about it. She needed to move with greater mobility and care. She needed to clothe the scorn in positive ideas and concepts, a new direction, a new start. At the same time it was a necessary initial response. If a party loses a general election, something has gone wrong; it has failed. If a party loses two in one year, the failure is serious. If, between the two, a presentiment of defeat is read in the stars, the appropriate action by anyone ambitious for power is to combine scorn with the offer of an alternative. In her own way Margaret Thatcher did better than that; she recognised, even before the February 1974 general election, and confirmed in all her public attitudes swiftly enough after it, that the simple transfer of the leadership from Edward Heath to some other worthy and senior member of the Conservative Party would only be pre-empted by herself if she could offer a new start, and a new direction. And in order for this to be achieved, the sense of present failure, and magnitude of it, had to be emphasised and hammered home, while at the same time new directions, new prospects, revitalised beliefs, were being constructed. The reasons for her success in this were embodied in the incapacity of the party to offer anything better. But it was a situation arrived at by contrivance rather than naturally. And the contrivance was substantially of her making.

She gave form and direction to the inescapable dissatisfaction with the leadership which followed the February 1974 general election, an election which invited the gloomy prospect of another dissolution in the near future. And she imbued it with ideological concern. For this to be possible, a well-judged measure of scorn for what had failed was essential. And he did judge it well. It was not directed, except implicitly, at Edward Heath, or at others who supported him and could be joined in the collective responsibility for Conservative Party policy. It was directed at the policy itself. The ideas, the thinking, the strategy for Britain, were her target. And this approach was followed throughout the crucial months between the two general elections of 1974.

Another issue to be handled was that of loyalty. In defeat, it becomes a burdensome handicap within a political party. There is an inevitable set of confusions between people and ideas, between the party and the groupings within it, between the leader and potential alternatives. As an outsider, as a woman, and as someone who had swiftly made public disagreement with the policies proposed by the Government of which she had been a senior member, Margaret Thatcher was well placed to disembarrass herself from any of the inhibiting elements of (dutiful respect to) loyalty in the aftermath of defeat. She owed Edward Heath very little. Though she had subscribed to the policies pursued between 1970 and 1974 as a member of his Cabinet, and had been a demanding burden, as Secretary of State for Education, on the public purse, she had no instinctive or natural sense of loyalty towards the policies as they had been shaped by circumstance. Nor did she have many senior associates within the party, Sir Keith Joseph excepted, whose attitudes on the question of loyalty, either to Heath or his team, on the central ideas, needed to be taken into account. She was remarkably free.

Until such time as they also were prepared to abandon the beliefs on which the 1970-74 Government had based its policies, including the belief in the 'necessary' U-turns of 1972-73, she had them all at a distinct disadvantage in terms of creating a mood in the party favourable to a new direction. And this was long before the question arose of a direct challenge to Edward Heath.

She was an outsider. She had been consistently under-rated by Heath. He had excluded her from the area of responsibilty she most wanted to occupy, and for which she had demonstrated her suitability. And he continued the process in the period after losing power. In effect, he scorned her endeavour and disdained her ability. She responded in like fashion, withdrawing her loyalty to his policies as a prelude to the withdrawal of loyalty to his leadership. In both respects it made it possible to take the leadership from under the noses of many who considered themselves more worthy, more senior, more appropriate, but whose freedom to act was inhibited by the inflexibility of their interpretation of loyalty, and their misinterpretation of the nature of failure.

In time she would demand, and get, the same sort of loyalty from a different group of politicians. It would create the same apparently impregnable structure of power within the party. And its survival would be directly dependent upon success in power. To get power, and to keep it; that is the first requirement. Edward Heath's simple failure to do this invited a process of criticism and challenge which contained carefully judged elements of scorn and disdain. The remarkable fact was the extent to which these forces, combined with the determined ambition to be leader, became embodied in Margaret Thatcher more than in anyone else. There are several keys, the first of which concerns defeat.

The Conservative Party had failed in two successive general elections, the most obvious of its failures; but it had failed more substantially and more profoundly than that. It had failed in its ideology, its policies and its people. And it had done so against a political opponent in Harold Wilson whose skill was not matched by any very convincing ideology. If Heath had been faced by an uncompromising radical of the left, or a democratic socialist of the centre, with real beliefs about the government of Britain and real vision about its future, his failure might have been more excusable. But he had been defeated by a verbal technician and policy manipulator with dispatch-box beliefs and limited national vision. And this, for those courageous enough to open their eyes and see the truth, was inexcusable. It pointed the way forward, directly inviting that far greater degree of courage that turns a cool recognition of what is wrong into an even cooler recognition of how to put it right. The person who best exemplified that courage would be the party's favourite for the leadership. And courage in coming out was her initial strength.

It is to misunderstand the nature of power, and of the mind that seeks power, to attempt to fix upon its many candidates a reasonable, logical and ordered approach to its acquisition. Like the majority of other members of the House of Commons, but not all, Margaret Thatcher was ambitious; like a smaller number of them she had a well-developed sense of self-regard, had deployed her talent intelligently, enjoyed office from an early stage, anticipated higher office in the future, and had achieved, very belatedly, a position in the centre of the main arena, which concerned finance and economics, by the crucial shape of Conservative opposition in the aftermath of the February 1974 general election.

To say she was preparing for leadership is to pre-empt the progression towards power. Equally, however, to accept her own words – 'It will be years before a women either leads the Party or becomes Prime Minister, I don't see it happening in my time' – is simplistic. From the day she entered Parliament in 1959, Margaret Thatcher's ambition and ability, her instinct for measuring life in terms of winning and of victory, and for protecting herself against the opposites, had conditioned her for the highest office one day. It was an inescapable and central part of her character.

Of her loyalty, and of her attitude to Edward Heath's economic policies at this time, two distinct interpretations are given. They are not very flattering. Those who served in Cabinet with her do not recall her as outspoken in terms of monetarism or rectitude, or particularly clear and determined on economic issues at all. She was not rated as all that important in the economic sphere, and was seen as basically loyal, in Cabinet. To those outside Cabinet who were critical of Heath's 1972-73 U-turn, she gave the deliberate impression that she was with them, and would have resigned, only she believed she could better influence things and change Government direction from within. Heath's leading critics were none too sure of her. One of them, now a member of her Cabinet, expressed the view that they had hopes but no great expectation.

By any standards it was a tricky period for a prospective leader, watching the slow disintegration of loyalty in the wake of defeat and the rising tide of vengeance. It was necessary to retain relations with different groups, and identify the direction in which the main body of the Conservative Party might move if it dumped Heath. And this Margaret Thatcher did quite skilfully, safeguarding potential support and organising herself sufficiently well to be in the running when the time came.

*

One endeavours to reconstruct the mind of Margaret Thatcher, during the summer of 1974, by way of disdain. It is not an unworthy emotion, embracing indignation and anger as well as contempt. 'Nature never fram'd a woman's heart of prouder stuff. . . . Disdain and scorn ride sparkling in her eyes, misprising what they look on.' And she had much to misprise, all around her. If all the years she had been a member of the Conservative Party, in the House of Commons, a junior minister, a member of the Cabinet, meant anything, they meant that she had a duty to turn her misprision into action. Something was fundamentally wrong in a Conservative Party which knew what had to be done on coming to power in 1970 and yet turned from its obligations in 1972-73. Something was wrong in a party which could lose an election against the policies of a Labour Party led by Harold Wilson, and with such men and women at its head as James Callaghan, Denis Healey and Barbara Castle. And as is always the case with political parties, the main thing wrong is to be traced to the leader. He defines and manifests policy, direction, vision, philosophy. He chooses people and gives them jobs. And if the mix doesn't work, then he has failed.

By the summer of 1974 Edward Heath had fought three elections as leader of the Conservatives and lost two of them. He looked as though he might lose a third. He was beginning to look like a chronic loser. Worse still, he was traduced by his own inconsistencies. In policy terms, having once indulged in the wasteful luxury of U-turns, he had both de-stabilised the basis of Conservative economic policy and, in the process, divided the party. The division was unequal; but it was nevertheless serious, since economic unrest, in the form of high inflation and deep industrial relations strife were raising steadily the demand for a tough and unequivocal political approach. And Edward Heath was precluded from offering this, during the frozen political summer of 1974, by the very actions when in power which

Margaret Thatcher now indicated she most disdained.

She did so dishonestly. The perception has been firmly established, not least by herself, that, together with Keith Joseph, she stood out against the economic changes of 1972-73, and as a bulwark of rectitude against public expenditure cuts. She was not. As Secretary of State for Education she made repeated and excessive demands for money. She was prodigal in her policies, and left-wing in her leanings. She likes the 'no milk' decision to be remembered; what is conveniently forgotten is the fact that she introduced more comprehensives than her predecessor or her successor in Education and she demanded heavy spending increases. Nevertheless, she successfully sold the idea that she had been a model of economic rectitude between 1970-74.

It was a moment in her career deserving of that much overused word, 'seminal'. The final and fullest germination of ambition took place in a period of personal political frustration. After the first 1974 defeat, Margaret Thatcher had been appointed spokesperson for the environment. In this responsibility she had dealt, in the early summer, with mortgage rates, and been the chairperson of a shadow policy committee responsible for a populist set of proposals about public mortgage subsidy with which she claimed she did not agree. She said that it was not part of her reading of how to get back into power that the Conservative Party should compromise on what the country and the economy needed in order to win votes. Votes would be won by doing what was economically right. Moreover, she had anticipated a more central role than the shadow responsibility for Environment, and this added to the sense of frustration. Nor did it go unrecognised by Edward Heath. Belatedly, after the second general election defeat in October, in the reshuffling of his Shadow Cabinet, he transferred her, on November 7 1974, to the position of assistant to the Shadow Chancellor, Robert Carr. It was too little, and it came too late. It was an act of self-defence by a beleaguered leader, not good in his judgment of talent, toughness, and that even more elusive quality, sheer ability, and handicapped furthermore by a species of his own kind of disdain.

*

In June 1974, Margaret Thatcher said: 'It will be years before a woman either leads the Party or becomes Prime Minister. I don't see it happening in my time.' She was not yet fifty. She could expect between ten and twenty years more in politics, and near the top of the Conservative Party, which at that stage she had actively represented for fifteen years. She was an ambitious and dynamic woman who had not had an easy time under Edward Heath's leadership, was in an area of responsibility which was neither to her liking nor of her choice, and she seemed set for a basically marginal role. She was emerging as a supporter of harder economic policies than those which the party had pursued through 1973-4, and on which it had been defeated. Was she speaking the truth, whistling through a graveyard, or offering hostages to fortune?

To her former confidant, and later her biographer, Patrick Cosgrave, she had said enough, following the February general election, to inspire an article by him in the *Spectator* suggesting that Margaret Thatcher might succeed the defeated Edward Heath as leader of the Conservative Party. The subsequent disowning of such ambition in the *Liverpool Daily Post* in June 1974 as well as in other newspapers was the natural response to speculation, and a nicely calculated form of humility and disinterest. But it was no more than that.

Implicitly, she claimed that her biggest opponent for the leadership of the party was Keith Joseph, in that he was the only person against whom she would not stand. Keith Joseph was not really another contender for the leadership at all; he was a defence mechanism for Margaret Thatcher, from behind which she could build up her own standing as an eventual contender without ever declaring herself. She could be a dominant part of the process by which Edward Heath's leadership was challenged without being or becoming the challenger until a remarkably late stage in the sequence of events.

Was this intended? Was Keith Joseph a stalking horse for Margaret Thatcher between the summer of 1974, when he deliberately led the challenge against Heath on policy grounds, and that much-recounted winter afternoon visit to Margaret Thatcher's small office in the Palace of Westminster, November 21, when he told her he would not be a contender for the leadership? Only one person knows, and he declines to say.

Keith Joseph cast himself, and was cast by others including Margaret Thatcher, as the leading critic of Edward Heath's economic policies. He had been a senior member of the 1970-74 Cabinet, but not directly responsible , as Secretary of State for Social Services, for economic thinking. He had however, like Margaret Thatcher, been responsible for heavy departmental spending demands. He had been a member of Parliament for two years longer than Margaret Thatcher, and had more ministerial esperience than she had. He was also eight years older. But in periods of opposition, unlike her, he pursued considerable business interests, and this had been the case in the period 1964-70. He had been founder, in 1974, and was the chairman for the next five years, of the management committee of the party's Centre for Policy Studies. And he was respected as a right-wing political thinker, logical and fundamentalist in his beliefs in a Conservative Party philosophy which regarded economic 'solutions' to social ills as valueless unless they formed part of a wider moral regeneration of society.

It was a general belief which had developed a much sharper edge as a result of experience in government between 1972 and 1974. In that period he had witnessed the detachment by Heath of economic objectives by means of various control mechanisms from the more fundamental political objective of a society which believed in the principle of self-help. In a less precise way than was subsequently evolved by Margaret Thatcher, in the years between becoming Conservative leader in 1975 and the election of 1979, Edward Heath had developed in opposition his 'Selsdon Man' approach, so named following a Shadow Cabinet policy conference at the Selsdon Park Hotel in 1969 out of which the successful 1970 general election manifesto was constructed. This combined private enterprise expansion with public sector control, and would have continued to work if the 1973 oil crisis had not punctured economic growth and caused Heath to lose his nerve. Economic protection and intervention followed, culminating in an attempt at setting prices and incomes within government-dictated guidelines. The confrontation which followed this, and centred on a dispute between the National Coal Board and the National Union of Mineworkers, led to the February general election initially fought on the theme: 'Who Governs Britain?'

*

Numerically, the electorate decided that Edward Heath should go on governing Britain. Unlike the October 1974 result, in which the Labour Party polled a million more votes than the Conservatives, the February result gave the party in power a majority. However, by virtue of the constituency boundaries, this resulted in fewer seats. It gave a curious moral strength to Edward Heath, even in defeat. For the majority in the Conservative Party, it complicated the question of Heath's continued leadership. But for sections of the Conservative Party, including Keith Joseph and those supporting him, the central criticism shifted from electoral performance to the much more fundamental errors of policy which were denying the party power.

The view now presented with increasing publicity was that the policy change of 1972 had not only not been necessary; it had been a counter-productive and defeatist capitulation to an unforeseen oil crisis which, when it came, should have been used to reinforce the basic Selsdon strategy of monetary control. It was allowed to do the opposite, breaking political nerve and producing reversal. The subsequent defeat, in February 1974, was made painful by the ignominy which was an inescapable part of the abandonment of principle.

This was the theme pursued by Keith Joseph in the summer of 1974 in a number of speeches critical of Conservative Party policy on the economy. Following the October general election defeat which, though narrow (319 Labour, 276 Conservatives and 39 the rest, an overall majority of four), was real enough to presage a full term in office, Keith Joseph immediately returned to the attack with a speech in the Grand Hotel, Birmingham, on Saturday, October 19, just a week after Wilson's confirmation in power for a further term. It was a speech in which controversial elements obscured the more wide-ranging examination of Conservative thinking. His suggestion that 'our human stock is threatened' by the birth of more and more children to women in the lower skilled and unskilled social classes was seized on in advance of the speech, and became the object of outraged reaction from various groups and individuals. But also, though much played down, were the favourable reactions from the Right, including a number of Conservative MPs, one of whom said that the speech 'pinpointed several of the acute moral and social problems to which Conservatism can offer proper solutions'. It did more than that. It offered fresh principle and new direction at a crucial moment of doubt and uncertainty within the party in the wake of defeat.

Keith Joseph indicated, on the one hand, a degeneration of 'human stock' by too many births to those least fitted to cope, the unmarried, deserted, divorced, and those of low intelligence and low education; he did not quite say of lower moral stability, but it was implicit. And even the extension of birth control meant condoning immorality. Weak restraints on strong instincts were being further undermined by permissiveness: 'The worship of instinct, of spontaneity, the rejection of self-discipline, is not progress, it is degeneration.' He was deeply critical in his speech, both of educators and education, and of the media; only then did he turn his restrained and careful attack on the failures within Conservatism. The central fault lay in the belief that economics was something which could be detached from the 'sound body politic', and then manipulated and altered for electoral purposes. While blaming Labour for doing this, and winning power by promising the earth, Joseph implicitly criticised the leadership of the Conservative Party. It had been Edward Heath's error to make economic policy central as well as changing its basis, thereby weakening the philosophic certitude in the service of which economic strategy was merely a tool.

Keith Joseph was recommending an extensive and profound re-questioning; a range of basic social assumptions, all of them founded on human expectations which the State funded, and for which economic policy was constructed, had produced, in his opinion, a society in which delinquency, hooliganism, vandalism, illiteracy, drunkenness, teenage pregnancies and abortions, sexual offences, crimes against property and the person, were all increasing, many of them at unprecedented rates. It was necessary to question university expansion, the rapidly rising budgets for social services and other facilities which made easier the attitudes and actions responsible for the degeneration which it was Keith Joseph's primary purpose to attack.

The most remarkable thing about this speech was the fact that the man who made it should have walked into Margaret Thatcher's office exactly a month later to tell her that he would not be standing against Edward Heath for the leadership of the party. Variously put down to domestic difficulties – his marriage, which ended in 1978, was in difficulties, and one of his children was suffering from mental illness – and to the unfavourable reaction to the speech, including demonstrations outside his house, any careful reading of its content must dispel the idea that Joseph had taken leave of his senses, or was in danger of some kind of emotional breakdown. Central and fundamental to the argument in favour of a return to his version of 'true Toryism', which was Margeret Thatcher's version as well, was the belief, implicit in his attack on degeneracy and profligacy among the lower classes, that one reaps what one has sown. The only real help which society could give to the disadvantaged individual was self-help, and this theory was offered with conviction, and as part of a comprehensive outline of what was wrong with the system and how it should be put right.

There is some evidence that Keith Jospeh wanted to be seen as a possible candidate for the leadership of the Conservative Party during the summer of 1974, and increasing evidence that he wanted to be seen in the role of a right-wing thinker testing political attitudes and beliefs. There is less evidence that he considered himself seriously as an alternative leader of the Conservative Party, and fairly strong circumstantial evidence, in his political performance between June and November of 1974 that he was proving certain ideological points and clearing the way for another kind of party leader, who would propound another form of Conservatism to which he was deeply committed but for which he was not necessarily the best spokesman.

In that same period, consciously or not, Keith Joseph performed an invaluable service for Margaret Thatcher. Her own venture into self-promotion, as a challenger to Edward Heath, via the pages of the *Spectator*, had not worked because her attitudes on central issues, including the economy, were not well known, and her political weight was not established. More seriously, the general movement towards the Right in the country was far from being an established fact with which the Conservatives looking ahead to future elections could identify. In a calculated way Sir Keith Joseph was actively performing the function of encouraging and confirming this shift in public speeches, and in the Centre for Policy Studies. Did he do this, one is forced to ask, in order to step back at an early stage in the leadership contest, only to step forward again immediately afterwards, and take on the key spokemanship position with overall responsibility for policy and research from 1975 up to the 1979 general election? And after that, Secretary of State for Education and Science? Did he recognise, in the wake of that comprehensive Birmingham speech, that he had faltered and made a mess of things, ruining his chances of becoming party leader? Or had be never entertained those prospects, running, instead, in order to test the ground, shift opinion, and move support behind a deliberately unidentified product of the Right, the only source for a leader who would change things sufficiently strongly to win a convincing victory for the beliefs which Joseph held dear, and which he wished to impose on the Conservative Party? And moreover, which he believed would succeed.

This task was the critical one which Sir Keith Joseph assigned to himself during the summer of 1974. Was it his motive to become leader of the Conservative Party? Was it purely ideological, the shaping of new ideas and a new direction? Or was it more subtle, the arrival from the wilderness of a preacher, paving the way for one greater than himself who would offer salvation to the defeated Conservative Party? If there were rhetorical questions, these are they. Even if Keith Joseph were to answer, would he tell the truth? Would Margaret Thatcher? There is a visible orchestration about the events which can only be construed through speculation on the motives concerned with very real and very substantial power. An enormous amount was at stake, and very few people of high intellectual quality were committed to the job of winning the Conservative Party round from the growing flabbiness of Edward Heath, Anthony Barber, Robert Carr, William Whitelaw, Francis Pym, James Prior and Peter Walker.

It is generally asserted by those close to the centre of power within the Conservative Party at this time that such an interpretation is over-complicated, and suggests a sublety not given to the politicians concerned. The majority of those asked have given an interpretation of events which leans heavily on the theory of accident rather than design. Some had good personal or political reasons for doing so. Most of the questions are unanswerable, except by individuals who refused to answer. Nevertheless, the point has to be made that one is talking about the transfer of power within a great political party in a major world democracy. If its leading political figures maintain that it is all more or less accidental, so be it; my own conviction is that it was quite the reverse, and that many critical questions leading up to Margaret Thatcher's defeat of Ted Heath have yet to be answered, and most of them never will be answered.

CHAPTER TEN

'Pride will not let me fail'

One must consider carefully the relationship between Sir Keith Joseph and Margaret Thatcher, the joint architects of modern Conservatism, who effectively took over the Conservative Party between February 1974 and the second week of the same month a year later. Whoever else may be a part of the equation – and Airey Neave has an obvious place of honour in it, perhaps Enoch Powell as well – the central position must be occupied by the two contenders for party leadership from the Right. Moreover, that is the way to see them. On the one hand the wealthy, distinguished patrician baronet – war service in the Italian campaign as an artillery captain (wounded, despatches), fellow of All Souls, Middle Temple barrister, an alderman of the city, under-writer at Lloyds, liveryman of the Vintner's company – who is prepared to deploy his forceful and distinguished mind in the service of Conservatism. He is of the Right by birth, by persuasion and by conviction. And his independence of mind is backed by sufficient acumen to determine the direction in which not only he but a substantial body of Conservative Party members as well as the general public would like Britain to move, and the courage to chart the course.

In contrast, Margaret Thatcher is the proud plebeian product of the system of self-help which is central to Joseph's beliefs. Had she belonged to her natural guild in the city, the Grocers, or Pepperers as once they were called, she would have been a member of a group believing since the Middle Ages in the equality of women. And if her career has a place in any study of Margaret Thatcher's grasp on power, then it is here, as a golden and perfect example of everything for which Sir Keith Joseph, as he expressed himself in his Birmingham speech, was seeking to preserve Britain.

It was under assault from degeneracy deriving from a bewildering multitude of sources, including the left-wing intellectuals in the education system and the media who were weakening 'the national will to transmit to future generations these values, standards and aspirations which made England admired the world over'. The fact that Margaret Thatcher was a product of the system who had conquered all its inherent handicaps, made her a vital figure in his eyes. She was sharply in contrast with the majority of members of the Conservative Party, not so much in being different in her political origins, which were independent in upbringing and in philosophy, but because she retained the main body of this primal conviction, and had not subscribed to the more natural Conservative Party philosophy which, while it believed in a 'one-nation' theory, sought to deliver it through an élitism best represented through the intelligent and provoking mind of Sir Ian Gilmour. He belonged to a worthy tradition which was out of date and could no longer be relied upon to achieve power. It was a tradition which lacked mass appeal.

While it *appeared* from the general reception to Sir Keith Joseph's speech on October 19 that what he stood for also lacked such appeal, he believed it to be far more central to the Britain he knew; on many occasions he had apparently been persuaded not to express such views by his advisers and speech writers. He did so because the climate of opposition to the kind of socialism he deplored was growing, while at the same time finding an inadequate set of answers in a Conservative Party led by Edward Heath.

This perception, that it was the element of compromise in Conservative policies as presented to the electorate in February and October which had brought about the double defeat, and that it would have been otherwise had there not been the 1972 U-turn, was shared no more clearly and fundamentally than by Keith Joseph and Margaret Thatcher. They both abhorred the centrifugal force in British politics by which principle and belief were modified in order to capture the 'centre'. It was clear at that time that it no longer worked: the kind of majorities won by the Conservative Party in the past, notably and most recently the 100-seat majority won by Harold Macmillan in 1959 of which Margaret Thatcher was a part, seemed to be of the past, and depressingly so in 1974.

What was at stake was the Britain in which Joseph believed.

Margaret Thatcher was part of that belief. She had been bred in domestic circumstances positively committed against degeneracy when it had been but a pale precursor of the kind of moral collapse which seemed to Joseph to be poisoning 'values, standards and aspirations'. Long before she became a committed Conservative, Margaret Thatcher had, on her own evidence, been a natural conservative. And the virtues of self-help and moral rectitude were fundamental to her nature, and had been deeply and genuinely imbued. Small-town shop-keeping, Methodism, community politics, teetotalism, hard work at school, personal independence consistent with the principle of self-help are all part of the early life which has been covered extensively in a number of well-written books about a person, a study of whom has been of a delayed and limited kind.

*

The biographical details which are relevant to an examination of her acquisition and deployment of power are of a different order, and concern Margaret Thatcher's *use* of her origins and upbringing as part of her essential armoury.

There is nothing inherently good or virtuous about small-town grocers' shops and sub-post offices, about dedicated Methodist preachers and local politicians. The twitching lace curtains of Grantham in the 1930s neither concealed nor harboured anything better or worse than was producing embryonic politicians in the industrial streets of Liverpool, the shipyards of Belfast, the rolling hills of Gloucestershire or the suburbs of London. Yet Margaret Thatcher makes them both virtuous, and politically important.

The first chapter of *Margaret Thatcher* by Patricia Murray (London, 1980), which is really a long monologue by Margaret Thatcher about her early life in Grantham, establishes to a degree that is extensive to the point of exhaustion, as well as being 'perhaps more vivid than most', the wholesome goodness of 'a very regulated pattern of behaviour'. Her parents 'were described by the inhabitants of Grantham as people who were always true to their principles and beliefs'. In company with her sister, helping her parents, looking forward to Christmas, getting excited about the purchase of the first grocery delivery van, and serving in the shop, lead on to higher things: family shopping, church work 'a large part in our lives', the strict upbringing with no films on Sundays, nor even 'games such as snakes and ladders'. 'We didn't go out very much for pleasure', but when it happened it 'was a tremendous treat and I used to look forward to it for days on end'. Piano lessons, lectures on current affairs, dependence on the radio for home entertainment, helping with the shop accounts on Sunday (work was okay, sport and pleasure forbidden), and her own growing involvement in her father's political career as a local independent councillor, were the early ingredients of Margaret Thatcher's life. She doesn't tell us she was known at school as 'Snobby' Roberts; she doesn't tell us *everything*.

From this, her later biographers, Nicholas Wapshott and George Brock,* deduce that she is 'a "conviction politician", by which they mean that she depends for her inspiration upon a profound set of beliefs. She is guided by an inner mechanism which instinctively tells her whether she considers an action is right or wrong. She does not need to ask whether a new set of circumstances suits a particular body of doctrine. She is confident that the deep conviction which guides her will keep her on the right track. She acquired this deep-rooted conviction, by her own admission, during her childhood in Grantham. . . .' This lively parade of abysmal clichés about the Prime Minister is demonstrably wrong, inaccurate, or at best unprovable. There is no evidence, in anything she has said on the record, of 'a profound set of beliefs'; those of her beliefs which can be defined are determined ones, but shallow, rigid and questionable in their integrity and value. The 'inner mechanism' is clearly and demonstrably a political one, for which the use of the words 'right' and 'wrong' had a distinct and precise meaning unrelated to beliefs other than those in oneself. She needs repeatedly to check circumstances against a particular 'body of doctrine', and does so with a laborious attention to detailed precedent, both personal and political, rather than conviction; and it is this, more than anything else, which 'will always keep her on the right track', the 'right track' being the political one of remaining in power.

It is an admirable end result of intelligence, skill and judgment; it has little if anything to do with 'a profound set of beliefs'. Indeed, there is a banality, as well as a woolliness, when

---

* Nicholas Wapshott and George Brock: *Thatcher* (London, 1983).

she does talk of belief. The equating of Methodism with methodical is an example; so too are her comments in reply to Laurens van der Post's questions, in a film shown by ITV in expectation of the general election, where her references to the Old and New Testament are those of someone who regards them as telephone directories in which one looks up names and numbers.

This does not preclude belief in hard work and determination, consistency and the simple statement of basic ideas – all acceptable material for establishing principles by which one lives – but a long way from belief in any religious or philosophic sense. The very readiness with which she talks about it should alert one to the questionable nature of what we hear. Would Gladstone, Macmillan or Pitt have dreamt of divulging such stuff? For her, the heart of the Christian message was that 'each person has the right to choose'.

The beliefs of politicians on the whole, however, are political ones, just as the beliefs of writers are generally literary ones; God's presence is part of the instinct for nostalgia innate in most of us. An occasional exception, like Enoch Powell, may emerge, but tends by so doing to prove the general rule. Margaret Thatcher presents herself as true to a basic set of principles, acquired early, valued, and retained, to make belief a good ingredient of leadership. How real or profound is another matter altogether.

*

To this presentation of early and constant belief one adds ambition, and comes to the second and equally vital phase in her life: the education and evolution of her intellectual capacities. From the scholarship to Kesteven and Grantham Girls' School, which she took up in the late summer of 1936, in her eleventh year, right through to the end of her pupillage as a barrister in 1955, ambition and education went hand-in-hand. Marriage and the birth of her two children were covered by that period, as were her early and direct involvement in Conservative Party politics as a conference delegate from Oxford, and her more direct participation as an unsuccessful candidate in Dartford in the atrocious winter election of 1950 and the autumn of 1951.

The character displayed is not exceptional, the achievements modest. The best part of her, not to be under-rated in the career towards which she was working, was her dogged determination to succeed in the face of difficulty and setbacks. She was not lucky. She fought for everything she got. She did not give up. When entering her papers for the Bar finals from her hospital bed, after the Caesarian delivery of the twins she said to herself, 'If I fill in the entrance form now, pride will not let me fail.' *

Ambition rather than ability dictated the next phase, which was the application of achievement to political advance. 'Essentially a critical mind and not a creative one, but with a remarkable facility for taking a brief and with the minimum of changes, making it her own' (the judgment of a civil servant who worked with her later, and paraphrased by Wapshott/Brock) Margaret Thatcher shifted away from the doomed pursuit of a Conservative seat in Dartford, for which she would have been obliged to wait until 1970, to Finchley, a comfortable Conservative seat (though by no means triumphantly so, and never, under Margaret Thatcher, the scene of any great personal triumph). In her first run as party leader there, in 1979, the swing to the Conservatives was below the national average.

The switch to Finchley came after the break, between 1951 and 1954, during which she married and had her twin children, Mark and Carol. Even then, the road to getting a nomination was a rocky one. She worked extremely hard as a supporting speaker in various constituencies in the 1955 general election, she tried, unsuccessfully, against Philip Goodhart, to get the nomination in Beckenham for the 1957 by-election, though she was short-listed, and she was short-listed for Maidstone, but again turned down. She then tried for Oxford and, simultaneously, for Finchley. She did not come top in the preliminary ballot for the four candidates short-listed, but in subsequent votes she was adopted.

*

Now it was the turn for ability rather than ambition. And the road ahead was a long, hard slog. She had inherited from her father a capacity for incessant work and an inability to relax. Yet this did not rule out the possibility that she could waste away her parliamentary days in precise acts. Her grandmother had offered

---

* See Laurens van der Post programme

her a familiar cliché which she was, and is, fond of using: 'If a thing's worth doing it's worth doing well.' Her father had offered her a slightly more interesting, if clumsy, basis for a political career: 'You do not follow the crowd because you're afraid of being different. You decide what to do yourself, and if necessary you lead the crowd, but you never just follow.' This also she was fond of repeating. For what it was worth. But when, on October 9 1961, she was offered her first job by Harold Macmillan as Parliamentary Secretary to the Minister of Pensions and National Insurance, a more down-to-earth pragmatism of her own emerged: 'When you are offered a job you either accept it, or you are out,' was what she told her sister, Muriel. She had accepted her first political appointment; her foot was on the treadmill of parliamentary service; it was also on the first rung of ministerial advancement.

She had already made her mark in a minor area of legislative change. She had won a parliamentary ballot for the introduction of her own private member's bill. She had then been frustrated over her first choice for legislative change, affecting the law of contempt; she was steered in the direction of another bill which the Government preferred should go through private members' time to avoid any direct consequential embarrassment should it have failed. She was amenable to this, and found herself, ironically one might say, on the side of greater press access to local government meetings. This was the background to her maiden speech, on Friday, February 5 1960. It was also the basis for her early friendship with Keith Joseph. He was Parliamentary Secretary to the Minister for Housing and Local Government (Henry Brooke), and therefore directly involved in the issue of press rights to attend local government council meetings. Though the bill itself was a private measure, it had government backing, and government representation during the committee stage, on which Margaret Thatcher and Keith Joseph worked together.

The occasion is significant for two reasons: Margaret Thatcher's definition of the first obligations of Parliament being the defence of civil liberties, and the clear indications also of Sir Keith Joseph's warm regard for her, and close working relationship with her at this time. There was evidence of abuse of the law as it then stood, on press access to local authority meetings, in spirit and letter, and because of this, she said at the end of her speech in moving the second stage, 'there is a case for safeguarding the rights of the citizen. I hope these honourable members will think fit to give this Bill a Second Reading, and to consider that the paramount function of this distinguished House is to safeguard civil liberties rather than to think that administrative convenience should take first place in law.'*

She was assured, diligent, and well prepared in her handling of the rest of the Bill, and at the end of the committee stage, which effectively completed the measure, Sir Keith Joseph gave Margaret Thatcher credit for a number of significant improvements in the committee stage, and congratulated 'most warmly my Hon. Friend the Member for Finchley on her achievement. This has proved a delicate and contentious Measure, perhaps not ideally suited for a first venture into legislation, but the House will remember from all the stages of the Bill the cogent, charming, lucid and composed manner of my honourable Friend. I am sure that we must all hope that this will not be her last venture into legislation, and we must hope it all the more because she has had such concentrated experience of legislation with this Bill.' It signalled publicly a close friendship.

She also impressed William Deedes, then largely responsible for the Peterborough column in the *Daily Telegraph*, in which appeared a short but enthusiastic paragraph about her 'uncanny instinct for the mood of the House', as expressed in her thirty-minute speech 'without a note'. More than 23 years later, writing a major profile in the same paper at the beginning of the general election, Deedes was disposed towards the view that political commentators, biographers, interviewers and pundits over-complicated her, whereas, from ordinary men and women a more sharply drawn portrait emerged. It was the draughtsmanship of Topolski against that of Thurber. She was, to Deedes, who rightly claimed knowledge of 'the earnest and talented Margaret Roberts of more than a generation ago', essentially uncomplicated, offering the consistent message that there was no such thing as a free lunch, and essentially unchanged in that fundamental view of life after a quarter of a century in politics.

She had clearly made her mark elsewhere. She had come into early and mild conflict with the Government Chief Whip, Martin Redmayne, over the choice of her private member's bill content matter. As well as involving Keith Joseph, his cabinet superior,

---

*HANSARD, February 5 1969, Col. 1358.

Henry Brooke, was also involved, and she made an early impact on the Opposition.

In subsequent and early contributions to parliamentary debate, she extended this. On home affairs issues she had expressed a decided belief in punishment as an end in itself, and had rejected the woollier 'humanitarian reform of offenders' as an exclusive objective. She subsequently became less certain about this, moving towards a belief in deterrence as an objective rather than, or in addition to, the end-product of punishment. This was presented as a basis for her argument in favour of capital punishment in the 1983 general election.

She had been equally precise and determined in the presentation of her views on the economy, and in her speech on the 1961 Budget, given on April 19, shortly after Anthony Barber, who was then Secretary to the Treasury, she had demonstrated considerable skill and knowledge as well as forceful views on the issues of interest and importance to her. The first of these concerned legal powers over speculation in capital gains, which she regarded as adequate but ineffectively deployed by the Revenue Commissioners; secondly, she stoutly defended companies against individuals in the tax realm, deploring the habit of successive chancellors of loading profit tax against companies, which were the 'Cinderellas', in order to alleviate personal taxation; thirdly, she dealt with the overall taxation structure, and its simplication. Most interesting of all, however, in the light of subsequent developments, were her views on government expenditure. She was well read, and offered the interesting contrasts of government spending rising from 9 percent of gross national product in 1890 to 42 percent in 1952, and back to 37 percent in 1959. This provoked the first interruption in her speech which she handled curtly. She went on: 'The Government have control of 37 percent of the expenditure of the total gross national product. It is extremely high, and it brings us to the heart of the problem, that we, as new hon. members, cannot begin to tackle the burden of tax until we have some means better than we have at the moment of controlling the size of Government expenditure. . . . At present, the system of control of Government expenditure is very dangerous in that it gives all the appearance of control without the reality, and that is about the worst situation which one can possibly have . . . until we manage to solve this probem of controlling the amount effectively by Parliament I do not think that we shall be able to devote our attention to considering how the burden is to be distributed as between one kind of taxation and another.'

It was an impressively balanced speech, good both on principle and detail. Like much else that she was doing at the time, it contributed to the degree of notice taken of her, and the steady building of her political personality and reputation. More importantly, it provides further evidence of the perceptive judgment made by Deedes then, and echoed again much later. In essence, she acquired early a set of simple principles and stuck with them. Monetarism is a sophisticated translation of the cottager's statement that the family cannot afford meat on particular days in the week, and she was enough of a political realist to perceive that the underlying message was valid, whatever the language used to convey it. It was politically attractive in 1960 in a limited way only. But it contained also a visionary element, in that anyone considering the boom which was then getting under way, and applying to it even a rudimentary sense of history – in her case, personal experiences growing up in Grantham were enough – must have known that the basic cottager's philosophy would inevitably come more and more into its own. Consistency was the key; being true to herself was paramount.

She had accepted the first promotion offered, on the principle that 'you are out' otherwise. She had aligned herself with the slightly more senior right-wing intellectual force of Keith Joseph. And she was now established a couple of rungs up the ladder, with determined and more than just competent views of her own.

The exercise of talent was not as widely noticed as perhaps it should have been. Colleagues who have worked with her in Cabinet are dismissive of any idea that she made any substantial impact then or later. Margaret Thatcher as an economic force in the early sixties is discounted. Yet the record is moderately impressive. She knew her stuff, and delivered it with confident determination.

It is not the purpose of this book to trace in detail that parliamentary and political career. Its relevance, on the road to power, is a collective one made up of a number of ingredients, the most constant of them being negative: not to blot one's copy book in ministerial and party terms. She of course did better than that. Wapshott and Brock are wrong in ascribing her ministerial debut to March, 1962. She handled with skill and a remarkable grasp of detailed material the report stage of the Family Allowance Bill in December 1961, letting drop a minor but characteristic pointer to her debating method: 'Members will never find me reading selected passages out of paragraphs without trying to give the whole picture.' It was also the occasion for her first clash with Barbara Castle, a more experienced politician who came to respect Margaret Thatcher, and to favour her in the leadership struggle thirteen years later.

Meanwhile, she served her time under Macmillan, then under Alec Douglas Home, who she thought should have stayed on, and she supported Edward Heath for the leadership when Home stepped down.

*

In his first general election as Conservative leader in March, 1966, Edward Heath was defeated. He moved Margaret Thatcher to the Shadow Treasury team, under Iain MacLeod, whom she impressed. In her Budget speech that May, notable for the derisive reception she got for claiming to have read all the Budget statements and Finance Bills since 1946, she clearly demonstrated that she had, and used the knowledge to show policy changes by Labour, and then to attack them. But she also used the knowledge to establish policy alternatives which were fundamental to the principles to which she adhered. Later, she was to put them together in a more measured and more flowery dissertation at the Conservative Party Conference in Blackpool in October 1968, when she was invited to deliver the annual lecture to the Conservative Political Centre, later published in pamphlet form, and began with well-rehearsed quotations from *King Lear*, Richard Brinsley Sheridan and Anatole France. But on May 5, 1966, in the heat of parliamentary debate against the Labour Chancellor, James Callaghan with whom, among others, she clashed, the general presentation of a position – a set of attitudes on economic philosophy – had the added sharpness peculiar to the House of Commons and to the combat of debate. And Margaret Thatcher brings to that arena a considerable weaponry: sardonic, acid, extremely good on detail, verbally dextrous, even witty, she was a competent match for the instinctive challenge to the right-of-centre Conservative views.

What is apparent in the speech is that it represents a continuation and development of economic and social thinking discernible in the April 1961 Budget contribution. Like the sowing of the teeth from which sprang forth fully armed men, the implantation of Margaret Thatcher in the Treasury team under Iain Macleod in the Spring of 1966 merely released within her a force the direction and structure of which was mature and thought out, even if it was also representative of a minority view. She addressed herself to a number of issues: strong opposition to economic subsidy, and a belief that the inefficient should go out of business; strong and well-informed views on the introduction of taxation in order that it should benefit enterprise; an attack on the number of forms people have to fill up, and the bureaucratic mish-mash resulting from this; a detailed chronology, from her genuine reading of past Finance Bills and Budget statements, of past tax reliefs in order to demonstrate what she saw as a central fault in the Budget, a failure to encourage enterprise, and the use of tax to bolster social commitments.

But most important of all were the sections of her speech on inflation and prices. She came at the issue first, in practical terms, in the context of meat and groceries, and from the woman's point of view; but then she dealt with it in what are now familiar economic terms. Labour's proposals favoured inflation because they put the average growth target between 1964 and 1970 at 3.8 percent with the increase in public expenditure at 4 percent a year; 'This is a blueprint for inflation,' she said. 'But when to that is added the performance of the rate of growth, about two percent over the past year, it can be seen that inflation is built into the economy, and we shall get it more and more under a Labour government.' The remaining five minutes of her speech were a sustained attack on Labour's basic economic philosophy of subsidies, rising taxation and greater State control, contrasting it with an equal and opposite Conservative approach compellingly demonstrated with references to Budgets from 1947 through to the early sixties.

Edward Heath was present, a witness to her clear and obvious ability in the field, not just of taxation, but of economics generally. And it was not just command of the fiscal and business implication; she displayed a political aggressiveness strongly in keeping with the demands of circumstance at the time. Following the March 1966 general election Harold Wilson was riding a tide of popularity which was unsupported by the necessary economic stability. He could only sustain it by being irresponsible, and the Treasury was not going to permit that. The actual choice was between devaluation and savage cuts, and Wilson chose cuts. Margaret Thatcher's style was suited in opposition to the Wilson-Callaghan combination, and, if one is to judge from her parliamentary performance, her most productive period in opposition was between March 1966 and October 1967.

*

Edward Heath moved her in the autumn of 1967. It was both promotion and a sideways shift, away from her first love, economics. Though she became part of the 'Shadow Cabinet' it was as principle spokesman on Power for a year, to October 1968, then on Transport for a further year before taking up the Education spokesmanship in October 1969, at the time of the Selsdon Park shadow cabinet meeting at which election strategy was discussed. Although Margaret Thatcher described herself as 'Selsdon Woman', the flippancy concealed, or perhaps emphasised for those sharp enough to see it, her basic isolation from the central economic team within the Conservative Party. And this isolation was confirmed when Heath formed the 1970 Cabinet with Margaret Thatcher keeping her shadow responsibility for Education and Science.

Cause and effect deserve some comment. Iain Macleod thought Margaret Thatcher exceptionally able; she herself was engaged in her preferred area on Treasury matters; yet the party leader excluded her on formation of an administration from precisely that area, putting both herself and Keith Joseph into high-spending ministries controlled by, rather than being part of, the financial management structure. Jealousy? Fear? A reluctance to be challenged on the hard options? An inability, like hers later, to work closely with people other than those of a like persuasion? Edward Heath declines to answer any of these questions, indeed any questions at all, threatening us with eventual memoirs. If comprehensive, they will be stimulating.

CHAPTER ELEVEN

'A Voice like Tinkling Glass'

Excluded from her first option, but included in the Cabinet with senior responsibility, Margaret Thatcher was consigned to the wings. It is a dangerous approach. To have people of one's own persuasion responsible for the central policy issues is all right if the policies work. To make critics and potential opponents directly party to the same decision-making process is the art of politics and indicates the presence of the true adrenalin of power, most necessary should things come unstuck. The critics and opponents are then less able to dissociate. It is part of the failure of Edward Heath – and, for all his qualities, his record of failure, by the rough and brutal measure of whether one wins or not, is fairly massive, losing as he did three out of four general elections – that he either failed to recognise Margaret Thatcher's political qualities as expressed through clear, right-wing policies, or that he simply could not stomach that particular road towards rectitude. However it is regarded, his consignment of her to Education contained within it the seeds of his own undoing.

He could not possibly have been conscious of this. What he must have been aware of, since the 1966 speech already referred to it, was the general drift of her mind on economic matters, and its increasing relevance to the uncertain and opportunist handling of the economy by Harold Wilson which led the British electorate to replace him in 1970, basically because his apparent wizardry had not paid off. Much of what she had said then was right; much of it was incorporated, following Selsdon Park, in the 1970 Conservative Manifesto, which was detailed in its commitments. A situation was therefore created by Heath in which he needed to be right on the economy, but also right in political terms. Otherwise, he faced forces within the party more right-wing than he was, ready to judge adversely any inability on his part to take firm hold of the running of the country.

It is cosy and comfortable to see her 1975 victory as the result of 'a succession of accidents', 'a surprise to her supporters, even to herself', which is the view in Wapshott and Brock. But it is credible only if one believes the word of ambitious and totally dedicated politicians who publicly engage in self-denying ordinances of the 'I don't see it happening in my time' variety. In her mind's eye she saw it happening all the time. In her political actions she made it happen.

It was, and indeed still is, politically advantageous for the period between 1970 and 1975 to be seen as one in which she worked hard at departmental administration, learning French, being patient, and familiarising herself with the names and natures of the three hundred and more Conservative members of the House of Commons whom she would one day lead. But it is a rose-tinted view of what politics and power are about. Heath had been a witness to her potential ability, and had shunted it into a succession of sidings, not really acceptable to her. She was a witness of his failure of nerve in 1972, failure of judgment in early 1974, and failure of leadership as the year proceeded.

Although Wilson was in power from February, the autumn background to the leadership struggle – a background of inflation at 17 percent, and rising, and wages and salaries moving at an even higher rate of more than 19 percent – was an indictment more of Edward Heath's failure between 1970-74. It is curious how failure attracts loyalty.

Following Keith Joseph's Birmingham speech, eagerly taken up and attacked by Barbara Castle, three Conservative Whips resigned. The following week the 1922 Committee debated the question of rules for a leadership election. Heath indicated that he was willing to accept a reform in the system for electing the party leader, but in a sense this put off into the new year the actual contest. It provided vital time for Margaret Thatcher to establish herself. For Heath it represented an important breathing space, but one which could only provide him with the opportunity to demonstrate that there was no alternative, always the strategy of the beleaguered leader who had failed, never an adequate defence.

On November 3, Peter Walker made a speech at Droitwich

which clearly indicated fears in the party about a shift to the Right, in the wake of two general election defeats and the inevitability of a leadership election. Conservatives believed in appealing to 'all sections of society', he said, and went on to oppose monetary policy. At the end of that week, Edward Heath, in a Shadow Cabinet re-shuffle, moved Margaret Thatcher back into mainstream economic responsibilities, but *only as deputy* to Robert Carr, the Shadow Chancellor. All the other changes, which included the promotions of Nicholas Scott and Timothy Raison to the Shadow Cabinet, and the internal promotion of Geoffrey Rippon to replace Alec Douglas-Home on Foreign Office responsibilities, favoured Heath men. In effect, Margaret Thatcher was being demoted, and restored to the position she had occupied under Iain Macleod more than eight years earlier. At the same time, she was being given a central parliamentary platform from which to exercise her proven talents in the realm of economics at a time of growing crisis for the Wilson Government, and for just as long as the newly-formed shadow structure of the party under Heath's leadership was to last. It was an extraordinary decision.

*

It was exactly a week later, on Thursday November 14, that Edward Heath had his first meeting since the general election with Conservative backbenchers, and agreed to a new procedure for electing a leader. He would play no part in deciding what it would be. His reception was respectful, unenthusiastic and at times icy. Though the fact was not articulated, it was clear that many felt he should go. Many also felt that the election should be then, under existing rules. But these could only come into force if Heath resigned first. He made the mistake of not taking up the challenge then and there.

One week more, on Thursday November 21, and Keith Joseph visited Margaret Thatcher in her office in the House to tell her he would not be contending for the leadership. She then informed Heath that she would be challenging him. It was the fateful day of the IRA Birmingham bomb blasts, which swept other stories from the pages of newspapers, but by the weekend Margaret Thatcher, not just as a contender, but as a potentially successful one, was being promoted in the papers. At that early stage, with no leadership election rules drawn up, it was openly the view that Heath's strength lay in the unwillingness of Cabinet colleagues to stand against him. Once again, it represented a negative form of defence.

There followed immediately all the speculative and mainly negative articles about her. Women attract a different vocabulary of assessment, and it is demeaning: 'peaches-and-cream complexion', 'voice like tinkling glass', set going a process which then switched to a widespread denunciation of her 'hoarding habits', as revealed in a magazine called *Pre-Retirement Choice*. As every politician knows, all publicity is good publicity, and Margaret Thatcher needed it more than most. She won the approval of at least those believing in 'prudent' hoarding; she then won the approval of at least some of her critics by a carefully-worded justification for what she had advised.

By mid-December, with Wilson giving way, before the Paris Summit, on continued membership of the EEC 'if the terms are right', and with virtually all economic news within Britain bad, Heath signalled his determination to stand again for the leadership, and his conviction that the Shadow Cabinet were all working well. On the same day, December 15, Keith Joseph reasserted his economic arguments of the summer about controlling the money supply.

Two days later the leadership election rules were announced, proposing that the leader has to stand for re-election each year, and get an absolute majority plus fifteen percent to remain; otherwise, a second and subsequent ballot follows, with eliminations, until an absolute majority be achieved by a new leader. Once again, good advice, though not intended to sustain Heath's leadership, came from the Bow Group magazine, *Crossbow*, in an editorial which pointed out that Heath's inability to communicate personal warmth prejudiced the party's prospects for regaining power. Heath's response was to launch a major attack on Labour's economic mismanagement the next day in the Commons.

The leadership elections procedures were debated in mid-January, and approved. On January 20, Hugh Fraser's name went forward. On January 22 it emerged that both James Prior and William Whitelaw would stand on the second ballot, in the event of Heath failing. It turned the first ballot into a vote of confidence in a leader who had lost two consecutive general elections.

Margaret Thatcher set a determined pace. On the Monday of the week before the first ballot she handed in her nomination papers to Edward du Cann. At that stage there was moderate confidence that Heath would survive as leader – his supporters gave him 120 of the 140 votes he needed – and equal assurance that if he did not, the winner would be an as-yet-undeclared contender. When nominations closed there were the expected three candidates, Heath, Fraser, Thatcher. There was also growing confidence among Margaret Thatcher's supporters combined with a 'prudent' determination to continue the further search for support, just like hunting the shops for more tins of meat to put away as security. Too late, a scramble by others, including Sir Geoffrey Howe, Maurice Macmillan and Julian Amery, was signalled on the eve of the first ballot, indicating, more than anything else, that support for Heath was not sufficient for his survival.

The vote on Tuesday February 4, of 130 for Margaret Thatcher, 119 for Edward Heath and 16 for Hugh Fraser, led to Heath's departure and signalled a sufficient Conservative Party wish to move towards the Right to handicap alternative, second ballot moves. Those who had supported Margaret Thatcher cannot have been displeased at having a winner, and would have faced difficulty in turning their votes into 'tactical' ones. The concept is too theoretical. It implies too much 'head' and too little response to the enthusiams of the heart and instincts. Her determination and guts prevailed.

Margaret Thatcher won the most important contest of her life when she defeated Edward Heath. She went on a week later to defeat William Whitelaw, on Tuesday February 11, by 67 votes. She polled 146 out of a total of 274. William Whitelaw received 79 votes; James Prior and Geoffrey Howe 19 each, and John Peyton 11.

She won because of her instincts about power. She recognised the need for momentum, and the appeal of challenge. She created what appeared to be a credible and different 'policy' for the Conservative Party. She offered opportunity to the disaffected and the ignored. She tackled a whole range of traditions and shibboleths about the transfer of power within the party, and the benign, clubbable instincts which too many of its members had for too long thought they believed in. In this she represented a dose of honest realism, and a majority faced up, in different ways, to the fact that politics is about getting and keeping power, and about winning. Once she had set that relatively obvious perception before their eyes, she was more secure than even she believed. The underlying consistency in her character prevailed. So, too, did a set of simple perceptions about politics, and essentially about Edward Heath, since he was the most significant figure on her political horizon for as long as he remained leader. When his failure manifested itself in the February 1974 general election it became failure of a kind necessitating his removal. In her eyes that meant herself replacing him.

Since Harold Wilson had pulled the double election trick in 1966, following his insecure 1964 victory, the same process was anticipated, and came to pass in the autumn of 1974. It did not prevent, within the Conservative Party, the necessary corollary to Heath's failure, that it had been a result of policy changes and weakness as well as misjudgments about the confrontation with the miners. The latter was a personal problem, stubbornness, judgment, tact. The former, however, was a party problem. Policy failure demands a change of direction, if only a change back to what had prevailed and then been abandoned. This brought into being the Centre for Policy Studies, which in turn provided a focus for alternative thinking about the direction the party should take. What became crucial, and ultimately dictated the course of Margaret Thatcher's victory, was the presentation to the Conservative Party of an alternative to failure, which was the promise of success in both a new face, as well as new policy directions. The predictable other offer, belatedly made by William Whitelaw, but only when he had assured himself that Heath really *had* failed, was party unity. This was compromise. It stood no chance against the far stronger clearer prospect offered by Margaret Thatcher, that tough, new, uncompromising, re-stated Conservative values would lead to electoral victory under her. Politicians do not *want* unity; it is an incidental acquisition, of limited importance, rather than an objective. They want victory. They want to win seats and majorities. And their instincts tell them when they have found a winner, just as surely as those instincts expose, often cruelly, the inescapable indications that they are led by a loser.

In democratic states, potential winners demonstrate their capacities within parliaments. She had already done this convincingly on a number of occasions more effectively than her enemies like to admit. She had further opportunity after becoming Treasury spokesman once again, and she used it particularly well immediately before the leadership election in confrontation with Denis Healey. The Chamber is a more significant arena on such occasions than those outside can perceive, or those within care to admit. Even the most extrovert of politicians become seduced by its exclusive atmosphere and their rights within it; and no mechanisms, except perhaps those of fiction, have managed both to convey and reveal its workings in terms of power struggles. Particularly to a party in which the elected member had retained his central position in deciding on succession was this the case. The Conservatives had strengthened this still further by the setting up of democratic procedures for the election or confirmation of its leader. Being in Opposition gave added muscle to the backbench members at the expense of Shadow Cabinet authority which had been weakened by two election defeats in a year. Margaret Thatcher had always recognised the importance of this. While it is perhaps not possible to claim that she never made a foolish speech, it is clear, from a study of her contributions to the legislative process over the previous fifteen years, that all her innate qualities of hard slog, determination, attention to detail, consistency in both research and presentation, and the enunciating of a solid body of ideas, even obvious and mundane ones, constituted an impressive record which, if it did not have much impact on the minority of Conservatives more senior to herself, represented a fine example to the majority who were more junior. And she gave a convincing and sustained example of this at the very time of the leadership contest, in the debates on the Finance Bill.

She schooled herself to be a winner in the eyes of those who would elect her, setting aside the far less important hunt for public popularity, party consensus, policy compromise. She emphasised simplicity and directness, on what she wanted, the beliefs on which it would be based, the personality by which it would be achieved.

Winning is the essential objective in politics, as it is wherever happiness is fulfilled through ambition. It dwarfs all other achievements. Margaret Thatcher had won the most important prize of all on the road to power, leadership of her party. She could now devote all her energies to winning the next prize, power itself.

CHAPTER TWELVE

'The Next Name on the list'

Margaret Thatcher became 'the next name in the list' of Conservative Party leaders, and used the phrase 'stamp of greatness' to describe the quality of leadership given to the Conservative Party by Macmillan, Home and Heath. It was important to her that there had been 'open electoral contest', and she then emphasised the unity needed by the Opposition as it addressed itself to the main task; returning to power. Her mind was set, not on the list to which she referred, but on a longer and more varied list, of Britain's Prime Ministers. That was where she wanted to append her name next.

She described the whole process of becoming leader, at her euphoric press conference on that February afternoon, as 'like a dream'. Wapshott and Brock describe it as being achieved through 'a succession of accidents'.* Patrick Cosgrave is more conscious of her 'warrior' instinct, both in the planning and execution of her dual struggle to remove Heath *and* become his successor.** Allan Mayer *** is also conscious of the necessary level of tactic and strategy rather than of 'accident', though he does underestimate the tacit support by Airey Neave, and the active canvass by others committed *to* Margaret Thatcher, rather than merely *against* Edward Heath.

The reality, like most things in her career, was far from being 'a dream'. There is a hard, slogging quality in her approach to power, and it had paid off. Consistency, which is at heart an inflexible characteristic, is the enemy of imagination, and there-

---

* Wapshott and Brock, op. cit.
** Patrick Cosgrave: *Margaret Thatcher, Prime Minister* (London, 1978).
*** Allan J. Mayer: *Madam Prime Minister: Margert Thatcher and her rise to Power* (New York, 1979).

fore of the inspired and brilliant act in politics. And in the period which now faced her, looking forward from February 1975 to an indeterminate moment in the future when the next general election would be called, it was to be her dogged determination, her will to succeed by hard work and application, that would dictate her course.

The underlying approach would relate to the economy. It was her strong suit as a politician. It was the principal reason for the most significant support she enjoyed within the Conservative Party. And its ingredients were likely to be enhanced steadily by the performance of the administration led by Harold Wilson and, in due course, by his successor, James Callaghan.

But the economy, central to public life, central to everyone's domestic existence, is also politically boring. It is *always* there. It is generally gloomy. It does not always, even often, follow predictions, particularly those about things getting better. It is statistical. It is national rather than personal. Its undoubted primary importance does not readily relate to the man in the street. Doing the 'right thing', or doing the 'wrong thing', on employment, inflation, borrowing, taxation, incentive, the unions, while it may be crucial to the very existence of the state, and certainly affects everyone's life, needs the added dimensions of other and often only marginally related, issues to give that whiff of excitement and colour to leadership and popularity.

It has already been argued that this was critical in the general election of 1983, with 'the Falklands spirit' providing the extra dimension of excitement and colour which achieved victory. The possibility has also been argued, circumstantially, that Margaret Thatcher recognised this well before the election, indeed before the outbreak of hostilities in the South Atlantic, and deliberately engineered the necessary dimension by which victory could be assured. It will be at least thirty years, more likely never, before any final judgment can be made on decisions which ultimately were her own. But the circumstantial nature of the evidence surrounding her performance in leadership between the summer of 1981 and the invasion of the Falklands in April 1982 is paralleled elsewhere in her career, and to a large extent removes the element of luck or accident which is far too often attributed to politicians who are adept in power. Margret Thatcher studied to succeed and to win. She set out to be leader of the Conservative

Party deliberately, with key supporters operating on her behalf. She did so earlier than is generally recognised, and with infinitely more skill and instinctive judgment than that with which she is credited. And, having achieved this goal, she applied herself to the next target, of adding her name to the ultimate list, with the same deliberation.

She chose issues which gave an extra dimension to her political appeal. These included race and immigration, standing up to the Soviet Union, standing shoulder-to-shoulder with the United States. On all of them she was conscious that, side by side with the potential handicap of augmenting division and prejudicing the democratic consent which was a traditional part of Conservative philosophy, she was catering also to an alternative view which itself was gathering strength, and on which a future electoral victory could be based. It was a silent, moral majority view, not just about who governs Britain, and how firmly it is done. It was also about an interpretation of the crying need for government itself to be carried on by the traditional democratic process once again, and not by the uneasy partnership of the bureraucracy and the trade unions, with politicians and the people they represent standing in a futile frozen wasteland in between.

This definition of a new order had been fumbled by Edward Heath in the February 1974 general election, and thrown away. It had never really been tackled by Harold Wilson, nor was it going to be tackled following the October 1974 mandate which gave him an overall majority of three, and a more comfortable effective working majority.

The shape of the new order was already inherent in Margaret Thatcher's economic policy. Sound, consistent and logical, this provided the ground bass for the increasingly volatile economic conditions in the latter half of the 1970s. But it was not enough. Colour and style in leadership, that physiognomy and index to mind and character, particularly if its basis is consistency, needs the combative dimension of a series of issues which touch upon more than the housekeeping responsibilities of life. Issues like Western defence, a place in the world balance of power, a role in Africa, in Commonwealth affairs, on the issue of immigration, even if these were negatively constructed, as in the case of race and immigration, provided the necessary quality and shape to her leadership which, confined within the realm of economic competence, would be seriously circumscribed, particularly in view of the very considerable experience of the man to whom she was now opposed, Harold Wilson. And, even when he was succeeded by James Callaghan, the comparative levels of political experience were heavily weighted against her.

Wilson had Cabinet experience, albeit in the War Cabinet Secretariat, back in the early 1940s. He had direct Cabinet experience from 1947, and he won his first general election as Labour leader after only eighteen months, against Alec Douglas-Home in October 1964. His basic background was economic. So was that of James Callaghan, who had been Wilson's Chancellor of the Exchequer as well as occupying the Home and Foreign Offices before succeeding Wilson in April 1976. This formidable range of experience induced the second important strand in what she set out to do in early 1975, which was to establish herself in world terms.

The third strand was, in a sense, the negative one, of needing to play down rather than capitalise on the fact that she was a woman. While this was an important asset, in terms of novelty and potential electoral appeal, as well as setting different standards in public relations, debating techniques and the presentation of her personality, it was an asset to be husbanded for a time when it would really matter with the British public, and not squandered among her predominantly, but not exclusively male colleagues at Westminister.

These, then, are the broad aspects of the political character of the new Conservative Party leader: a sound and consistent economic philosophy, a good and reliable practical demonstration of the philosophy, mainly confined to opposition; the need for self-education in almost every other area; the will to educate herself; the instinct to make opportunity out of limited material; and the considerable asset of being underestimated from the very beginning.

This last was common to her own party as much as to the Labour Government, and to Harold Wilson and James Callaghan, both of whom adopted a patronising approach towards her which indicated more clearly than anything else that they were making the elementary mistake of underestimating her ability.

She had to deal with Wilson as Prime Minister for just over one year. During that time she addressed herself to three key issues:

parliamentary technique, particularly the vital business of Prime Minister's Question Time; world affairs, with the initial emphasis on the United States; East-West relations, with the two basic problems being Anglo-Soviet trade, over which she clashed with Wilson in April, 1975, and the objective of détente, which provoked an important but largely ignored speech in July 1975, but which was more fundamentally central to her political future than was apparent at that time.

Harold Wilson resigned on March 16, 1976. James Callaghan became Prime Minister on March 23. On the same day the death of a Labour backbencher deprived the party of its overall majority, and the defection, two days later, of another Labour backbencher to the Conservative Party further weakened Callaghan's position.

It encouraged in Margaret Thatcher another deep and instinctive characteristic, the urge for positive combat. Restless, impatient, disdainful, unwilling to rely on a providence which had been less than kind to her, she was determined, warrior-like, to assault the citadel of power again and again, knowing that in time it would fall, and knowing that the image of such impatient determination would stand her in good stead in the resultant electoral contest.

*

The importance of Margaret Thatcher's first visit to the United States, as leader of the Conservative Party, lay in several directions. She had an affinity with certain aspects of American culture: it was a society for the strong, not the weak; it rewarded enterprise and endeavour; it was overwhelmingly committed to a concept of defence and the overall balance of power which favoured détente only along lines where cutbacks were bargained for equally; it valued the participation of Britain and of Europe, but on the basis of a special relationship with the British people who represented the most secure ally in Europe. Even domestic culture – the way the United States tackled health and welfare, crime and poverty, unemployment – was of direct interest, since it charted an alternative approach to the proper role of government and the extent to which it should intrude upon and redistribute national income.

What she did while she was there was even more interesting

than what she felt. She delivered in her speeches a serious and well-reasoned critique on Britain which was clearly and emphatically political. It was characteristic of her to reject convention, at least when it suited. And she was unaffected by the mildly lecturing reproof she received from the Foreign Secretary, James Callaghan, who pointed out, as reports came back of her criticisms of British socialism, 'when we are abroad all of us submerge our individual party policies in the interests of the country we come from'. She was incapable of that. While the main profile of her presented to the American people was a frivolous one, mixing an emphasis on feminism which she repudiated with one on her being a new, original and refreshing phenomenon on the British political scene which she welcomed, the real purpose of her visit was also successfully achieved. This was to begin to establish her potential position as a world leader. While having the right answers on defence, détente, and NATO was crucial, so also was the presentation of intended domestic policies which would lead to the recovery of Britain as a trading partner rather than as an economic burden to the Western world. And it is significant that the only two speeches from that United States tour which Margaret Thatcher chose to republish in her selected speeches from the first two years of her leadership, *Let Our Children Grow Tall*, are about political economy.

They examine political discretion in the gathering and spending of the Government's share of national wealth, and how and why this should be changed in Britain. Her arguments went to the very centre of political controversy, and represented a fundamental challenge to the convention which Callaghan, as well as an irate press in Britain, wished to see preserved. She was right, too. The convention, in the world of GATT, NATO, the EEC and the IMF, is out of date. She breached it very substantially, however. She sought to displace the pursuit of equality of opportunity. She believes people should have the choice to be both unequal and different. And from an obscure American Middle West saying, she abstracted the idea for the title of her book, a cumbersome but accurate reflection of the central message in her political philosophy: the remaking of the balance between the state and private enterprise in favour of the latter, and in order that the individual – particularly the children who would form the next generation – exercise the choice to 'grow taller than others, if they have it in them to do so'.

She carried the argument a stage further in a lecture at Roosevelt University in Chicago on September 15, which began from the provocative if negative standpoint that politicians, who seem so often to get wrong their intrusion into the management of economy and market, are at the same time pathologically driven to continue along the same course of interfering, with ever renewed desires to counter the charge of incompetence levelled against them by economists who are not answerable to the same constraints.

She compared, in the same speech, the United States' capacity to bring down its inflation rates to 'tolerable' levels with the incapacity of the United Kingdom to do the same. One of the reasons she offered for this failure derived from incorrect value judgments made by politicians about their priorities. For her, the first was unquestionably the reduction of inflation. This was in marked distinction to the priorities of the Wilson administration, which put the issue of unemployment before rising prices and regularly rising wages. It was one thing to criticise this at home, quite another to use the criticism as part of a mutual invocation of values – those of American society with those which she sought to promote as domestic Conservative policy.

She justified what she was saying in the third strand of her Chicago theme: interdependence. The polite convention of not washing domestic linen abroad was overthrown by the relevance of domestic policy internationally. One country's inflation spilt over into the economies of other countries, distorting trade and undermining trust and security. And there was no remedy, in her view, in loans and grants from the IMF; they merely brought time and put off the solution to the problem.

The serious messages contained in these lectures and in other speeches, though not as widely reported as her more popular impact on the American people, nevertheless filtered through sufficiently to provoke Labour Party attacks on her, a sure sign that her impact was a moderate worry.

There was a consistency and cohesion about her economic doctrine to which Anglo-American accord lent weight. She knew it, and focused attention on it. The same was true of other trips she made in her first two years as Opposition leader. There were few Western democracies to which she paid visits which were in a sorrier economic and social plight, nor more run-down in terms of morale, than Britain. And it was her deliberate intent to emphasise this in order to chart the Conservative alternative to socialism.

*

She displayed assurance, and she learned assurance. Intellectually, she made a greater impact than emotionally. And the mild controversy which she had set in train by her criticisms in the United States of Britain under a Labour Government provided her with an important theme for her first speech to the Conservative Party Conference as leader in Blackpool in October 1975. The crisis which was the main concern of that conference was the crisis of capitalism; how to present to the British electorate a convincing set of Conservative economic policies which would defeat the Labour Party. But, publicly, Margaret Thatcher rejected this perception of the crisis altogether, and offered another: the crisis of socialism, against which she then launched a detailed assault. It began with the words, 'Whatever could I say about Britain that is half as damaging as what this Labour Government has done to our country?' It then went on to list the economic flaws: price inflation at 26 percent, failure of the social contract, rising unemployment, production below what it had been during the Heath three-day week – 'We have really got a three-day week now, only it takes five days to do it' – public spending and borrowing at record levels. the Labour Government, she said, had 'the usual Socialist disease: they have run out of other people's money.'

She was equally blunt about the Marxist takeover of the Labour Party at constituency level, 'infested' by left-wingers as Harold Wilson is quoted by her as saying. The same infestation is detected in other fields, such as education and industry, constituting a moral and political challenge to be tackled side by side with the economic ones. The country faced a conspiracy, made up of 'brainwashing' and 'intimidation designed to undermine fundamental deliefs and values. . . .'

'Let me give you my vision,' she asked, rhetorically, of a party which had spent most of the week at Blackpool still divided in its loyalties between the new leader and the old. By the time she came to this point of confession and exhortation, Edward Heath had left. But he had left behind him a degree of disaffection some of which had been made deliberately and divisively public in comments to journalists about Margaret Thatcher and Keith Joseph being 'fanatics who would hurt the country and ruin the Conservative Party'.* This was ineffectually denied. His own speech to the conference had been rapturously received, as had he – a typically Conservative, indeed very British, gesture of atonement for his irreversible departure from the leadership. But it was nothing more, and his own foolish and ill-judged response to it made easier the decisive way in which Margaret Thatcher turned the latter half of her own major speech, at the end and climax of the conference, into a major emotional watershed, cutting off the past, *his* past, and designating a new beginning based on her own 'vision': 'a man's right to work as he will, to spend what he earns, to own property, to have the state as servant and not as master: these are the British inheritance. They are the essence of a free country, and on that freedom all our other freedoms depend.'

The speech was very British: vulgar, tub-thumping, emotive, simplistic. It contained cheap music-hall humour: 'I sometimes think the Labour Party is like a pub where the mild is running out. If someone does not do something soon, all that is left will be bitter, and all that is bitter will be Left.'

It divided society into two camps, one free and one state-owned; and it set them in opposition to one another. It sought also to re-draw the line of division: 'When the next Conservative Government comes to power, many trade unionists will have put it there,' and in order for this to become a reality, she advocated the same tactics of infiltration and rule-book manipulation of unions as had been carried out by the far Left.

It was a sensationally successful speech, and deservedly so. Her audience sensed that 'will to power' which born winners exude. It was not that she was right, but that she had conviction. She was deliberately doing what Edward Heath had equally deliberately accused her of, which was to divide the country by narrowing down the Conservative options, and the party's eventual electoral target. For him, this should have been the country's good; for her the country's good, above all else, lay in her own success: this was victory, a simple, clear mandate to govern and to go on governing for a very long time. Her starting point

---

* Allan J. Mayer, op. cit.

needed to be the strong conviction of her own party that she could do it. And she achieved this indisputably at Blackpool, in October 1975.

*

Margaret Thatcher had become leader of the Conservative Party because she offered a change of direction. Yet the change of direction was not something new. It was a change back, to certain basic principles fundamental to elementary housekeeping: the stabilising of money as an item the constant value of which could be trusted, the stabilising of work practices, so that labour also could be trusted in its input to productivity, the encouragement of enterprise and initiative in order to make capital out of the stability through competitiveness and the natural superiority with which Margaret Thatcher consistently endowed the British people.

The newness lay in the determination and simplicity of her approach. What is genuinely refreshing about her economic speeches after becoming leader, two broadly comprehensive examples of which have been cited, is in their confident restatement of a set of policies which inescapably would require nerves of steel to sustain through a full period of opposition, and then deploy in order to win power. Post-war British politics had produced a succession of leaders disposed to fudge issues and blur the edge of definition. If they did not do it to the electorate, and most did, they certainly did it between elections; and Edward Heath was the biggest casualty of that. But after sixteen years in parliament, with limited experience in dealing with economic issues, and virtually none on other issues, Margaret Thatcher's economic stand was, of itself, a thin foundation for overall leadership of the Conservatives. And the principle behind it, of restating, adopting and then sticking with a simple formula, that you reap what you sow, seemed ill-suited to other issues.

Yet it was to her credit, in terms of judgment, that she sensed the mood in Britain to be ripe for an era of principle over expediency in politics, and that she applied exactly the same basic thought processes to foreign affairs as she had done to economic affairs. From her first months as leader she grappled with the key question of détente. Her basic approach is well documented. All the biographies deal succinctly with her first confrontation with Harold Wilson, in April 1975 on his return from Moscow after the signing of a new Anglo-Soviet trade agreement, when she expressed doubt over the desirability of such a pact. Wilson treated her with condescension. In July 1975 she made a speech on détente in which the emphasis placed on it, during the previous decade, as a desirable objective, was contrasted sharply with the *fact* of steady Soviet military expansion during the same period. The speech made no great public impact. In the United States, and at the Conservative Party Conference in October, she dwelt on the border issues of East-West relations, defence and Soviet aggrandisement, with denunciation of Marxism and socialism which were treated as essential political fulminations. It was not until January 18 1976, in a major and hard-hitting anti-Soviet speech given in Kensington Town Hall that she achieved the desired domestic impact, combining it however with an even more significant impact on Russian opinion. The Soviet press launched an attack on her, calling her 'Iron Lady', and effectively created the political reputation on international affairs which, by their dismissal, her Labour opponents had denied her, up to that point.

By stating the obvious, by invoking the basic fears of the Cold War, by substantiating them with facts about armaments, and by turning her anger against the Government for its weakness and uncertainty, she established herself on three vital fronts: *against* the Soviets, *for* the free world, and on one clear side of an ideological divide at home the extent or balance of which had yet to be tested. It was untested precisely because it did not exist as a dominant political issue. The prevarications inherent in an over-reliance upon détente as an answer for everything had fogged the issue without bringing any reliable or clear advantage to the West. It therefore needed to be challenged. Why not by her, a female Parsifal, available to redeem the corrupted and enfeebled Knights of the Grail of Western freedom? Successive Governments, including Heath's, had gone along with détente as a broad policy which seemed to meet with a consensus support. And this had swallowed up the clear idea of right and wrong, black and white, as applied to the complicated world balance of power.

Much is made of the influence of Robert Conquest on Margaret Thatcher's ideas about Communism and Soviet ambition at this time. He became an adviser following her July 1975 speech, and

1 The Mask of Ambition, October 1970

Accident, not art, reveals the mind's construction in the face. Since 1970, when she became Secretary of State for Education, Margaret Thatcher's face has been increasingly a matter of public record; yet on the whole inscrutable. The following pages represent a chronological sequence tied to the key political events in her career. Of her, at the time of the leadership struggle (*see numbers 4, 5 and 6*), Barbara Castle wrote: 'What interests me is how blooming she looks — she has never been prettier. I am interested because I understand this phenomenon . . . She is in love: in love with power, success — and with herself . . . if we have to have Tories, good luck to her.' — *The Castle Diaries 74-76*, 5 February 1975

2 Summoned to Office,
   June 1970

3 Pre-election Cabinet,
   January 1974

4 Leadership Candidate,
   October 1974

5 Wins first ballot,
   February 1975

6 Becomes Leader,
   February 1975

7 After US Tour,
   September 1975

8 Opposing, 1976

9 Workload, 1977

10 Crucial Vote,
    28 March 1979

1 Election Victory,
   May 1979

12 Conservative Conference,
    October 1980

13 Rethinking the Economy,
    April 1980

4 Conservative Conference,
   October 1981

15 Falklands Stress,
    April 1982

16 Falklands Spirit,
    October 1982

7 Launching Manifesto,
   May 1983

18 Eve of Victory, June 1983

19 'Round and About',
    Summer 1983

20   The Face of Power, Summer 1983

'In 1982, she had a number of teeth capped, which slightly changed her enunciation and removed a distinctive gap between the teeth at the front of the right side of her mouth.

'She has long abandoned the extravagant sculptured hair-dos of the Opposition years in favour of a more manageable, more dignified, less severe style.

'Thatcher dislikes blow drying. Her hair is so fine that it needs to be set in rollers after it has been permed to give it body. She also dyes her hair. She was originally fair, but by 1976 the hair was white. Now she is a brunette . . . .' — from *Thatcher,* by Nicholas Wapshott and George Brock undoubtedly brought a substantial amount of knowledge and well-informed judgment to bear on her mind. Much is also made of her 'discovery' of Solzhenitsyn's *The First Circle*, and her extensive reading subsequently of modern Russian writing in order to inform herself about a culture which denied the basic freedoms for which she stood. Perhaps not enough is made of her instinct, which recognised the reinforcement provided from these sources for convictions which were well formed and absolute. It is probable that a certain shrewd intent lay behind the picture of herself conveyed in Patrick Cosgrave's comment about her 'transformation': 'Certainly, the Chelsea speech was the beginning of important things for her, and nothing gives her more pleasure than the fact that since she became leader she had made a world-wide impression in the field of which she was most ignorant at the outset.' It was ignorance of detail, a relatively minor omission and one easily remedied; it was not ignorance of the right course to pursue, in terms of establishing a reputation *and* appealing to potential majority of the British people.'

To this central aim Robert Conquest was an adjunct, someone who endorsed her beliefs and filled in the detail, but not necessarily a modifier of the beliefs. These did not diverge from being simple, and, in basic terms, not open to modification. A revulsion for totalitarianism, an admiration for the principles of freedom within the law, which is both logical and emotional, are central to her stated political beliefs. The word 'freedom' is used as an economic touchstone, and applied to choices about work and social advantage. But it is equally applicable to defence and the world balance of power in her eyes. And having grown up through the European shadows of Nazism and fascism she had an equally well-developed objection to modern régimes like that of the Soviet Union, which deprived people of freedom and were ideologically opposed to Western democratic systems under which such freedom worked tolerably well.

Her belief was that the Soviets were a potential, if not actual, enemy and should be treated as such. They would respect power and strength set against them; and that is all they would respect. An imprecise road towards détente could turn into unilateralism, and it would be Chamberlain's policy of appeasement in 1938 all over again.

There was a more important if more general force at work here, to which one adds the label of principle with a slight hesitation.

Margaret Thatcher was moving away from the idea of consensus. Broad agreement that détente as an objective was not just the most realistic and sensible approach to East-West relations, but was the only logical peaceful approach, had dominated political thought since the traumas of the Cuban missile crisis. Instinct told Margaret Thatcher that consensus was always a handicap in the pursuit of power. Heath's double defeat in 1974 had been occasioned by the abandonment of the Selsdon Conference line on the economy in favour of one that approximated to the British post-war political consensus that all governments have a responsibility to 'manage' economies in the interest of maintaining employment.

She challenged this. She went for the leadership on the basis of that challenge, and won. She constructed her initial year's political performance also on the instinctive challenging of consensus as well as abandoning convention and carrying the challenge abroad. That also worked. On Anglo-Soviet, East-West relations, whether in the context of trade or defence, the same basic challenge emerged. It was supported by logic. Any Western moves on détente over the last two decades have been from a reserve position of basic militancy. The offer of the olive branch was made under the shadow of the unfired but not unprimed missile. It had not worked too well. The Russians showed a marked reluctance about taking hold of the branch, and everything that was known about them, whether it derived from political, military, literary or intelligence sources, suggested that scepticism, in the end, was the most judicious approach. Yet for politicians scepticism is too negative; for politicians in opposition this is even more the case; and, for politicians of Margaret Thatcher's make-up, it offers an unacceptable route. She changed the emphasis, making détente the reserve option and bringing forward an enmity which was equal and opposite to what she believed was the basic, ideological enmity of the Soviet Union towards the West. 'We must add deterrence and defence to détente,' she said in Hanover on May 25 1976, in a speech to a meeting of the Christian Democratic Union, 'for unless we do, we in the West will find ourselves constantly accommodating ourselves to Marxist values, instead of making the world safe for our own. We should not be timid or uncertain in proclaiming our values; we must build a world in which freedom is on the offensive.'

She went on to berate the Soviets for their failure to honour a basic provision of the Helsinki agreement – the free flow of ideas – contrasting the West's laxness in letting extreme socialism gain currency and popularity, while Western ideology was kept firmly out of Russia.

The fight against extreme socialism, which had been her theme in the United States the previous autumn on a mainly economic argument, was being clothed with the extra dimension of being part of the struggle between a totalitarian ideology and a democratic one. It was being extended logically into the realms of defence and into education. She invoked the threat to the West of Marxist Left domination in school and universities, which had run as a strong tide in the late sixties in various European countries, but since had been countered by the growth of alternative right-wing views, notably in Britain by the rising membership in universities or Conservative societies and clubs.

On defence, and in defiance of traditional expectations where there could be such expectations of so new a phenomenon as a woman political leader in Britain who might one day be prime minister, she evinced interest, not just in broad international policy issues but in the military implications as well. She wanted to be a soldier's woman, and was by no means averse to service publicity, including those stimulating shots of her head and shoulders emerging from the cockpits of military vehicles. It gave human substance to the idea of reversing the priorities of détente with military alertness and defence spending. It made real and personal, in terms of her own increasingly clear commitments, the relationship between forces on the ground, defence alliances and pacts, ideologies and beliefs, economic and social policies, the philosophies being taught in British schools and universities, and the combative framework in which these all came together: the political arena of the House of Commons.

When Margaret Thatcher is described as a divisive force in British politics, this is what is meant: the deliberate choice of one direction for her thoughts and actions which rules out, or sets up in opposition, the alternative direction; she precludes that consensus which has been regarded for so long as an essential part of the body politic, and seeks out instead the confrontation which is a required element, indeed a central one, in her combative nature. Having sought it out, and established it with firm and well-researched credentials (this is where the Robert Conquests of her political career come in) she applies to it her fundamental political attribute of consistency.

Margaret Thatcher was formidable on the road to power. She changed attitudes within the Conservative Party about the major problem areas. One of these was the media. From a low point at the time of the leadership struggle, when she suffered indignity and dismissal or disdain at the hands of the media, she organised a press lobby which became increasingly vociferous on her behalf. She developed a media-management approach which could also be said to have brought out some of the worst instincts in journalistic attitude and judgment. But it was undoubtedly a basis for favourable attention when the 1979 general election came along. It was different, more manipulative and less natural than under previous Tory leaders. But it worked. She carried out a comparable reconstruction of Conservative Party policy organisation and also of her personal 'team'. The importance of publicity and promotion, advertising and speech-writing, briefings and formal press conferences set against actual ideas and performance, policy and intentions, changed. It was subtle and careful. As with the media, it worked. A focusing of the leader with growing emphasis on personality and character generalisation at the expense of a team with detailed policies to implement was the main intent; and it worked, too.

CHAPTER THIRTEEN

Defeating Callaghan

The check upon Margaret Thatcher's urgent and aggressive pursuit of power was the frustrating and obvious reality of James Callaghan's marginal but effective majority. If one examines the issues which dominated British politics between April 5 1976, when he became leader of the Labour Party in succession to Harold Wilson, and March 28 1979, when she finally achieved his political demise through the humiliation of a no-confidence defeat, they are almost all issues on which he was in retreat while she advanced, like a Wellington or a Napoleon, on his ill-defined position. Yet he managed to survive. Twisting and turning for support here, there, and everywhere, his survival was, of itself, a form of defeat, since it involved the growing exercise of expediency, trimming, compromise and policy reversal, in order to satisfy the various groups whose support was essential. And, by the same token, her relentless pursuit of him, severe, combative, uncompromising, and well organised, represented more than a succession of political victories; if the process fell short of the ultimate achievement of forcing dissolution upon him, it nevertheless emphasised the sharply defined, uncompromising substance of what she offered. And this was not just a question of making the best of Callaghan's games with numbers. She needed a full term in opposition to establish herself. And whatever the cosmetics were, apparent in the portrayed frustration of various accounts of the period, she needed all the time she could get. The important individual issues, such as race relations and immigration, devolution, Northern Ireland, defence and disarmament, European elections, must be set against the economic background, as individual and heroic engagements are fixed within the wider framework of the larger and less easily determined war.

The economic war had been progressing so badly that in September 1976 there had been a run of the pound. Denis Healey had sought a loan from the IMF of up to £2,300m and had imposed economic measures, with IMF approval, which aimed to cut back the public sector borrowing requirement from its forecast figures of £10,500m in 1977-8, and £11,500m in 1978-9 to £8,700m and £8,600m respectively for the two years. As a percentage of gross national product it would be coming down from 9 to 6 to 5 percent. Current plans would also be adjusted by figures of around £1,500m for each of the two years, the mechanisms being public spending cuts rather than increased taxation since tax levels were already too high. In addition, Healey announced a range of other cuts.

Politically, this set of measures, which represented a substantial new Budget and was announced just before Christmas on December 15 1976, represented a serious blow to Margaret Thatcher, in that it implemented Conservative policy, and deprived her of the grounds for combative attack which were her first instinctive tactic. Healey was folding away past prodigalities and choosing the path of rectitude, and this could only meet with approval from Margaret Thatcher's Shadow Chancellor, Sir Geoffrey Howe, and silence from herself, her normal way of expressing endorsement of the actions of her political opponents. There were things that were wrong, of course, like continued price control measures; but even there Roy Hattersley, the Secretary of State for Prices and Consumer Protection, announced relaxation proposals in early 1977 which again represented a movement towards Conservative policy which could be met only with grudging approval.

In anticipation of this being even more the case with the 1977 Budget, the Conservatives moved a motion of no confidence the week before, and effectively forced the Liberals into a formal agreement with the Callaghan Government which would last to the end of the Parliamentary session in the first instance and, while not a formal coalition, would allow the Liberals to make regular proposals and suggestions, with regular meetings taking place between David Steel and James Callaghan. A commitment to proportional representation in the European Assembly elections was part of the price. The pact was 'in the national interest' in the Prime Minister's view; it was 'in the pursuit of economic recovery' in the words of the joint statement. It ensured the defeat of the no-confidence motion on March 23 by 322 votes to 298, and a week later Denis Healey introduced his Budget, which included a substantial reduction in income tax, and a further shift towards indirect taxation. It was hoped that this would lead to moderation in pay demands, thereby checking inflation. Grudgingly, Sir Geoffrey Howe had to approve.

It was Britain's turn to host the 1977 economic summit, in which the United States, Canada, France, Germany, Italy and Japan participated on May 7 and 8, at Downing Street. The twin and, some would argue, opposed objectives of bringing down inflation and sustaining employment were stated as priorities, and the message, at the end, was one of 'confidence', and of 'substantial agreement'.

Government anti-inflation policy, announced on July 15, and related to joint Government-TUC pay guidelines, which Denis Healey said had been of 'immense advantage', won from the Liberals a renewal of their pact with the Callaghan administration. It would continue 'into the next session of Parliament for as long as the objectives set out in the Chancellor's statement of 15 July are sustained by the Government'.

Though two by-elections that summer had seen the seats retained respectively by Conservatives and Labour candidates, the latter – in Birmingham, Ladywood – had been a lucky survival. It left the overall totals underlining the importance of Labour's dependence on the Liberals. From its general election total of 319 seats, the Labour Party were down to 310. The Conservatives had gained only three, at 279, though with a likely additional win from the vacancy in Bournemouth East. The balance was held by Liberals (13), Scottish Nationalists (11), Unionists of various persuasions (10) and miscellaneous, including 3 Plaid Cymru, a further 7. Healey was in a position to talk about Britain's financial transformation at the IMF meeting in late September. Sterling was strong, inflation coming down, and official currency reserves at a record level. And his speech a month later, at the Mansion House, was a catalogue of Government successes. It was followed by a positive White Paper in January 1978 which proposed an additional £1,000m on public expenditure, aimed at creating more jobs, and in April James Callaghan spoke of Britain's economic prospects being better than at any time since the first energy crisis produced the economic reversal of the early seventies. When the Budget followed on April 11, there were further personal taxation cuts representing a £2,500m stimulus to the economy aimed at raising growth, bringing down unemployment, and contributing to the concerted international effort to deal with the problems of the world economy.

The record of the Labour administration, in mid-1978, was good. Inflation over the 12-month period had come down from 17 percent to 8 percent. A 5 percent wages guideline was established for the year beginning August 1 1978, and there was to be a further year's extension of the 10 percent dividend ceiling. All Sir Geoffrey Howe could do was endorse 'absolutely the need for realism, moderation and responsibility in pay bargaining' which was contained in the Government policy statement in the House of Commons which coincided with the publication of the White Paper on July 21. Howe wanted less rigidity. The scope for rewarding work, skill, enterprise and success, measured in profitability, was hampered both by the 5 percent wages ceiling and the 10 percent dividends ceiling. But David Steel committed the Liberals to supporting the White Paper proposals, and they were approved on July 25 with a Government majority of 15. The TUC took exception to the central determination of pay.

Expectation of a general election in the autumn of 1978 was high. Not only were the economic indicators strongly in favour of the Labour Government; in addition the party's popularity was ahead of the Conservatives by some four points, and James Callaghan's personal standing was a massive twenty percentage points ahead of Margaret Thatcher's. The Conservative Party fully expected a general election, and on Gordon Reece's advice to Margaret Thatcher a publicity campaign, using the slogan 'Labour Isn't Working', was launched in the late summer.

But the purpose of that advertising campaign was precisely the opposite of what it appeared. The Conservatives were not ready for a general election, and certainly did not want to fight one on Denis Healey's record during 1978. They could easily have been defeated and probably would have been. Though the advertising campaign generated a great deal of interest, it did not produce a sufficient swing in public opinion poll predictions about swings in voting intentions away from the Government and towards Margaret Thatcher. But it did achieve the far more important objective of frightening James Callaghan and the

Labour Party leadership into putting off the general election into which so much careful work and planning, of a solid and balanced kind, had been ploughed by Healey. She played the part of a leader ready for battle and certain of victory with consummate skill. The vivid portrait of her encounter with political commentators given by Allan J. Mayer is fascinating when read against the background of a Conservative Party publicity machine frantically working for an objective which was the reverse of what it *seemed* to welcome, and what Labour *seemed* to intend:

> For their part, the Tories were gearing up for a full campaign. An airplane was chartered to carry Mrs Thatcher around the country, and the dozen or so reporters who planned to accompany her were invited to an informal reception in her offices at the House of Commons. Mrs Thatcher appeared at the gathering in dazzling spirits, keyed up and ready to go, much like an actress on the eve of an opening night. Earlier that day, Callaghan had hurriedly summoned his cabinet to No. 10, and the BBC later announced he had requested five minutes of air time for a ministerial broadcast the next evening. It seemed clear to everyone that the election date was finally going to be set. 'I don't know what he's going to say,' Mrs Thatcher grinned, 'but I don't imagine he is making a Ministerial broadcast to say he *isn't* going to hold an election.'
>
> A reporter at the reception was intrigued by Mrs Thatcher's certainty. 'What if the Prime Minister doesn't call an election?' he asked her, somewhat perversely.
>
> She smiled indulgently. 'Of course he will,' she said, 'He has to.'
>
> 'He has to,' she repeated. Her smile was gone now, as if she were considering the question seriously for the first time. 'My God, if he doesn't, it would be a disaster,' she finally said. 'We're all ready to go.'

But when James Callaghan went on television in October, against the mounting expectations of a dissolution, it was to reassure his political opponents and astonish those closest to him within the Labour Party by declaring that the Labour Government would continue its fight against inflation, un-

---

* Allan J. Mayer, op. cit., pp. 160–161

employment and low productivity. Part also of this fight would inevitably be with the unions over the 5 percent wages guideline, to which the TUC were opposed. Callaghan was funking an election at a time when private opinions polls were actually favourable. And he was doing so because of effective public relations and advertising.

In soldiering on, James Callaghan had to reconstruct the basis for his support in the Commons. He commanded 308 of the 631 effective seats; the Liberals had pulled out of their formal pact; the Scottish nationalists wanted the devolution referendum finalised; the Northern Ireland Unionists wanted greater representation at Westminster; the Conservatives wanted blood; nobody wanted harsh economic measures. Blandness and compromise were the order of the day.

The policy programme announced at the beginning of November 1978 directed Government action broadly towards inflation control and employment creation. Adverbs like 'vigorously' and 'closely' were used in the Queen's Speech to describe intended actions which were not clearly defined. The most specific undertakings were those on devolution and proposals for greater Northern Ireland representation.

Thus it was that James Callaghan ushered in his own political demise. As the TUC had warned, it was a winter of discontent. The 5 percent ceiling was widely ignored; pay awards soared into double figures, and within the Government there was disagreement about the exercise of control. Greater price control was brought in while wages were allowed to mount. The key strike of the winter was that of the tanker drivers. Petrol, diesel and heating oil supplies were all disrupted, bringing cold, hunger, immobility and widespread frustrations to every sector of the community. Schools closed because of the cold, and it was a bitter winter anyway; queues formed at petrol stations; agricultural feeding stocks ran short; cargoes piled up at the docks for want of road transportation; and factories were forced to close.

It represented the break for which Margaret Thatcher's combative instincts had prepared her. The key lay outside strict economic policy. In principle, she and the Conservative Party supported the free collective bargaining which was being applied by the unions in total disruption of the 5 percent wages guideline, and was leading to the industrial chaos. It was the

Defeating Callaghan

chaos deriving from unrestricted trade union power which was the target for her speech in the one-day Commons debate on January 16 1979, on her own motion to adjourn, which in effect was defeated. She sought to 'redress the balance of trade union power', the ending of intimidation by pickets, the protection of workers who did not wish to belong to trade unions, and the introduction of 'no-strike' agreements with key unions. Necessity had forced the outlining of a major Conservative election plank. The debate ended in a Government majority of 24, mainly because of abstentions (the vote was 301 to 277). But it marked the beginning of the end for Callaghan's administration. The joint Government-TUC agreement on industrial relations, announced on March 7, represented a woolly compromise, a patching-up of discontent, not a solution, nor even a basis for credibility. The Prime Minister had given too many hostages. He had paid off the Liberals, the Unionists, and on March 1 he was forced into the position of losing his last group of supporters, the Scottish Nationalists, when the complicated machinery which Parliament had set up for devolution saw its implementation defeated, not by a 'No' vote, but by apathy.

In a low turnout less than the required 40 percent of the registered electorate supported the idea of a separate Scottish Assembly, and the Scottish Nationalist Party, who had earlier threatened that 'unless Callaghan makes sure the referendum is "yes" he's out', withdrew support. The direct nature of the challenge to his survival came first from the SNP with a motion of no confidence. This was then supported by the Liberals. With their commitment against him assured, Margaret Thatcher put down her own motion of no confidence. On March 28 1979, the Labour Government was defeated 311 to 310.

James Callaghan had demonstrated a mixture of poor political judgment and selfishness. From the day on which he became Prime Minister he had been faced with a minority position in the House of Commons, where the combination of non-Labour members, if they could have been got together against him, would have defeated him. While this is by no means a unique situation, it should have the effect of ringing muffled alarms for the future. While the reality is that the collective self-interest of varied minority groups rarely brings about active cohesion, it does eventually respond to instinctive laws about every parliament being finite. Yet in Callaghan's case it was as if he wanted the single term and cared nothing for the succession. It made him identifiably a loser.

It must have been particularly galling for Denis Healey. By the late summer of 1978 he had delivered the correct economic strategy for Britain; the housekeeping was right, and paying the wages for it lay in the future. He had Howe's grudging approval for virtually everything he was doing, and the conditions likely to undermine this had not materialised. Only when they did was Margaret Thatcher able to introduce her telling addition to the equation: trade union reform. This was put forcefully in the one-day debate of January 16 1979, and became central to the Conservative manifesto.

The emergence of trade union reform as a major plank in the March manifesto is indicative of a certain thinness in the fabric of Margaret Thatcher's mind. It denotes more opportunism in the struggle for power than it does any broad Conservative strategy for an alternative overall handling of the major problems of inflation and unemployment, on which Labour were perceived by the public to be better. Indeed, in absolute terms, comparing the Denis Healey achievements of mid-1978 with the Geoffrey Howe handling of the economy by mid-1982, when he had exchanged 8 percent inflation for 4 percent at a cost in increased unemployment of two million, they were better. But the grim events of November-January 1978-9 offered a critical gap in Labour defences through which Margaret Thatcher drove her limited but appropriate proposals, backed by the offer of support for Government if they were adopted. They included 'any action' to end intimidation by pickets, to protect workers not wishing to belong to trade unions, and to protect by 'no strike' agreements the essentials of life which had been so cruelly impinged on by a trade union movement which many judged to have run out of control.

Instinctively, she had struck a winner. She had done so after a curiously numb period. The frustrations of Callaghan's adroitness in surviving by means of pacts and alliances with minority groups, combined with Healey's more than adequate handling of the economy, had brought about an undoubted faltering in her approach, and a somewhat awkward hunting-around for 'issues' on which her combative character could express itself, though they were not necessarily issues at all.

One example was devolution, another race and immigration.

On the first of these she took a tough line against the 1978 Scotland and Wales Bill. The two countries should not be covered by the same set of proposals. Wales did not, in her view (which proved correct), want an assembly, Scotland could hardly want one which equivocated over the location of real power; the separate but supervised assembly was 'giving power with one hand, and taking it back with the other. It will satisfy no one, and will lead to the very discord and conflict which it is our purpose to avoid.' She seemed at odds, in her views, with Francis Pym. While she repudiated the breaching of the unity of the United Kingdom, Pym expressed support for a third, Scottish chamber as an extension of Westminster north of the Border, and with the function of serving as 'the focus of all issues affecting Scotland'. The differences, and indeed her views generally, were cut short by the defeat of the measure on a procedural vote on February 22 1977, and by a Government decision to hold bi-lateral talks aimed at a new, agreed approach. This was not forthcoming. In the mid-summer it was accepted that no progress could be made before the next session, when *two* bills were to be introduced, meeting part of Margaret Thatcher's and the Conservative party's objection. The new Bills came before Parliament at the end of 1977 and were both opposed by the Conservatives. In January the important amendment requiring 40 percent of the *electorate* to vote in favour of devolution in order for it to be implemented (and eventually the cause for its defeat in Scotland) was carried. The stage was set. The Royal assent to the Bills did not follow until the end of July. The referenda took place on March 1, 1979, as part of James Callaghan's already doomed programme of measures designed to sustain SNP support for his floundering administration. The defeat in Wales was overwhelming: 46.9 percent to 11.9. In Scotland a small majority, 32.8 percent of the electorate (well short of the legislative requirement), voted in favour of devolution, while 30.8 percent voted against: modest proof of Margaret Thatcher's sound instincts and political judgment. She was much more opportunist about race relations and immigration, which emotionally go together, while legally being separate issues.

The Labour Party's handling of race relations during its period in office following 1974 had been sensible. Laws against discrimination had been strengthened by the 1976 Race Relations' Act, covering, among other things, discriminatory advertising. A new Commission for the Racial Equality had been set up, to replace the Race Relations Board and the Community Relations Commission. The Act came into force on June 13 1977.

The net political effect of the situation covered by this legislation was of polarisation. Minority extremism had bolstered support for the National Front; majority feeling favoured the general policies enshrined in the legislation. But racial tension in January 1978 in Wolverhampton, which led to rioting, had persuaded Margaret Thatcher to seize upon the opportunity for a restatement of views. Her words were imprecise and, in the circumstances, highly emotive. If she was 'making policy as she went along', which was claimed by party officials explaining to political journalists what she had said, she was pandering to the least worthy instincts in the Conservative rank and file by her suggestions that 'if you want good race relations, you have got to allay people's fears on numbers'. 'We are not in politics,' she said on this occasion, 'to ignore people's worries, we are in politics to deal with them.'

The row which followed was a major one. The shift in opinion poll support for the Conservatives was marked. The personal mail sent to Margaret Thatcher, supporting her overwhelmingly, was very substantial. Party officials claimed it was in excess of 10,000 letters. And in the March 1978 by-election in North Ilford, which in 1981 had only 8 percent black and Asian voters, the Conservatives took back the seat from Labour, with a 12 percent lead. She used then, and continued to use, the word 'swamped' to describe the way people were feeling about immigration. Merlyn Rees, the Home Secretary, took a moderate line in response to the parliamentary select committee's report on immigration which was published three weeks after the by-election, committing the Government to 'firm and fair immigration control', saying that 'primary immigration' was over, and good race relations were the main priority. Fall in immigration ruled out the need for new quotas. The Conservative Party response was given by the Home Affairs spokesman, William Whitelaw, on April 7 1978, in a speech at Leicester which enshrined what subsequently became the eight-point manifesto section on race relations and immigration: an entry quota system for all non-EEC countries; a register of Indian wives and children eligible for entry; a limit on parents, grandparents and grown-up children; restrictions on those seeking

Defeating Callaghan

work; an end to the transfer arrangements from temporary to permanent residence; greater vigilance against illegal entry; and new nationality legislation defining entitlement to British citizenship. The Conservatives, Whitelaw said, wanted 'certainty and finality' so that the 'constant and widespread preoccupation with levels of immigration' – the fact that, in Margaret Thatcher's words, 'people can feel they are being swamped' – should be brought to an end.

Government policy was slightly modified in July. A three-point policy statement stressed the continued commitment to the access of close dependents to their relations already settled in Britain, but emphasised that in future the country's immigration levels would be more strictly related to humanitarian arguments, and to the need for particular skills. There would also be a more vigorous approach to evasion, or the abuse of controls. It was a partial tightening up, a movement towards the Conservative position, in response to the obvious favour with which, according to opinion polls, the public regarded their policy.

*

The Conservative Party advertising campaign launched in the summer of 1978 with the countrywide display of posters depicting a queue of unemployed and with the message 'Labour Isn't Working', demonstrated clearly enough that the kind of campaign Margaret Thatcher would run would be based on a mixture of slogans, publicity stunts, and carefully weighed responses to the public's demands, as far as they could be ascertained from opinion research. Policies and issues, in any serious sense, would be kept to a minimum. So would detailed undertakings. It had already been decided that the Conservative manifesto would be sharply reduced in length, and 'simplified'; in other words, clear and precise commitments would be edited out in favour of the offering of broad 'solutions'.

The whole approach was a marketing one. When Harold Wilson had resigned in March 1976 Margaret Thatcher had expected a general election to be automatic. It was a futile, if attractive expectation. Though the two changes of leadership in the Conservative Party during Margaret Thatcher's own time in parliament had taken place while the party was in opposition, the historical precedent for such changes to be accomplished smoothly enough in power as well were there to demonstrate the absurdity of Wilson both resigning as Prime Minister and dissolving for an election; nevertheless her instinctive fervour at the news is revealing of the aggressive urge for contest which is deeply ingrained in her nature. The same, but far more theatrical, display of fervour occurred following Callaghan's television appearance in the autumn of 1978. Behind it was blankness. There were also the 'huge' resources of Gordon Reece, Saatchi and Saatchi, Ronald Millar, a successful playwright who wrote speeches for her, not to mention the Conservative Party machine. But apart from race and immigration, the modest success in shaping the devolution legislation to make the setting-up of separate assemblies more difficult, there was no clear platform established for the Conservatives; and in the most important area of all, the economy, Denis Healey was substantially moving towards the high ground which Margaret Thatcher would normally occupy. Nevertheless, she was armed and ready for the fight; and with her attendant sales staff, seemed resolutely determined to treat the whole exercise as a marketing operation. She was this new commodity, a female Mars bar, ready to be launched upon a British public never before asked to buy a woman Prime Minister. That was the offer, and instinct repeatedly would suggest that its potential for success was such as to rule out the need for well-reasoned argument.

There is a serious side to the marketing approach. In a manner not previously attempted by the Conservative Party, Margaret Thatcher had cultivated press, radio and television personalities, raised the whole tenor of public relations thinking, and devised an overall strategy of advertising and salesmanship unprecedented in British politics. It was peculiarly *hers*, and lay side by side with the more traditional party machine, represented by Conservative Central Office. In due course this would swing in behind the marketing approach, and the two become synonymous. But at this stage it was a somewhat dubious phenomenon, very much on trial, very much associated personally with her.

'The winter of discontent' added a substantial dimension of bitterness and acrimony to the Conservative's sales package. The offer was underwritten by the collapse of the marketing potential on the other side, and Margaret Thatcher's naturally aggressive nature was able to seize on envy, extremism, division and irresponsibility as the hallmarks of her opponents.

The chosen vocabulary for the important opening paragraphs of the manifesto referred to a Britain that had 'lost its way', and was 'shaken' by loss of confidence, self respect, common sense, 'even our sense of common humanity'; society 'seemed on the brink of disintegration'.

Division in British society was laid squarely at Labour's door, and had been achieved by encouraging 'the politics of envy' and discouraging the pursuit of wealth. Individualism and enterprise had been sapped by the expansion of the State's role. And concessions to trade union power had been irresponsible, leading to the undermining of liberties and the country's prospect of economic success.

A message that would have been very difficult to sustain in October 1978, had ripened to perfection by March 1979, not as a result of anything done by the Conservatives, but simply in the fading light coming from Sunny Jim.

PART THREE

Power

CHAPTER FOURTEEN

Promises, Promises

Harmony, truth, faith and hope were offered by Margaret Thatcher on her first day as Prime Minister of Britain in her most famous, and most fatuous, quotation out of the past. She offered them in place of discord, error, doubt and despair. Five years later there is greater discord in Britain than there was then; truth has been placed under stricter and more rigorous control; the sneaking, shifting marginal doubts about her have grown; and whatever despair existed then, diverse and puzzled, looking as much at her as it looked in other directions politically, has now focused all its intense feelings upon this woman.

Five years ago she offered to restore economic and social health, create new jobs in an expanded economy, reduce inflation and public expenditure, reduce taxation, raise standards of education, and reform and redefine services for those in real need. She has failed in many of these areas.

Five years ago she defined more specifically the ills facing Britain in three ways, all of which related to the socialism which she so openly and aggressively despised and attacked. The first of these three was 'the politics of envy'. By discouraging the creation of wealth, she claimed the Callaghan Government had induced a bitter struggle in Britain, with opposing groups seeking to gain the lions's share in a weak economy. There is no easy measure of fairness nor of envy, but statistically the differentials in salary scales in a range of incomes from £5,000 to £30,000 when taken in the context of tax, social welfare payments and other charges, have led to greater divergence, not less. The directions in which the envy is felt may have changed; the intensity of the envy is at least the same if not more bitter. And the essential axiom about monetarism – that it is 'extraordinarily beneficial to the rich and extraordinarily punishing to the poor'* – has contributed, not just to the discord, but to the doubt, despair and error as well.

The second definition concerned the balance between the state and the individual. The former was seen by her as having enlarged its role under socialism, diminishing that of the latter. The measure of this was polyglot and ill-defined. It embraced the level of public expenditure, public ownership of industrial enterprise, public involvement in housing and education, all of which could be presented as *opportunities* for the redress of imbalance. But it embraced also certain darker areas of conflict between the state and the individual, such as health, welfare and law and order, where the possible shifting of the burden could represent a reduction of safety, security, well-being and contentment, or where the intention was actually to shift the burden in the opposite direction, increasing the powers of the state to impinge on the rights of the individual.

From whatever point this complicated equation is viewed, it has not worked out in such a fashion as to give the 'prosperous country' which was promised as its direct result, nor has it led to the 'improving social services' which were also offered as a direct response to its implementation. Public expenditure increased over the five years; the transfer from public to private ownership concentrated prosperity, increased the divergence between rich and poor, and did not contribute to the key problem of unemployment; and in housing, education, health, social welfare, the basic dependence on self-help – whatever its moral and spiritual value may be in the restoration of the fibre of the British people – has been revolutionary in its impact, possibly with disaster as the eventual outcome. As to law and order, the state's intrusion is undoubtedly greater now than it was five years ago; it is so in legislative terms; it is so in human terms.

The third definition of a wrong to be righted concerned the trade union movement. This was, and remains, the most complex of all. With considerable justification the Conservative Party under Margaret Thatcher could look upon its victory in the general election of May 3 1979 as having derived more from its manifesto proposals on trade union reform than on any other issue. Whether one believes in accident or in design, in a pro-

* John Kenneth Galbraith, interviewed in the *Sunday Telegraph*, December 11 1983.

phetic definition of trade union unrest before the 'winter of discontent', or merely the seizing of a golden opportunity, the reality of March 28 1979 was that the country welcomed the prospect of a Government that promised to end the abuse of privilege and of power by Britain's trade unions. But more was at stake than that. The key area of discretion lay between breaking trade union power, or reforming it.

The Conservatives under Margaret Thatcher freely acknowledged the force of trade unionism in British politics. They referred to the movement's past value and its historical contribution, using indeed the emotive reference that it 'sprang from a deep and genuine fellow-feeling for the brotherhood of man'. Well, the test for such emotionalism lay in the careful definition of a route towards reform rather than combat. In this area, more than in any other, a diversity of forces meet, affecting profoundly Britain's future.

On the Right, within the Conservative Party led by Margaret Thatcher, her policies on trade union reform, which were absolutely central to her acquisition of power in May 1979, raised essential questions about adversary politics as opposed to the politics of consent; in other words, traditional conservatism, as preached by Sir Ian Gilmour, Christopher Patten and others, against the more radical text coming from Margaret Thatcher's pulpit, which five years later was to wring from her the sardonic challenge: 'how pathetic the party you support, how pathetic you are'.

On the Left, a similarly sharp dichotomy emerges between constitutional socialism and a form of radicalism equal and opposite to the right-wing radicalism which is manifest in Margaret Thatcher's every utterance. It was there before she came to power, and helped to bring her to power. It was the dark force in British trade unionism which she was to combat, 'the single powerful interest group' which had Labour in its thrall, and was pushing a once honourable British political tradition towards self-annihilation. The way Margaret Thatcher tackled this single issue of trade union reform was, and still remains, the most vital area of all. If pushed in one direction, militancy would triumph over tradition and the demoralisation would be complete; the trade union movement would split in two or more directions, those on the Right moving away from the Labour Party and breaking the traditional liaison which had been responsible in the first place for the creation of the party itself; those on the Left of the trade union movement would continue to grow in strength, and in militancy; they would also shift the Labour Party in the same direction.

The stated objective, in 1979, was for 'free trade unions . . . (to) flourish in a free society'.* 'Government and public, management and unions, employers and employees, all have a common interest in raising productivity and profits, thus increasing investment and employment, and improving real living standards for everyone in a high-productivity, high-wage, low tax economy.' This utopian view, panglossian in its simplicity, required two things: the willing co-operation of the trade union movement, together with full agreement about the conditions; and, secondly, success in implementation. Without one of these, problems were inevitable; without either, divisiveness was inescapable. Neither was ever really forthcoming.

Worse still, however, the very reforms which were promised added to the problem and have worsened the future prospects. What had all the appearances of a necessary package in 1979 – reforming picketing, the closed shop and wider participation in union affairs by rank and file – had become, by 1983, a different and more threatening area of union-state conflict.

Far from Margaret Thatcher bringing external legislation, or internal administrative reforms to trade unionism compatible with the trade union movement fulfilling its proper function in British society, she has deployed the direct pressure of legislation, and the indirect pressures of unemployment, taxation changes, shifts in industrial emphasis and the encouragement of a free market economy to weaken traditional trade unionism, thereby encouraging its more extreme forms. Deliberate or accidental, it is the reverse of the objectives laid down when she sought and got power in 1979. It is the opposite of the free trade unions flourishing in a free society. It is the negation of the harmony, truth, faith and hope asserted on May 4 1979. It has led to the discord, error, doubt and despair which were all then recognised, against an emotive and unreal backcloth induced by 'the winter of discontent', to become real and rational in the present seasonally unchanging wilderness of leadership by public relations.

* The Conservative manifesto; see *Campaign Guide*, p. 504.

It is the purpose of this book to see Government and party policy in the arguably distorting context of power. It is arguably so because of the permanent dichotomy which exists in interpreting every action of a politician: Is it for the public good? Is it for self-advancement? If it is a mixture, what is the ratio? How do we arrive at it? What judgments do we make about it?

In the period under consideration, from May 1979 to June 1983, there is the continuous issue of the economy, a constant overall responsibility, to get it 'under control', to get it 'right', punctuated by a set of economic and fiscal variables.

There is then the equally constant issue of overall foreign policy, again with a basic responsibility to serve Britain's security interests, and her economic ones, punctuated more wildly by external events wide in both variety and predictability.

Then there is domestic security, law and order, social reform and stability, trade union reform, and the huge, inexhaustible burden of desirable, necessary, or essential legislation. In an ideal world, in which some utopian concept of Britain is promulgated, and towards which the energies of British politicians then direct the machinery of the State, the overall policy of the party in power becomes central to the examination of the deployment of that power. In less ideal circumstances, the threads which tie power and policy together become stretched to breaking point, and then break.

The past five years have been less than ideal. The majority of policy objectives laid down in 1979 have not been achieved. The quotient of prosperity and contentment has not been augmented; quite the reverse. If Britain is a country, as Margaret Thatcher then claimed, 'rich in natural resources, in coal, oil, gas, and fertile farmlands', then something has gone lamentably wrong in the management of that wealth. If the people, as she also asserted, are rich in 'managerial skills of the highest calibre, with great industries and firms whose workers can be the equal of any in the world', then something equally sad has gone awry in the deployment of all that skill and capacity in the service of a country then seen by her as having 'lost its way' and being faced 'with its most serious problems since the Second World War'.

Part of what has gone wrong is undoubtedly to be found on the other side of the British political divide. Poor leadership by Michael Foot, complacent leadership by David Steel, and aimless leadership by Roy Jenkins, Shirley Williams, David Owen and William Rodgers, have all contributed to the creation of a power vacuum which Margaret Thatcher has filled with skill and determination. Their failure has led to the fragmentation of the whole political structure Left of the Conservative Party, depriving it of focus and shape, and setting in motion still more fragmentation, so that, within each political party the wings, groups or factions are themselves divided, over policy, over leadership, over internal constitutional issues, over the relationship between Liberals, Labour and the SDP.

It would be less than human not to capitalise on all of these disasters taking place with the Opposition. It is to Margaret Thatcher's political credit, and a mark of her well-developed instinct and judgment, that she did just that, turning around the normal evolution of power, whereby Governments generally manage to lose elections. They do it by a combination of error, and the fickleness of human nature in a democracy, 'wanting a change', usually out of boredom. Instead, the alternatives were rejected, mainly out of fear.

Fear played an important part in the 1983 general election. It was not direct fear, of the possible combination of leadership which could emerge as an alternative to Margaret Thatcher's leadership. It was fear of the potential instability, and of what lay behind the different degrees of failure already referred to: Michael Foot dominated by his left wing, and overshadowed by the threatening mass of words in his cumbrous party manifesto; David Steel apparently unable to say or do anything memorable or effective; and the 'gang of four' constructing policies the relevance of which were increasingly open to question. But handling this, while admirable as an exercise in political opportunism, is a very long way indeed from the undertakings and commitments made by Margaret Thatcher on coming to power. It is also a long way from Government based on policy and performance, leading to a general election fought at that level.

Seen in reverse, from the standpoint of Margaret Thatcher's confirmation in power for a further full term of five years, with an augmented majority unprecedented in British politics in the twentieth century, the period 1979-83 is one of broad policy failure salvaged by the Falklands, by adroit public relations, by the failure of alternatives, and by one woman's outstanding deployment of will, instinct and charm. Yes, indeed, charm too, that much misused word which encompasses the idea of magic and fascination, of bewitching or subduing by supernatural powers, of conjuring or attracting powerfully the otherwise indifferent or unconcerned. Hers may be lifeless charm, without the heart, or sinister charm, manufactured on a drawing board, by committee, under the hair-drier, or at the desk of a playwright directing the energies of a troupe of speech-writers. But in a lacklustre and indifferent world where disillusionment and fear are there to be played on, charm of a manufactured variety – and the word implies that by definition – can work wonders. She brought off a coup with the British people by the exercise of charm, making them 'love the precepts for the teacher's sake'. And it was a major achievement.

No word has been more frequently on the lips of those with whom I have discussed her, over the last two years, than 'fascination'. She exercises it over friend and foe. It is the general descriptive term for her power, both to attract and repel. It is a bridging term to encompass the extremes of love-hate which she manages to provoke in people. And it is, of course, a central ingredient in the word which few people use about her: charm.

This is a long way from policy, and deliberately so, on her part. It was always necessary, from May 1979 onward, to lead people away from policy. No matter how generalised, the policy objectives on which the acquisition of power had been based were only remotely within prospect of achievement. They had been given, in manifesto form, before the general election; they were given in the more neutral language of the Queen's Speech at the opening of the forty-eighth Parliament of the United Kingdom on May 15 1979; they were repeated in the triumphant language of victory on October 10 1979 at the Conservative Party conference in Blackpool, and thereafter. But they were increasingly generalised and repetitious, attenuating the linkages between power and policy to a point where they were stretched so far as to undermine credibility or raise the threat of unprecedented unpopularity. It was almost fortuitous when circumstances, as in the case of the Falklands, severed the link altogether, allowing policy to be dumped in favour of history's most popular road to power, by way of military victory. In the process, other policy objectives, some of which were responsible for a massive decline in Margaret Thatcher's popularity, were reconsidered in the light of her personality, and totally fresh judgments made. On foot of this she was able to go to the country and win a second term with resounding conviction.

Yet the policies were the same. Her very consistency, which had isolated her by the autumn of 1981, bringing the Conservative Party's standing below that of the SDP/Liberal Alliance and Labour as well, was based on the same policies offered to the people in the early summer of 1983, and willingly accepted. It cannot therefore be claimed that policy played either a positive or negative role; it was rendered incidental by a combination of other forces, will, instinct, charm, personality, public relations, the absence or failure of alternatives, accident, deception, chance or good luck. And it is in the context of these different forces that policy becomes relevant to the continued possession of power. On its own it is generally tedious, and never more so than in the field of economics. Just as one's own domestic economic circumstances, involving bank overdrafts, mortgage repayments, household budgets, and the funding of one's leisure pursuits are essential but boring means towards ends, so, at national level, are the details of control of inflation, money supply, interest rates, borrowing requirements, and the failure to control rising unemployment and declining services. But extract an issue from a policy document, and make it personal and combative within the arena of power, applying to it human personality and timing, and the ingredient is transformed.

Margaret Thatcher transformed a number of issues in a number of different ways. She altered fundamentally the way in which Cabinet and Conservative Party were handled. She brought to the former a debilitating authoritarianism and to the latter a flamboyant sense of theatre. She managed to combine these two quite distinct approaches in her handling of the media by dividing it from top to bottom into the elements which were deserving of frosty reserve, combativeness, or silence on the one hand, and those favoured editors, broadcasters and interviewers who had frequent and indulgent access.

What is important is how she governed the country and the directions in which she led the British people. What is less important is how she managed her Cabinet team, her party, and how she presented herself to the public; these are means, not ends, and occupy in statecraft a modest enough management of money, trade unions or the old and sick. At least, this is how it should be. If power becomes an end in itself, the order is reversed. The presentation of self to the public, the management of the media, the emphasis on image, words and appearances, dominates. And its domination spreads into, and infects, the behaviour and performance of those who surround the central figure of power. In the public domain these are Cabinet Ministers; in private, they are the team of Cabinet servants, speech writers, press secretaries and the like. But the domination is like a virus, and spreads beyond, affecting party and public. The examinations which follow represent a selection from the awesome range of responsibilities and achievements of her first period in power. In each case a dual interpretation is possible.

To take one example, on Rhodesia nothing can detract from the ultimate achievement, which is Margaret Thatcher's, and by which that country was brought to independence by Britain. Yet in reaching it she had to pass through a sequence of learning and revision which is exemplary of her skills as a power politician. Starting from ignorance and misjudgment she was steered by far more skilful and selfless politicians than herself to a state of political grace. When it was in sight, and she recognised it, she seized upon all the advantages and made them her own. She was ruthless and self-centred in the way she did this. She turned a whole tangled web of diverse energy and toil to her political advantage. Few denied her the credit, because the real achievement, of a new state in Southern Africa which was politically organic in its composition, was the true benefit. And to allow her the political scalp, or the notch on the gun of power, was a comparatively small price to pay in the minds of Commonwealth and other world leaders who are serious about countries working internally, working with each other, and playing a part in the balance of power.

But each such experience, judged on its merit, must also be *seen* in the accumulative sense. Margaret Thatcher, on Zimbabwe, Europe, Ireland, the EEC, the Falkland Islands, the economy, Grenada, to take the chosen issues, and Margaret Thatcher on the handling of her Cabinet, of talent generally at the top of her Party, of crisis issues like Parkinson, of the grassroots, and of her opponents, has lived a politically schizophrenic existence in which the shadow and substance of her merit seem to be in uneasy conflict. What she tells us she has achieved cannot be taken on trust. We have to investigate, first, whether it has actually been achieved; secondly, if it has, whether she was responsible; thirdly, what price we pay, in political terms.

CHAPTER FIFTEEN

Cabinet Management

It was the general perception of commentators, after she had come to power, that the real struggle for loyalty and party cohesion in a difficult period for the country was going on at the highest level, between 'wets' and 'dries'. It was a neat and tidy perception, closely confined, easy to monitor, amenable to the normal conditions under which parliamentary lobby-writers work. Conditioned to absorb and interpret the fluttering of Edward Heath's eyebrows, the latest quotation carved out by Sir Ian Gilmour from the inexhaustible mineshaft of Conservative philosophy, the sparkling witticisms delivered by Norman St John Stevas, and the further vast resource of unattributable and at times unprintable lobby comment about Margaret Thatcher and her leadership, the political commentators failed to acknowledge two things: her basic impregnability as prime minister, and her enormous popularity as a leader. And though she demonstrated both repeatedly, and with very great skill, the tide of speculation about internal challenges to her continued occupation of the position of prime minister and leader gathered momentum against the evidence of her strength.

She encouraged this. Instinct told her that a beleagured leader, threatened at the top, can rely on increased support from rank and file. It told her also that to be the subject of criticism and opposition from senior members of her own party, while in power, shifted the centre of gravity of such opposition away from her more serious critics in the Opposition. For much of the time between May 1979 and the low point of her popularity, in the winter of 1981-82, the main focus of conflict was *within* the Conservative Party, and only marginally embraced the alternative and conflicting claims to be heard from Labour under Michael Foot (after he became leader on November 10 1980), and from the SDP/Liberal Alliance which, even at its high point of popularity, lacked any precise alternative focus either in people, or in policies.

Yet she was never seriously threatened by any of the opponents to her policies within the Conservative Party. And she handled those opponents with consummate skill, beginning with the formation of her Government in May 1979. This demonstrated her political instincts at their keenest. From her decision to include Edward Heath if she could, down through the successive layers of opponents and potential opponents for whom she found places, the construction of her first administration was a sustained exercise in appeasement and in balance.

It was intuitive rather than reasoned. But, with women, intuition is a skill. Most of the assessments of that period quote Margaret Thatcher's comment, during an *Observer* interview with Kenneth Harris in February 1979, shortly before the general election. In it she gave two options to Cabinet formation: one was to have 'all the different viewpoints'; the other to have 'only the people who want to go in the direction in which every instinct tells me we have to go. As Prime Minister I couldn't waste time having any internal arguments.' The rather elementary mistake is then made of believing that she would do what she said. What she said to Harris was part of the instinctive pre-election presentation of herself to the public as a strong, single-minded leader who would deliver precisely what she was expected to deliver, including a disciplined and single-minded Conservative Party, fully behind a short, simple, uncompromising election manifesto which by then had been worked over through the long winter of discontent. But the idea that the stance adopted in February should be sustained after May 3 represents a misreading of her political character. Nevertheless, it governed judgment about Cabinet formation. Hugh Stephenson gives up half of the first chapter of *Mrs Thatcher's First Year** to Cabinet choices, and in general his judgments are negative. Her power was 'most absolute' at the start, and yet she failed to use it and her choice was 'circumscribed' resulting in a Cabinet 'almost entirely devoid of major surprises', and 'extremely conventional and cautious'. His is the most detailed and reasoned assessment. But Wapshott and Brock also suggest that

---

* London, 1980.

she faltered and 'missed her chance to design her Government without the breaking mechanism which the traditional liberals would represent'.

Hugh Stephenson also claims that 'by the time of the election there was never any question of Mrs Thatcher offering Heath a job'. This is not so. Margaret Thatcher wanted Heath, sought to include him, but could not get him on her terms. He is an important exemplar for her attitude to all the other appointments, and the failure raises in a telling way the question of loyalty. I have said earlier that her sex is an important discriminating factor, and that questions about her ability to work as a member of a team, even to understand how teams and committees work at all, are critical in understanding also her management of power. This extends to the realm of loyalty and judgment in appointments. She was feminine in her loyalty to ideas rather than people, even if her comprehension of ideas lacks depth and subtlety, which it does. In her own words, 'I believe you should be loyal to the things which put you in power – *totally loyal*. I couldn't bear disloyalty to those things at all because that would be tantamount to getting in on a false prospectus.'*

To a considerable extent her formation of her first Cabinet derived from this basic perception. The Conservative Party had been elected on a manifesto which was simple and clear. She was its guardian and would lead the Government which would implement it. While not indifferent to whom she should have beside her, the question of their loyalty to her and to the policy-outline of the manifesto was a logical prerequisite which they could argue about if they so wished, but which they would breach at their peril. Once in power, she knew that the logical outcome of challenges against her could have only one of two conclusions: either the departure of a member of her Government, or a split in the Conservative Party. She judged, rightly, that there was not, and would not be, sufficient stomach for the latter eventuality; and she was entirely confident that she could deal with the former. And it is in this context that her choices must be seen. She needed talent, experience, weight, and party cohesion. She needed to be seen healing breaches, not provoking them. She wanted the public, and Conservative rank and

---

* Murray, op. cit.

file, to recognise appeasement and unity in her vital early decisions about the team she would deploy. And, for the future, she wanted to place the onus of division, disruption, disloyalty and eventual revolt on men to whom she had given high office.

She did not know whether they would be Heath's men, or others. She was new to the game, just as she had been as party leader, sticking mainly with her Front Bench team, and making no substantial changes in it between 1975 and 1979. And so too, in power, she made the apparently conventional but correct judgment of including potential opponents fully behind a package of measures which she knew would make life difficult in two or three years' time, when the real dangers of a badly balanced administration would come home to roost.

She was rewarded for what many would describe as uncharacteristic loyalty by disloyalty of a remarkably sustained and intense kind. It reached astonishing proportions in the autumn of 1981. It was eventually stifled only by the invasion of the Falklands in April 1982, and has since become little more than a memory, to be read in the increasingly sad and embarrassed and tired faces of her former party adversaries.

First, the facts. Margaret Thatcher made no fundamental Cabinet changes between May 1979 and the beginning of 1981. Then, on two separate occasions, she took initiative in reshaping her Cabinet. She did so with effective economy and minimum fuss. It was painful for some; such occasions always are. But it was sensible and measured, with considerable forethought. In January 1981 she dropped from her Cabinet Norman St John Stevas. Angus Maude retired. She moved Francis Pym out of Defence, where he was obstructing cuts, and replaced him with John Nott. She promoted John Biffen from Chief Secretary to the Treasury to Trade, brought in the articulate and strongly monetarist Leon Brittan to replace Biffen, and promoted Norman Fowler from Minister to Secretary of State. It was a modest set of changes. Of the two senior resignations one was on health grounds, and none of the four junior resignations was politically significant.

Much more significant, both in its timing and in the actual changes, was the re-shuffle of September 14-15 1981. Three senior members of the Cabinet were dropped: Lord Soames, Sir Ian Gilmour and Mark Carlisle. It was a tougher operation altogether. All were opponents of her economic policies, and

Soames particularly took his dismissal badly. In their place she promoted Nigel Lawson, Norman Tebbit and Lady Young, respectively to Employment, Energy and the Chancellorship of the Duchy of Lancaster. More importantly, she moved James Prior from Employment to Northern Ireland; he retained, at his own insistence – and incidentally it was an indicator of his power in the party – his position as a member fo the Cabinet's economic sub-committee. But with a great deal of his time necessarily spent in Northern Ireland, and even more of it taken up with the very real and intractable problems of the Six Counties, his input on economic decisions was weakened.

For Francis Pym it was the second move in a year, in theory of neglible significance, since he retained his basic, and somewhat pedestrian, 'spokesman' role of Leader of the House of Commons, while shuffling between the nominal jobs of Chancellor of the Duchy of Lancaster and Paymaster General, held from January until September, when he took on the equally nominal job of Lord President of the Council.

All the important Cabinet moves involved Margaret Thatcher's supporters. Keith Joseph went from Industry to Education and Science. Both, in her judgment, were key positions, but the shift represented the rescuing of a highly-strung occupant of an adversarial and at times controversial responsibility and his appointment to a job much more in line with his talents.

To replace Keith Joseph in Industry she chose Patrick Jenkin, limited in talent, but loyal. She shifted another close lieutenant, Norman Fowler, into the sensitive job of the Social Services. And, as has already been indicated, gave to two close and loyal aides the important tasks of Energy and Employment. Arguably, the latter of these two was the most important Cabinet position for the forthcoming two-year period.

Margaret Thatcher made no other Cabinet changes until the resignation of Lord Carrington in April 1982, following the Argentine invasion of the Falklands, when yet again poor Francis Pym was shifted into the by-then unenviable post of Foreign Secretary.

She lost Humphrey Atkins at the same time, and brought into the Cabinet Cecil Parkinson and Lord Cockfield. In the context of her handling of her own Cabinet and other appointments, the moment from which to view her abilities and judgments is the major reshuffle of September 1981 rather than the subsequent and imposed change which followed the Falklands crisis. While she handled the latter with political skill, the former was more conclusive and far-ranging in terms of power, and represented a well-timed exercise in pre-empting opposition at a moment of maximum threat.

She was within one month of the Conservative Party's annual conference. Her standing in the country was lower than it had ever been. In electoral terms the Conservative Party was lying third, behind both the Social Democrat-Liberal Alliance, and the Labour Party. Most of her promises had come to nothing. Inflation was substantially higher than it had been under Labour. Interest rates and mortgage rates were also substantially up on the figures when she came to power, and personal incomes and company profits were down. Worse still, both investment and productivity had fallen under Margaret Thatcher and the level of unemployment had gone up by 1.4 million.

In such a climate, the real test of her power and authority effectively lay wherever it was challenged. In other words, in the upper echelons of the Conservative Party if there was anyone to lead such a challenge, or at the grass roots by means of a back-bench revolt, or simply as a result of the crumbling of her credibility. She therefore carried out her major hatchet operation when she was, in general terms of policy and performance, most vulnerable, but also when, in a much more specific short-term way, she was approaching an occasion – the Conservative Party's annual conference – at which endorsement for her actions, whatever they were, support for her policies, however badly they seemed to be progressing, and acclamation for her person, with all the misunderstanding of it then current, were almost inevitable. Her timing was part of her instinctive understanding of power, far more sensitive and assured than that of all her opponents, from Edward Heath down through the Conservative Party.

She invited a challenge from the 'wets' which then became the major focus of political comment for the autumn. But if she was most vulnerable in public opinion terms, as well as in respect of the very apparent failure of her policies, she knew that the timing of the reshuffle was, in a populist sense, entirely safe, since no leader in power, however statistically unfavourable her standing, will be challenged before or during the annual 'hosting' ceremonies. She set up the two forces against each other, knowing in advance where the real political strength lay. And of course she survived.

She did so against an unremitting leakage from senior Cabinet colleagues to the press about the wrongness of her actions (though 'madness' and 'insanity' were closer to the vocabulary of abuse and disaffection then used). Rank disloyalty was the order of the day, and it continued to fester in the autumn of 1981, with absurd speculations about a change of leadership, and the 'drafting' of Geoffrey Rippon. Ironically, the economic background for this was of continued concessions to the very people who were covertly opposing her leadership. To a considerable extent the stringency implicit in the 1979 manifesto had not worked out, and the spending ministers had, to a substantial degree, been able to sustain levels of spending well above the cuts which monetarist principles required. Even so, they continued to resent and block her leadership, and to do so with a disloyalty which bordered at times on the outrageous.

Her own response was to be consistently loyal to them. Her propriety about Cabinet decisions and collective responsibility was absolute. So was her use of constitutional power in deliberate and precise moves against critics and opponents. The sequence of dismissals, beginning with Norman St John Stevas, and continuing with Lord Thorneycroft, Lord Soames, Sir Ian Gilmour, Mark Carlisle, was unimpeachable in party or national terms. It was also limited enough and carefully timed enough to keep the shock and possible instability that might follow to an absolute minimum. But those dismissals, together with the consequent changes, were extremely effective. Contradicting the general perception that she did not use power effectively when she should have done so, at the beginning of her tenure of office, Margaret Thatcher was intelligent enough to judge that the time for such exercising of the ultimate discretion of the leader, to hire and fire at will, was a far more effective weapon when the going was really tough, as it was in the late summer of 1981.

The negative legitimacy by which she steadily disposed of opponents or critics was combined with an equally steady strengthening of the more positive objectives of prime ministerial government. With every reshuffle Margaret Thatcher strengthened her own position vis à vis the team which increasingly took on the character of a collection of acolytes.

Simon Jenkins described this in the *Economist* as 'high-risk politics',* which it certainly was. But then Margaret Thatcher has always been a high-risk politician, not in the obvious sense, such as going for broke in May 1979 with a Cabinet of like minds, a recipe for swift and absolute disaster, but in the instinctive, feminine, introverted decision-making about people and issues, which reveals her striking down vulnerable opponents when least they expect it, and seizing upon policy initiatives also when such actions are least expected. We shall come shortly to some of these, but first it is necessary to deal with her chosen antidote to the kind of upper echelon treachery and conspiracy against her leadership which manifested itself in the summer and autumn of 1981. That antidote is her appeal as a politician to the public, and more specifically to the grassroots of the Conservative Party. She is, at heart, a populist. She knew that her power derived from the electorate, of whom the favoured representatives were the delegates attending the Conservative Party annual conferences. Whatever magical charm she possessed was tested best on those occasions, and no matter how banal and trite the annual speeches may seem, in cold blood, read over and over with a fitting bewilderment at their impact, that impact should not be underestimated. It was the force that turned bitter as bile the resentment and disaffection of 'wets' who were half-hearted and pessimistic in their wish to remove her and put forward another, more moderate leader who would reach for consent rather than combat.

* October 10-16 1981.

CHAPTER SIXTEEN

The Grassroots

Conference speeches give the entirely false impression that power derives from personality. It *seems* that words and ideas sway people. Applause and standing ovations are a succession of instant, and at times overwhelming, responses to personality; or so it seems. In reality, a good political speech is invariably designed in simple direct terms to maximise feelings and convictions which are already there. And this reverses the phenomenon of personality convincing people. The successful, populist politician simply gives expression to belief and convictions which are already there. The crowd creates the leader.

Margaret Thatcher was willing, indeed enthusiastic and accomplished in her response to this unsophisticated grassroots demand. It distinguishes her from her predecessors. She lowered the level of argument and ideas, brought down the intellectual tone, warmed up the emotions, augmented her economic proposals with rhetoric and homespun example, and generally simplified the message. For all her drawbacks as both speaker and woman, deploying appeal, language, tone, accent, even clothing and appearance, she nevertheless brought to the occasion apparently passionate conviction and resolute personal consistency. It would be unfair to call her a demagogue, except in the neutral sense already referred to: that she clearly and emphatically sought the populist bond with ordinary people, and hence at Conservative Party conferences with grassroots delegates rather than with the party leadership. She avoided what the OED calls 'the bad sense' of that word, and was neither openly factious, nor an agitator; in any case, what need, since she was democratically the leader, and democratically in power? Nevertheless, her principal skill was in identifying herself with the broad and simple wishes of the majority of her audience, playing upon certain basic loves and hates. The loves included Britain, and the restoration of Britain's greatness in the world, through economic recovery, world defence, personal freedom and independence, and resolute balancing of the accounts. The hates were socialism, idleness, immorality, Soviet communism, and disregard for the rule of law.

By October 12 1979 she had delivered four such conference speeches as leader, and was faced with the fifth. It was the first in power. It was followed in 1980 by a moderately triumphalist follow-on speech from 1979, more moderate, better-wrought and slightly more cautious. In 1981, a low point in her political fortunes, she made what was, for a near-demagogue, the most skilful speech of the four-year period in power. And she followed it, in the autumn of 1982, with a clever and exact statement of the overall set of prescriptions for the general election by which she would win a second term.

She used the 1979 conference speech as an occasion to summarise her own and her party's position just five months after their electoral victory.

The party had won the May 3 general election with the largest swing since the second world war, and the largest majority in votes. She told the party this well-known set of facts, and it was greeted with the pleasure it naturally deserved. She went on, with studied deliberation, to catalogue the fact that the Conservatives had an absolute majority of 43 over all other parties. The party had recorded, she said, the largest trade union vote in its history; it had gained the support of young people 'many of whom saw no future under Labour'. It had implemented, in a June Budget, its election promises: more pay for the police and armed forces; increases to pensioners which were 'the largest in cash terms ever paid'; reduced income tax; and the commencement of the sale of council houses and flats.

It was an earnest of endeavour, she implied, while at the same time detecting that, after only five months, there was evidence of an ingrained scepticism among the British people. Could the Conservatives, any more than their Labour predecessors, or any other administration since the war, really do it'? In good party conference style she answered her own rhetoric immediately, in the affirmative, and went on to identify the key problems: 'high inflation, high unemployment, high taxation, appalling industrial relations, the lowest productivity in the Western world'.

She dismissed any idea of a caring and compassionate society being inconsistent with a capitalist, wealth-creating one. The Tories could provide both. And she identified the support which had been registered in the general election, making her Prime Minister, as support for both an idea and an ideal – the Conservative one – rather than for a manifesto, which implied the giving of a precise mandate. The manifesto, in any case, was not precise enough to elicit detailed support for specific intentions. It had to be a general endorsement, and in her view it was for 'the principal policies we stood for . . . *all* those policies'. And she delivered, in popular form, an economic lesson about the interdependence of taxation, public spending, inflation and industrial relations. Britain was trying to pay itself German wages for British output, and borrowing to bridge the gap. Earnings and output were unrelated; competitiveness was lost; weak governments printed money to pay strong unions their swelling pay awards; and no one seriously considered, or else treated dismissively, the low growth and high inflation which were the inescapable result.

Well, not quite no one. The Conservatives had persuaded the British people in the May election that the time had come to put a stop to this drift into bankruptcy. It was not surprising that doubts were felt all round. If the Conservatives had won 13.6 million votes, the Labour Party had won 11.5 million. And given the straight vote system, support for rectitude was in an absolute minority. But this would in no way inhibit the Conservative Government from tackling industrial relations together with the other economic problems. It would require 'certain limited but essential changes in the law', and she devoted time in her speech to the regulation of conflict: not the coercing of people but the protection of people from coercion; in other words legislation on secret ballots, secondary picketing amd the closed shop. There had been a welcome from trade union rank and file for Conservative undertakings on industrial relations law; the union leaders had said they would 'work with the elected government of the day'. Margaret Thatcher gave notice of her intent to call in these broad undertakings during the lifetime of her administration. 'Trade union power is out of balance,' she said. 'That is why people are supporting us in legislating for trade union reform.' And she identified the secret ballot as central, the closed shop and secondary picketing as pernicious in making it 'possible for small groups to close down whole industries with which they have no direct connection'.

In immediate contrast with the dark spectre of trade union power, Margaret Thatcher presented to her audience a vivid personal example of enterprise from her own constituency of Finchley, a letter from a small businessman, unidentified, but quoted verbatim in a measured eulogy of Conservative policies which had led him to start a fresh enterprise: ' "the biggest factor in its creation has been the steps which you have taken to restore incentive to work at all levels of the community. Not only can self-employed proprietors of small businesses keep more of the profits of those businesses but, more important, those good and hard-working employees who are patently worth a high level of wages are also feeling the benefits of more cash in the pocket and it is now worth their while to work that bit harder or longer as the case may be." '

Margaret Thatcher made increasingly vivid the personalised anecdote on which she had embarked. ' "Please stick to your policy",' she quoted from this man's letter. ' "It is the only way that we shall eventually solve our problems. It may be hard to bear in the short term but I truly believe that the bulk of public opinion is now behind a return to the basic commonsense fact that the country as a whole cannot continue to be paid more and more money for less and less work." '

The sentiments were so close to Margaret Thatcher's own, and the actual wording so similar to her fundamentalist style, that the letter could easily have come from her own hand. Lest this unworthy thought might seize upon the minds of her audience of loyal Conservative delegates, the Prime Minister went on to give the lie to that possibility. 'Here we have proof,' she said, 'that the policy is working. It is creating more wealth and more jobs. This is exactly the kind of person whom our Government seek to encourage. We rang him up to ask him if we could use the letter because it was so good and said that we would not dream of embarrassing him by revealing his name or anything like that. "What?" he said. "Non-attribution? I want to stand up and be counted!" It is small businessmen like this who, given the chance, will provide more jobs and more wealth, and the only Government from whom they will get the chance is this Conservative Government.'

This was the climax of that section in Margaret Thatcher's Conservative Party conference speech in 1979 dealing with the British economy. And it represented two-thirds of the speech. She went on to deal with Rhodesia, and the work done by Peter Carrington. That was the Commonwealth dealt with. She spoke of Europe, of the June summit, and of the British taxpayers' reluctance to finance the budgets of the country's wealthier European neighbours. She spoke of freedom; of European and British defence; of NATO and Russia and Northern Ireland. And she concluded both her own speech and the conference itself with a homily about telling the truth, and about trust, about the country as a family, and about the Conservative Party as 'caring and united', and prepared to hold out the hand of friendship to socialists and trade unionists. 'They do not share our Conservative ideals – at least they think they do not – but they do want free and responsible trade unions to play an honourable part in the life of a free and responsible society.'

The 1980 speech identified the Government's task rather more simply than had been the case a year earlier; it was 'to change the national attitude of mind'. In a very simple and direct restatement of achievements, which included the commencement of trade union reform, the paying off of a sizeable part, and in advance, of Britain's debts, and progress towards the 'property-owning democracy', she included the memorable phrases: 'To those waiting with bated breath for that favourite media catch-phrase, the U-turn, I have only one thing to say: You turn if you want to; the lady's not for turning.'

1981 was a very different occasion. As we have seen, there was a good deal of private treachery; and publicly she was isolated and beleaguered. Not only had virtually all her ideological objectives been missed, such as bringing down inflation, interest rates and unemployment, but this failure had coincided with the substantial compromising of her stated remedies, in other words, public spending had gone up, instead of down, public pay during the early part of her term of power had been unacceptably high, and she had failed to put any real shape on the programme for changing the balance and relationship between the public industrial and commercial sector, in which nationalised industries' finances were in fairly chaotic condition, and the private sector whose interests she was meant to have at heart. It was a double failure. This woman, whose reputation was built on consistency, had compromised and prevaricated, and was reaping the short-term whirlwind. Underneath it, the ground-work was laid for future calm, if she could hold out. In the circumstances she made the most difficult of the four annual speeches arguably into the best, combining populism with a subtlety which had certainly not been a characteristic of previous speeches, and was not really something in which she trusted.

She had said at the beginning of her 1980 address, 'Challenge is exhilarating'; that was when she was least challenged. In 1981, faced with substantial revolt and discontent, she again welcomed it as indicative of the vitality and strength of the Conservative Party 'at an immensely difficult time'. She even welcomed Edward Heath's 'contribution', then consigned him, with 'delight', to the forthcoming Croydon by-election in which he had promised to help. Heath had attacked her in a comprehensive and highly political fashion only a week before, claiming that her policies would lead to Conservative electoral defeat; and at Blackpool he had been at the centre of alternative consensus murmurings. She used the nautical language so loved by politicians who are weathering stormy seas, and verbally she seemed to give an impression of being rocked and tossed. Her paragraphs and sentences were short and choppy, her metaphors mixed: it had been 'the grand assize of the nation'. But she turned the tables by her carefully managed appearances of sincerity and sensitivity as she catalogued the concern of her critics and made it her own. If delegates, and particularly Members of Parliament who wanted to retain their seats at the general election which was beginning to loom ahead of them, were worried about 'every factory closure and redundancy', then so was she: 'I learned from childhood the dignity which comes from work.' She defended her strategy skilfully, with a combination of logic and of emotion bordering on, but seeming not quite to achieve demagogy.

It is that semblance which is a critical factor in Margaret Thatcher's political character. She gives to the weaponry of the demagogue a polite, drawing-room manner. She invests the 'mob' with an equally polite set of characteristics,. No firm grassroots supporter of her, whether politically active or not, would be other than horrified at the idea that they were swayed by unprincipled or bombastic oratory, or that Margaret Thatcher indulged in such oratory. Yet this is precisely her political strength. Though it is dressed up in polite language and expressed by the physical and emotional epitome of middle-class firmness of principle and belief, her major conference speeches are a new and highly effective interpretation of what the modern demagogue needs to be. They answer the demands of a new interpretation also of what the modern 'mob' is in Britain of the 1980s: a well-fed, well-dressed, well-educated majority which wants to keep things the way they are, hold to themselves the values and standards they have been taught to expect, and divide and discipline the forces which threaten them. She provided clear and simple recipes for doing that. She followed the emotive claims about her understanding of 'the dignity of work' with a brief, pithy and selective outline of specific achievements, leading her naturally into the statutory attacks on Socialism, and contrasts of the alternative scenarios of SDP and Liberal Party 'middleness'. It sufficed. Privately, she must have been looking around her, hoping for something to turn up. But, publicly, she had made an adequate defence, and there was really no challenge with any prospect at all of changing the fixed trajectory of her falling star. That 'something to turn up' might arguably be economic. Yet all options were open. An examination of these options must now lead us to consideration of her use of various alternatives in order to win the infinitely more difficult prize of a second term.

CHAPTER SEVENTEEN

'Authority from Britain'

In mid-January of 1979 James Callaghan told the House of Commons that no useful purpose would be served by convening any conference in the near future aimed at a Rhodesia settlement. There would be no likelihood of a successful outcome. At the end of the month, white Rhodesians voted by an 85 percent majority in favour of the Executive Council's proposed constitution leading to majority rule, and the Government's immediate response to this was to say that it 'represented no measure of the acceptability . . . of the proposals' because the referendum had excluded three million black Africans. In February, Government proposals to set up an inquiry into oil sanctions were passed in the Commons, but rejected by the Lords. Michael Foot told the Commons that its decision would prevail, and that the Government would come forward with proposals.

The British and Rhodesian elections almost coincided. The Conservative manifesto gave less than ten lines to Rhodesia, committing the Party to a lasting settlement, based on the 'Six Principles'* with the ultimate objective of restoring the country to legality, lifting sanctions, and making sure that the new independent state gained international recognition.

By the end of 1979 this had been all but achieved. It was the first of Margaret Thatcher's successes, and it is significant, perhaps ironic as well, that it lay firmly outside the economic realm, that it was essentially a Commonwealth achievement,

---

* 1) Unimpeded progress to majority rule; 2) guarantee against retrogressive constitutional amendment; 3) improved political status for African population; 4) progress towards ending racial discrimination; 5) acceptability of independence proposals to all Rhodesian people; 6) need to ensure no oppression of majority by minority, or minority by majority.

and that the credit due to her is substantially because she listened to advice and took it. Most of her judgments, to begin with were wrong. She underestimated the Commowealth, she underestimated the political strength of Robert Mugabe aand Joshua Nkomo, and she was both superficial and too responsive to the right wing of the Conservative Party in her initial attitude to Abel Muzorewa and, by implication, to Ian Smith. At the same time, her first responses, during the debate on the Queen's Speech in the new Parliament on May 15, were sufficiently ambiguous to keep open her options and conceal her uncertainty and lack of either knowledge or experience.

She had no sure Commonwealth touch; nor has she acquired one in power. But she had a shrewd defence mechanism to cover this weakness, and it expressed itself in such determined but unfathomable phrases as: 'we must and will recognise the realities of the present situation in Rhodesia. We must and will take into account the wider international implications.' Yet it was others rather than herself who really took account of the realities, and the international implications. What is substantially to Margaret Thatcher's credit, throughout 1979, is the degree to which she subscribed to this process. She became Prime Minister at a time when a number of critical shifts in power, and changes in perception, had already taken place. Ever since General George Peter Walls, Combined Operations Commander in Rhodesia since 1977, had said more than a year earlier that the terrorist war could not be won, the recognition that this meant not *just* a settlement in favour of black majority rule, but a settlement with Mugabe *and* Nkomo, had been growing. They had substance; Muzorewa did not. They wanted real power; he was prepared to accept a formula which compromised black Africans from the start. And a fair number of Conservatives, including Margaret Thatcher, were also prepared to compromise, their motivation ranging between strong sympathies for the Smith regime and a simple desire to be rid of the problem.

Britain's strength, in finding a solution, lay in the not too powerful area of continuing the trade sanctions, and in withholding recognition. Used properly, and supported by other Commonwealth countries at the 1979 Commonwealth Conference due to be held in Lusaka in the first week of August, an acceptable settlement, crucial to the future of southern Africa, might be worked out. It therefore caused massive consternation when Margaret Thatcher, on her way back from the Tokyo economic summit at the end of June, stopped off in Canberra for talks with the Australian Prime Minister, Malcolm Fraser, and then gave a press conference at which she indicated possible parliamentary 'difficulties' in renewing sanctions. She also expressed her belief in the likelihood of an early recognition of the Muzorewa regime hoping for other Commonwealth governments to support this.

At one stroke she had thrown away Britain's bargaining position. It needed to be recovered in less than a month. Rather too much credit is generally given to the Foreign Office for persuading Margaret Thatcher to change her mind on the Patriotic Front, and too little to the Commonwealth countries in those crucial weeks leading up to the Lusaka conference. Malcolm Fraser, who was firmly committed to a solution of substance, rather than one of shadow, in southern Africa, began a process of 'bush telegraph' Commonwealth consultations in which Michael Manley of Jamaica, Kenneth Kaunda of Zambia and Julius Nyerere of Tanzania were key figures, as was the Commonwealth Secretary General, Sonny Ramphal. Their clear conviction, supported by the Organisation for African unity and by a majority of United Nations members, was that no settlement which failed to recognise the Patriotic Front could work, and that everything possible to underline this should be done.

One important aspect was trade. Since the early 1970s British trade with Africa had passed a watershed, as it was now greater in volume and value with black African countries. As a timely reminder of political and economic muscle, Nigeria nationalised British Petroleum. Lord Carrington had been warned by the High Commissioner in Lagos that this was on the cards, but had ignored it. It overshadowed the opening of the Lusaka conference, and gave essential 'bite' to a situation that was in any case highly dramatic. It is argued* that Margaret Thatcher went through a substantial change of heart between her Canberra press conference and the Lusaka meeting. The evidence does not support this. The most that can be said of her Commons speech of July 25 was that it indicated a recognition of the mistake she had made, and a greatly increased measure of caution about committing herself one way or the other in advance of the talks.

* See Hugh Stephenson, op. cit.

It is equally possible that she still went to Lusaka thinking she could do a deal, and that Carrington went with her prepared to do a deal, but less confident that they could. There is no evidence that either of them went in the clear conviction that no deal with Muzorewa should be considered. What was admirable about her stance at the end of July was her clear recognition of the mistakes of Canberra, and her careful ambiguities which were, in turn, a recognition that she simply did not have the stature to dominate the conference, or to indulge in confrontational politics.

But it was still potentially an exercise in opportunism not inconsistent with her view of how power should be handled and deployed. What is not apparent is any deep understanding of, or concern about, either the Commonwealth as such, its leaders, or the delicate balance of power in southern Africa, involving East-West, and race, relations. And it was precisely these concerns which motivated the other Commonwealth leaders already mentioned whose energies, whether or not their own vital interests were at stake, were deployed before and during the Lusaka conference to persuade the British Prime Minister – if necessary, to force her – into the swift and correct resolving of the Rhodesian problem.

She became convinced by the arguments she heard. She also recognised the advantage, in terms of her own power, of accepting a course of action which would undoubtedly reflect well on her. This is where her innocence and lack of international experience was an advantage. Surrounded by passionately articulate and skilful leaders whose own futures and those of their countries were at stake, she became convinced in a way that put her ahead of her own Foreign Secretary. He remained more sceptical, in part perhaps because he would remain in charge of the subsequent negotiations with the Patriotic Front, and was not sanguine about success, but in part also because he carried the burden of Foreign Office caution and step-by-step diplomacy.

Margaret Thatcher plunged off the plane at Lusaka airport into the warm African night, with its noisy crowds and the intense focus of world interest in a war-torn situation, her dark glasses in her handbag 'in case they got rough and start throwing anything like acid', * but without a backward glance. What she was going

---

* Quoted from Hugh Stephenson, op. cit., p. 85.

to be determined about she did not know, and this is fairly clear in her opening speech on August 1, an anodyne presentation of platitudes about 'our shared history' and the heritage of common ideas about politics and democracy, expressed in a common language. This was followed by a lecture on the world economy, and one on Vietnam and its refugees.

That she was going to be determined, and solve something, however, is equally clear from the transformation in style and content by August 3, when she explained the basis of British policy on Rhodesia. It bore little resemblance to the explanations given in London in July, since she now unequivocally rejected as defective the constitution which had brought Abel Muzorewa to power. The blocking mechanism given to the white minority was inconsistent with anything previously granted by the British Parliament at independence, and went beyond the legitimate objective of encouraging that minority to remain in an independent Rhodesia; so too did it contain constitutional provisions about appointments. Furthermore, she said, any lasting solution required the involvement of the Patriotic Front, so that those living outside the country, but belonging to it, could return to political life. She concluded this unequivocal presentation of Britain's case by asserting Britain's authority and responsibilty in bringing about an independence on the lines proposed. Four key points emerged: the commitment to 'genuine' black majority rule; Britain's 'unique' role in bringing this about; the consistency on any new constitution with previous ones monitored by Britain; and the need to do it 'as quickly as possible'.

She concluded: 'Our aim is to bring Rhodesia to legal independence on a basis which the Commonwealth and the international community as a whole will find acceptable. I believe that we now have a chance to achieve this, and we must take it.' Rarely in her career can the word 'now' have been more apposite, nor so heavily charged with meaning that affected many lives and many reputations, her own included.

Between August 1 and August 3 she came face to face with the reality of hard work by Commonwealth leaders, and determination just as strong as her own, not just to 'do something', but to do what was required: settle the Rhodesian question in terms of real power. As a dedicated practitioner of power politics, Margaret Thatcher recognises its use by others. And at the beginning of August, 1979, she came face to face with the phenomenon among a group of serious political leaders, vastly more experienced than herself, and in power situations infinitely more difficult and dangerous than her own. Men like Kenneth Kaunda and Julius Nyerere guided her to a final position which encompassed the recovery of the mistakes made in Canberra, and the abandonment of what had effectively been a Conservative Party commitment to the internal settlement which was clearly not on. In the sober exchanges of the Commonwealth Conference she saw the six principles in a new light, and changed her own position to one which was realistic. Whether it could be made to work was a question requiring further months of debate. But the change of heart took place during those three days, and her willingness to submit to that change allowed her to claim, quite legitimately, the credit for a real achievement in her first year in office. A certain artificiality is implied in this analysis of Margaret Thatcher's handling of Rhodesia; intentionally so. Nothing done subsequently in the Commonwealth context has indicated any natural growth in her understanding and breadth of vision about it as an organisation, or about its leaders and colleagues in the joint effort at world peace or a better world order. If anything, events like the invasion of Grenada have indicated the reverse, a movement towards a more superficial handling of a critical situation. This is not inconsistent with a certain ferocity and determination to *solve*, if solutions offer themselves, but to ignore otherwise. It emphasises that the political schizophrenia which separates people primarily concerned with themselves, who treat actions as adjuncts, and the true statesman who, in the final account, will sacrifice self-interest for a major principle. She *seemed* to do this in Rhodesia. It was one of the semblances which did not last.

The rest is detail. Under Lord Carrington's chairmanship the Lancaster House Conference met on September 10, with the Patriotic Front leaders, Joshua Nkomo and Robert Mugabe, present. In advance of it Abel Muzorewa announced that the then current name for the country he represented, Zimbabwe Rhodesia, would be changed to Zimbabwe 'in the near future'. Agreement was reached in December. Lord Soames was appointed Governor. Elections were called in February 1980 and resulted in a landslide victory for Robert Mugabe in early March. The right wing of the Conservative Party regarded the result as 'a major defeat for the West', and Margaret Thatcher was criticised for omitting Robert Mugabe's name from those she had listed who deserved congratulating. She replied: 'We usually do that on the day that independence is given'. It was an ill-concealed error, but it did not detract from her earlier achievement. Its political purpose related to her own right wing, and to the fact that Rhodesia, in power terms, was both an achievement and a thing of the past.

On April 19 the independent republic of Zimbabwe became the forty-third member-state of the Commonwealth, with Robert Mugabe as Prime Minister and Canaan Banana as President. The Queen was represented at the independence ceremonies by the Prince of Wales, the British government by Lord Carrington. The four key points in Margaret Thatcher's Lusaka speech of August 3 had been fulfilled; she had ended fourteen years of illegal independence by handing back power to a black Marxist. Democracy, and the exercise of power, are not easy.

CHAPTER EIGHTEEN

European Power Games

She brought together in a more masterly, and much more lasting fashion, a complicated set of intellectual and emotional capacities in her dealings with the EEC. This was not something to be 'solved' or 'resolved' in the deft working out of a single, triumphant formula. It would be with her, as Prime Minister, throughout the life of Parliament, and neither she nor anyone else could foresee the extent to which it would be an election issue in a number of different ways. While the short-term objective, on coming to power, was to obtain 'broad balance' on Britain's contribution to the EEC Budget, the possibility of a whole list of other matters, like defence, trade with Warsaw Pact powers, Commonwealth preferences, energy, Anglo-American relations and NATO within Europe, including the siting of nuclear weapons, were all potentially there as motivators of conflict. Margaret Thatcher's immediate predecessors, Callaghan, Wilson and Edward Heath, who between them covered the leadership of Britain for the previous fifteen years, had all been either ambivalent or prevaricators on the central question of domestic house-keeping while at the same time adopting substantially firmer attitudes on the range of issues covered by the EEC umbrella.

Those firmer attitudes differed sharply as between the Labour premiers and the Conservative one. Heath was a committed European, Callaghan and Wilson were reluctant Europeans. But all three consented to the collective will of the 'club' to which Britain, after many years of trying, had gained access during Edward Heath's premiership. None of them seriously entertained the idea of making the EEC an electoral or political option. Wilson came nearest; but he suffered the handicap of not being treated entirely seriously when he expostulated about membership. And for the greater part of his time as premier he was simply not given the opportunity.

Almost from the start, Margaret Thatcher established a line on Europe which was deliberately ambiguous. She did so in the pursuit of her instinctive conviction that option politics is the surest route to power. No one would know for certain, at any time, precisely where she stood. The ultimate direction of her mind would remain obscure. Each issue would be judged on merit. And the criterion would be Britain's interests measured in close conjunction with her own political ones.

From the start, therefore, she set out to destabilise European perceptions of the route Britain would take, by varying the tempo and altering the direction. It was not an end in itself; that would have been irresponsible. It was a perceived route to actual power on the European stage, desirable in its own right as well as in the context of domestic power politics. Initially, the effects were disastrous. But, though advisers were appalled, and the lobby of 'Good British Europeans' greatly dismayed, the basic objective, which was to dominate Britain's European partners, was relentlessly achieved.

Consider the facts. In the summer of 1979 Geoffrey Howe brought in a Budget designed to stimulate production in a freer framework of corporate incentives and greater personal choice. The shifting of the tax burden away from earnings towards spending was begun, and was accompanied by expenditure cuts. A list amounting to £1,600 millions-worth was headed by two major items, a £300 million cut in the housing programme, and a £320 million cut in the energy area through the sale of Government assets. This kind of domestic strategy was, of course, visibly undermined by the £1,000 million deficit on Britain's account with Brussels. The great British public – as confused about the niceties of CAP 'beef mountains', milk and olive oil 'lakes', and the economic imbalance between EEC partners like Ireland and Denmark, as they were about M3, monetarism, and the impact of corporate taxation changes – could readily grasp what was at issue when a Prime Minister simply said she was going to ensure that what Britain paid into the EEC she would get back again.

It was not a logical position. Indeed, it ran utterly in the teeth of the whole European idea. But it was emotionally appealing, and it was simple.

To begin with, Margaret Thatcher held herself in check. She attended the first European Council, on June 21-22 in Strasbourg, and simply established there what she then told the House of Commons, on June 26, was 'agreement to tackle the inequitably high contribution that Britain at present makes to the European Budget'. She flew immediately to the Tokyo Economic Summit of June 28-29, where she 'particularly impressed' Chancellor Helmut Schmidt with her 'knowledge, authority and sense of responsibility'.*

Things were markedly different, however, in Dublin on November 29-30, where she managed to infuriate Chancellor Scmidt and several of the other European leaders. Even the tactful chairman, Jack Lynch, who was then under diverse and considerable domestic pressures of his own, was moved to describe her as adamant, persistent and repetitive.

In preparation for the Dublin summit she had delivered an important speech on October 18 in Luxembourg, the Winston Churchill Memorial Lecture, in which she had linked together NATO and European defences, involving Britain's willingness to meet the defence spending challenge, with reflections on the European Community as 'a dynamic and evolving organisation that would bring together the peoples of Europe'. But it had to bring them together on her terms, and she was equally emphatic that the £1,000m balance in favour of the EEC should be cut. 'I cannot play Sister Bountiful to the Community while my own electorate are being asked to forgo improvements in the fields of health, education, welfare and the rest. The imbalance is not compatible with the spirit of the Community. Its continuation would undermine the sense of solidarity and common obligation which lies at the heart of Community endeavour.'

It was a remarkably skilful platform from which to approach successive summits and council meetings. Workers in fields and factories would admire Maggie for sticking up for Britain where it mattered to them, in their pockets; retired colonels and brigadiers would see the logic of her tough stance on defence; committed Europeans would detect, if they were objective

---

* Schmidt's words to the Bundestag, quoted in Hugh Stephenson, op. cit.

enough in their judgments, that she was establishing a position of strength which was very much more effective as a bargaining position than the consensus inherent in Edward Heath's Europeanism, which had, for all its admirable idealism, the basic flaw of predictablilty and therefore prior consent. Margaret Thatcher, at the Dublin Summit was aggressive in her defence of Britain's virtue and her deliberate and calculated discomfiture of overbold admirers like Helmut Schmidt.

Most of the time was spent on Britain's contribution to the Budget, which had the twofold effect of making her the central figure and Britain the key country. In reporting to the House of Commons she suggested two prospects, the veto on other decisions until the right balance was achieved, or the withholding of contributions. Her summary, in power terms, was a classic: 'There are two schools of thought. Some people believe that to withhold contributions would be better and more direct, and others believe it would be better to disrupt. Let us hope that we shall move a great deal further before applying either of these suggestions.'

As a short-term exercise in playing off against each other domestic and international politics, Margaret Thatcher was showing she was no slouch. It was an approach worthy of any good demagogue. As an expression of principled leadership by one who wished to be seen as standing resolute against Soviet Russia, and whose very resolution was embedded in the professed political lessons of conflict during the thirties, Britain's greatness in the second world war, and the need for Western solidarity in the subsequent period, her behaviour over Europe was at times petulant, shallow and full of ambiguities. She placed economic considerations above all others, applied shopkeeping judgments in emulation of the majority of other EEC leaders, and in conflict with the idealism which had brought the community into being, and lost a great deal of the valuable ground won by her most considerable predecessor Edward Heath. For those who believe or believed in Europe, she set a level of leadership which was short-sighted and selfish. She did not endeavour to establish longer-term objectives, or to work towards the difficult target of political unity implicit in much of what had been done before, not just by Heath, but by two earlier heroes of hers, Harold Macmillan and Winston Churchill. Demanding this is perhaps to demand too much; yet, for a Prime

Minister with ambitions to occupy the world stage, Margaret Thatcher adopted towards the EEC a very self-centred attitude primarily concerned with money, and with Britain getting out again everything she put in. It is legitimately pragmatic; it is real politics; it has no whiff of statesmanship or serious leadership about it.

Of the three net contributors to the EEC Budget, Britain, France and Germany, Britain was by far the largest. In anticipation of the continuing economic war, a Treasury case was prepared in February 1980 ahead of the April 27-28 Council meeting. No progress was made, and no communiqué issued on internal EEC matters. Iran and Afghanistan dominated the talks. But on May 29-30, in Brussels, agreement was reached, and it represented, in economic terms, a genuine triumph. The British contribution for 1980 had a ceiling fixed at £370 million, and for 1981 £440 million. This meant a two-year total of £1,570 million in rebates.

By November of 1980, when Margaret Thatcher visited Germany and France, she was able to make British commitment to the European Community the theme of her visit; and she did it from a position of strength. Not only had she achieved budgetary equilibrium, but at the Venice summit of June 22-23 had managed to steer, or at least to be seen to have steered, other leaders towards measures essential to non-inflationary growth and increased employment, 'entirely in line' with British policy. She could more freely state, as she did on German television on November 12, that Britain was bound up with Europe and that EEC membership was crucial to employment.

She had a firmer European direction through 1981, and it was not just economic. Indeed, she seemed temporarily to recognise the need to raise things to a new, more stimulating, plane. After the early confrontation, she was faced with the tedious nature of economic achievement and this she decided to leave to Carrington, Howe and Walker. She kept to herself, however, the continuing confrontation elements. To Afghanistan and Iran was added Poland, on which she issued a warning to the Soviet Union, on April 8 1981, to respect the will of the Polish people and their right to express it.

She was generally muted on Europe during the period of Britain's presidency, from July to December of 1981, which coincided with the rapidly declining fortunes of the Conservative

Party and of herself in electoral terms. She initiated the six-month period with a speech following the Summit of June 29-30 1981 in Luxembourg, in which were reflected the gloomy, pessimistic but necessary agreements of the Ten that controlling both inflation and unemployment went hand in hand; she admitted, however, they had 'by no means been brought under control'.*
The same muted tones prevailed through to December, when a dispirited Margaret Thatcher summarised a multiplicity of difficulties which remained to be solved: milk, Mediterranean agriculture and such were making impossible the adjustment of the Budget 'so that no member State is put into an unacceptable financial situation'. And this general tone was sustained by her at the Brussels Council meeting of March 29-30 1982, the eve of the Argentine invasion of the Falklands and the beginning therefore of the sure but far from instantaneous turning point in her political fortunes.

Her achievement on the European front in less than three years had none the less been remarkable. To begin with, she had won the confidence of the two European leaders of most significance, Giscard d'Estaing and Helmut Schmidt. The former admired her strong, right-wing views, the latter her sense of Western solidarity; both admired her apparently sound judgment, grasp of issues and personal authority. Six months later, lest they should be under the illusion of having enrolled her within a world 'club' of top people whose main admission requirement was subscription to a policy of broad consensus, she blasted them out of their previous sentiments. She sustained this until she got her way, ameliorating it only partially, and only along lines which also fitted in closely with her bellicose interpretation of world defence, by linking together, in a European framework, Anglo-American, NATO and East-West issues. Last scene of all, to end this oscillating cycle of behaviour, she imposed, or seemed to have imposed, on her partners a British interpretation, indeed a Thatcherite interpretation, of economic policy; what had been central to her demands in Dublin, in November 1979, that British rectitude should not pay for European prodigality, became a credible mechanism for shifting, not just the fulcrum across which the European budget was balanced, but also the collective thinking within the Community on economic policy. And even

---

* Speech in House of Commons, July 1 1981; See Hansard Vol. VII, No. 132.

where she had not done this, she managed to create the impression that she had.

In terms of power, Margaret Thatcher, who was infinitely less seriously committed a European than Britain's leading Community protagonist, Edward Heath, had outclassed him in manipulating and dominating the community issues. By withholding, then changing, and never fully revealing, the content of her mind, she had exercised a real and dynamic force on Britain's major trading and defence partners. She had combined popular achievements – the easily understood and valued rebates – with more arcane ones, in the form of psychological victories at the many conference tables, and more debatable ones, in the arena of actual economic policy shifts.

She had done so, however, with very questionable regard for the fundamentals of the European ideal. Britain, in the eyes of Europe, was enviably rich in the most valuable commodity for developed countries in the past decade, oil. It was this which bolstered the British economy, not rectitude, and it should have been this, in a well-ordered continuation of the process of Europeanisation of member-states, which would have balanced out the inequities between the rich and poor nations. Instead, her policies during the period 1979-82 represented a distinct shift towards a bellicose brand of nationalism, instinctively correct in terms of her domestic popularity, but threatening in the wider sense. The age-old laws which had dictated down through the centuries the cycles of change between protectionism and free trade, between rivalry and harmony among states, between imperialism and nationalism, were working anyway, and were working, sadly, against the proper evolution of Europe as a comprehensive entity. Margaret Thatcher, while claiming the opposite, firmly shoved them along the road.

CHAPTER NINETEEN

'The Unique Relationship'

Ireland appeared to offer Margaret Thatcher both a challenge and an opportunity. One would have been sufficient bait for her; the two were irresistible.

There were additional factors, however. Irish terrorists had, in the murder of Airey Neave, deprived her of her close political ally and adviser. It had concentrated her mind on understanding the problem, and though, with anyone else, it might also have pre-empted flexibility and balance, with her combative nature it encouraged a wish for precisely that elusive resolution of the Irish problem which had caused her predecessors an unending headache for more than ten years. In addition, she was faced with a new leader in the Republic who combined inscrutability and apparent political skills with a moody and threatening form of old-style republicanism. From the start Charles Haughey placed Northern Ireland at the top of his own agenda and in terms which were quite different from what had gone before. Her political instincts told her that there were options here worth exploring.

She came at them slowly. Her first encounter of significance as Prime Minister was with Jack Lynch. They had no detailed discussion on Northern Ireland or Anglo-Irish relations at the June meeting of the European Council, but met for a Downing Street summit on September 5, which was followed by a somewhat frosty agreed statement, pledging 'determination to stamp out terrorism' and agreement substantially to improve cooperation. British interest in restoring greater political control to the people of Northern Ireland was countered by Republic of Ireland insistence that it should be acceptable to both communities.

Jack Lynch formed the distinct impression that Margaret Thatcher's view of Ireland was severely limited in terms of her knowledge and understanding, but not in terms of her will to take action. It was a dangerous combination, and it represented a potentially new disturbance in an already destabilised political situation. For a man who was generally passive and phlegmatic, and whose understanding of the Northern Ireland problem, from a Southern point of view, was truly immense, the concern with which he regarded her was startling.

His reign, however, was coming to an end. In early December he resigned while in office, and was succeeded by Charles Haughey. Fianna Fail then had two and half years to run, and this represented a period long enough to do real business, if such business was there to be done; it also gave to Margaret Thatcher, with a clear four years before her, an edge of sorts in manoeuvring. This outline of the prospects pre-supposes a more positive and aggressive view of the Irish potential than is generally put forward about Margaret Thatcher. Let us see if the record supports this.

In mid-February 1980 Charles Haughey announced his 'new' Northern Ireland policy. It was that the Six Counties had failed as a political entity, and that no internal solution was possible; instead, the whole matter had to be raised to a new plateau and resolved between London and Dublin. It was also urgent. The new Irish premier painted a stark picture of a society in Northern Ireland which could well 'deteriorate beyond recovery'. He used the word 'solution' repeatedly through the section of this major speech dealing with the North, and laid heavy stress on the despair, isolation, hopelessness, instability and underlying violence which were all permanently present in Northern Ireland which 'casts a long dark shadow into every corner of these islands'. He rejected the Constitutional Conference which the Secretary of State, Humphrey Atkins, had initiated in January 7 1980 in Belfast, and which was still going on, though predictably with only three of the four main political parties, Alliance, SDLP and Democratic Unionist Party, the official Unionist Party having boycotted it. All the conference could do lay in the realm of civil rights and equality, and the impartial operation of security.

The Conference itself cannot provide a conclusive settlement.

> We must face the reality that Northern Ireland, as a political entity, has failed and that a new beginning is needed. The time has surely come for the two sovereign Governments to work together to find a formula and lift the situation on to a new plane, that will bring permanent peace and stability to the people of these islands.*

He made two additional points of direct relevance to the Atkins initiative as well as to Margaret Thatcher, in her own assessment of whatever top-level relationship would emerge between them. The first was Haughey's moderate request for 'a declaration by the British Government of their interest in encouraging the unity of Ireland, by agreement and in peace'. This would lead to an 'entirely new situation' with 'real lasting peace . . . an attainable reality'. The second point was that the 'solution', whatever it might be, or become, would be worked out 'without a British presence but with active goodwill'. Put at its most brutal, Irish Protestants and Irish Catholics, on the whole territory of Ireland, would sort out each other's differences without British troops, but with British money. And it is probable that at least some of Margaret Thatcher's advisers put it to her in fairly brutal terms. After all, twelve years of a bi-partisan policy on the North, between all the political parties in the Republic, constructed mainly by Jack Lynch, and involving at one stage the dismissal of Charles Haughey and other senior members of Fianna Fail, had been abandoned at a stroke. Lynch had dismissed Haughey and Blaney on Wednesday May 6 1970 'because I am, satisfied that they do not subscribe fully to Government policy in relation to the present situation in the Six Counties as stated by me at the Fianna Fail Ard Fheis in January last'.**

Now, almost exactly ten years later, and using precisely the same 'platform' for enunciating policy, the approach which then was cause for dismissal was being reinstated. And this was openly claimed, on Haughey's behalf in respect of a speech which was 'of major significance' on Northern Ireland, and which, in the words of a close associate, brought to an end a 'shameful interregnum'.

In these circumstances, Margaret Thatcher's response to

---

* Presidential Address by the Taoiseach, Mr Charles Haughey, TD, at the 49th Fianna Fail Ard Fheis, RDS, Dublin, Saturday February 16th 1980.
** Taoiseach's Statement, May 6 1970.

Charles Haughey was remarkable. The two leaders met on May 21. As a prelude typical of Haughey, and probably intriguing to Margaret Thatcher, he gave her a present of a silver teapot. (Ironically, British diplomats are in the habit of using the word 'teapot' in place of the difficult Irish word, Taoiseach, with its diphthong 't', and its 'tee-shock' pronunciation. They got on well, much better than Lynch and Thatcher, and issued a statement which was markedly warmer in tone than the one issued the previous November. More important, at Haughey's press conference immediately afterwards, as well as in her statements, a genuine mood of a positive movement forward was engendered. With the exception of the Republic of Ireland actually going back into the British Commonwealth, virtually every other option was said to be under consideration, and if it could be used to bring about unity, even defence commitments were potentially 'on the table'.

'I think Mrs Thatcher is a practical politician . . .' Haughey said. 'I hope that I would be able to persuade her where the best interests of Ireland and Britain both ultimately lie, and that is in the unity of Ireland.' In reality, Haughey even failed to force Northern Ireland into the centre of the stage. It was decidedly one of several issues discussed. He came away with considerable admiration for this 'tough lady', pleasure at the friendly atmosphere, but puzzlement as well. For all his brave press conference statements, he had failed to lay bare her Northern Ireland intentions, and had been steered towards international issues.

Margaret Thatcher was publicly much more cautious. She simply reiterated the guarantee: no constitutional change without the support of the majority in the North. But both on the Unionist side and within the Provisional IRA serious shifts of direction were recognised beneath the surface. Ian Paisley identified the strategic relevance of defence and NATO being raised, as did members of Fianna Fail who were unhappy about Haughey's abandonment of the Lynch line on Northern Ireland. And the Provisional IRA also saw signs of a legitimate takeover of their policies for getting Britain out. This was the background for the Maze H-Block hunger strike which seven prisoners began on 27 October 1980, in anticipation of the promised winter summit between Margaret Thatcher and Charles Haughey, which took place on December 8 at Dublin Castle.

The tone of the joint communiqué seemed to confirm the

growing suspicion that Margaret Thatcher was engaged in changing policy in order to reach some kind of rapprochement with Haughey. New phrases, like 'unique relationship' and 'totality of relations within these islands' went side by side with an intensity of commitment – 'the discussions were regarded by both sides as extremely constructive and significant' – which was new on her side, and increasingly alarming. And when the Maze hunger strike ended, on December 18 1980, a climate of 'progress' seemed possible.

It was aggressively sustained by Charles Haughey, both in the Dail, and through his press contacts, and led to growing anxiety in Northern Ireland that a sell-out was contemplated. Then the 'unique relationship' began rapidly to fall apart. Haughey was prevented from going to the country in February, the real objective in his high-level debates with Margaret Thatcher, by the Stardust disco fire on the morning of February 14, the day on which his Ard Fheis speech was to be made, setting a general election in motion. On March 1 1981, the first of a new wave of H-Block hunger strikers refused food in the Maze, and on March 5, in a visit to Northern Ireland, Margaret Thatcher made a speech of reassurance about the North, putting into much more sober perspective the two meetings with the Republic's Prime Minister. The guarantee still held; there would be no sell-out; and anyone who interpreted the meeting between herself and Haughey was misunderstanding their purpose, which was basically 'a common interest in peace and reconciliation'.

From then on, relations deteriorated rapidly. Margaret Thatcher took a tough, 'iron lady' stance towards the hunger strikers, while Haughey adopted a line based on 'humanitarian concern' as a way out of a confrontation which would lead to death. It did. 'The unique relationship' between the two countries, and the implied closeness between the two leaders, failing to resolve a relatively confined problem on prison clothing and work, was exposed as much less than had been vaunted.

It was subsequently suggested, no doubt on Margaret Thatcher's own initiative, as well as that of others, that she had been betrayed by the Foreign Office. Simon Jenkins, writing in the *Economist*, October 10, 1981, says: 'Her special aversion is reserved for the foreign office, hating its "Eurospeak" and deeply sceptical of its true loyalty to British interests (a view she shares with Dr David Owen). She will never forgive the hatchet job she is convinced its mandarins did on her behind her back at the Dublin Summit.'

Yet the Foreign Office advice given her at that time was strongly in favour of caution, and was particularly so in regard to the new Irish leader. She chose, quite characteristically, to ignore it, as well as ignoring the advice coming from the Northern Ireland Office about the delicate political and security situation.

She did so for a number of reasons. She believed, like Haughey, with whom she has many political characteristics in common, in political 'solutions'; and Northern Ireland was no exception. Even if it proved too difficult, it was nevertheless an option to be explored. In the tense and essentially gloomy economic environment which faced her in late 1980, and which was already undermining her policies as well as her popularity, the silver teapot was a harbinger of positive opportunities from a man who, like herself, believed in his destiny, his judgment, his instincts, and his capacities. She was headstrong, and wrong-headed as well. And she was lucky to extricate herself with as little damage as she did. Not unnaturally, what damage there was had to be blamed elsewhere, and it fell to the Foreign Office to have to pick up the pieces.

There is an essential human truth: we hate those we have wronged. Probably more than any other British Government department, Margaret Thatcher has wronged the Foreign Office, blaming it for her own errors. And this was undoubtedly the case with Ireland between 1979 and the summer of 1981.

She reverted during the second hunger strike, which did not end until October 3 1981, to her true political colouring, which was essentially that of a Unionist, additionally motivated by strong strategic feelings about Northern Ireland. (Indeed these had provoked, in the first instance, in May 1980, the emphasis by Haughey on defence and NATO as issues to be reconsidered by the Irish Republic). The love-affair with the Republic, with the idea of a 'solution', with Charles Haughey's inscrutable approach, was over. His own leadership of the Irish Government was temporarily over as well. More normal, more restrained, more anaemic circumstances prevailed with Dr Garret Fitz-Gerald, concentrating on joint studies, and on security co-operation.

When Haughey returned to power in March 1982, at the head of a minority Fianna Fail Government, relations remained frosty and distant. The Republic rejected the proposed new Assembly, rejected Falklands co-operation, went back on the undertakings given under the umbrella of 'the unique relationship', and conveniently forgot 'the totality of relationships within these islands' which were to have been the subject of special consideration. And by the time Haughey had to fight his second general election, in November, it was dominated by allegations of British spying, interference in Irish affairs, and coercion of Garret FitzGerald. Haughey had come full circle, back to the kind of republicanism which had led to his dismissal by Lynch twelve years before. Margaret Thatcher could thank her lucky stars, which had always been sparing in the light they shed on her, for preserving her from greater damage. But Haughey survived all attempts by his own party to remove him, retaining in the political equation a handicap on any basic change by her on Northern Ireland policy.

CHAPTER TWENTY

Falklands

The British Foreign Secretary contributed to the debate on the Queen's Speech, in the House of Lords on May 22 1979, with a general statement of British Defence and Foreign policy. Lord Carrington claimed as the Government's 'prime purpose' the avoidance of war, and said that, in pursuit of this three objectives were necessary: the maintenance of effective armed forces, a network of alliances with friends, and a better understanding with enemies. He also said that a key element was continuity, 'a source of real strength and stability' which reassured friends and discouraged enemies. It was a sound and well-judged expression of policy and political experience, exactly what one would expect from the combination of Peter Carrington's own wisdom and the resources of the Foreign Office.

Yet, during the course of the four-year period of Government on which the administration led by Margaret Thatcher was then embarking, Britain deliberately set in motion military action leading to war which was costly in lives lost, and horrendously expensive in a variety of different ways. In the course of this, arguably in order to facilitate it, Britain also broke that continuity which Lord Carrington saw as a 'source of real strength'. In doing this, the 'network of alliances' was destabilised in the eyes of many of Britain's so-called friends, and the 'better understanding' with enemies, also dependent on this fundamental continuity of foreign policy, was prejudiced and permanently weakened. The basic principles were thrown overboard, and Carrington with them. And the loss to Britain has been substantial.

The character and extent of the damage was heavily obscured by a number of factors. The first and most obvious was exemplified in that first 'Rejoice', 'Just rejoice!', with which Margaret Thatcher greeted the initial and minor British military and naval success, the retaking of South Georgia on April 25. In other words, Britain contemplated and then embarked on a just war which subsequently turned out to be victorious as well. Whether it was necessary is another question.

The second factor which obscured the issues related to the Opposition. The Labour Party and the Liberal-SDP Alliance either failed to grasp the essential arguments, or turned instead to what they considered was politically opportune. They fumbled between principle and expediency in those critical twenty-four hours between knowledge of the invasion of the Falkland Islands by the Argentine military junta and the House of Commons debate on April 3; and they got it wrong. They were further handicapped by internal divisions and uncertainties, not just between parties, but within them. And they were inadequately briefed. In anticipation of an approaching election, both they and the Conservative Party had a very wary eye on the press; and the press, with honourable exceptions, responded in an emotional and prejudiced way, admittedly to an issue which, above all others, invites such response: naked aggression against British people, property, and territory.

Considerable attention has been given earlier in this book to one of the turning points in the evolution of the Falklands War. It is not proposed to go back over that ground again, but to turn to another and even more important point of decision where the changes noted above, as well as the failures, were concentrated into a brief and vital period of hours. And those hours represent a most convincing demonstration of Margaret Thatcher's capacities as a politician who understands power, wants power, can acquire and augment power, and enjoys using power.

In order to conduct such an examination objectively it is necessary to separate, as far as possible, the political motives from the diplomatic negotiations and military confrontations which culminated in a war, which if proved necessary, was certainly legitimate and just, as well as being successful. Such separation is difficult at any time, and extremely difficult in the circumstances which prevailed between April 2 1982, and the end of the war on June 14, when the Argentine Commande surrendered at Port Stanley. But it is not impossible.

In her speech to the House of Commons on Saturday April 3

1982, at the beginning of the emergency debate following the previous day's invasion, Margaret Thatcher was defending a Government decision that had already been made, 'that a large task force will sail as soon as all preparations are complete. *HMS Invincible* will be in the lead, and will leave port on Monday.' The situation, and therefore the debate, had already been pre-empted, locking military and political decisions together, narrowing the diplomatic objectives, and turning the occasion into a House of Commons endorsement.

Margaret Thatcher was at pains to establish, and narrow still further, the perceptions of Parliament, of the press, and of the public. She said, in the course of her speech, that the unprovoked aggression of the Argentine Government 'has not a shred of justification and not a scrap of legality'. She said: 'We have absolutely no doubt about our sovereignty, which has been continuous since 1833. Nor have we any doubt about the unequivocal wishes of the Falkland Islanders, who are British in stock and tradition, and wish to remain British in allegiance.' And in reference to the previous fifteen years of negotiation, or attempted negotiation with Argentina, she said: 'We have always made it clear that their wishes were paramount and that there would be no change in sovereignty without their consent and without the approval of the House.' And, in reference to the 'invasion' of South Georgia on March 19, she said: 'The incident appeared at the start to be relatively minor. But we now know it was the beginning of much more.'

Outside the confines of the House of Commons she was more emphatic. As Tam Dalyell points out in *Thatcher's Torpedo*, in answer to George Gale's question, 'Did the Falklands crisis come at you more or less out of the blue?' Margaret Thatcher, presumably looking him straight in the eye, replied, 'Out of the blue.' All the evidence, on the record, suggests the opposite. It also suggests substantial grey areas where Argentine justification and legality are concerned. It suggests doubts on the British side about standing over sovereignty. Though it supports the argument in favour of respecting the wishes of the Falklanders, it avoids mention of the consistent endeavours to alter that view. And it is a very questionable claim that the wishes of the islanders 'were paramount'; consistent efforts to change these wishes, and the sustaining of negotiations which could only have a positive outcome by a combination of a deal on sovereignty and the persuasion of both islanders and House of Commons to accept this, had been going on for many years as part of that 'element of continuity in Britain's foreign policy' upon which Lord Carrington set such a premium.

The continuity, as well as argument about it, and discussion of its relevance to the key decision announced by Margaret Thatcher on April 3, were prejudiced by the resignation of Lord Carrington as Foreign and Commonwealth Secretary on April 5, and his replacement by Francis Pym. Margaret Thatcher's timing of changes of this kind is impeccably economic in its appropriateness; at no stage in her leadership was this more clearly the case than with Carrington's 'unalterable decision' to resign, which she accepted 'with the greatest reluctance'. Clearly, somebody had to go; but Carrington? The question is put thus, because the second issue to be considered is the Franks Committee which, much later, was established with terms of reference which precluded consideration of the key questions of Margaret Thatcher's own thoughts and decisions in the hours following the actual invasion, and affecting the lives, not just of so many servicemen, British and Argentinian, but of politicians and populations within a far wider compass, whose security and confidence continued to be affected.

The committee, under the chairmanship of Lord Franks, was precluded by its terms of reference from going beyond April 2, and from considering anything other than 'the way in which the responsibilities of Government in relation to the Falkland Islands and their Dependencies were discharged in the period leading up to the Argentine invasion. . . . ' It is therefore not surprising, in the circumstances, that one of the shortest paragraphs in the whole report is number 258: 'At 7.30 p.m. the Cabinet met and agreed that the task force should sail.' Strictly speaking, this was outside the committee's terms of reference, as was the next and final paragraph of the report's penultimate chapter: 'On Saturday 3 April, the Prime Minister announced in the House of Commons that Argentina's armed forces had attacked the Falklands Islands the previous day and established military control of the Islands.'

The Franks Committee then posed two questions, which it raised out of many to the status of 'crucial'. The first: 'could the Government have foreseen the invasion of *2 April*' (my italics). The second: 'could the Government have prevented *that invasion'* (my italics). And, not unnaturally, the answer the committee came up with was an emphatic no. An equally emphatic yes would have been the answer had the question allowed for a wider period of expectation than the single day on which Argentine forces landed. And, of course, an equally emphatic yes would have been inescapable for the second question.

As the Franks Committee's report points out, in Chapter 2, dealing with the period of Conservative Government 1979-82 (March 19), in many paragraphs, the possibility of 'violent' or 'military' action, of 'harassment', of 'threats', and of 'invasion' is frequently mentioned*. These paragraphs are stepping stones through a relatively straightforward argument; at first wet and slippery, because they only just emerge above the moving waters of diplomatic argument and negotiation, they become progressively larger and drier, and more reliable. The argument is a relatively simple one: the British Government led by Margaret Thatcher had four options. The first was to abandon the islands and resettle the islanders; the second was to defend them as they were, the policy known as 'Fortress Falklands'; the third was to keep up negotiations which had been going on since January 1966, following UN resolution 2065 of December 16 1965, in the hope that something would turn up *acceptable to the islanders* and to their lobby at Westminster, which was mainly Conservative; the fourth was to move towards, and if necessary impose, the only compromise solution which had a serious prospect of satisfying the practical desires of the islanders with the emotional wishes of the Argentians, and this was to concede sovereignty while leasing back the islands for a long or indefinite period.

The first option was probably not possible in parliamentary terms, and psychologically not possible for Margaret Thatcher, whose political instincts in addition would have been against such a course. The second course of action, which now we have, was regarded as militarily impossible, and, in addition, *not necessary*. The third course, which was the one pursued, eventually failed for a number of reasons, perhaps the most important being that it was simply *not serious*. It had no ultimate objective. Yet, repeatedly through the Franks Committee analysis, it is the

*See paragraphs 73, 75, 77, 86, 87, 88, 91, 94, 95, 96, 100, 104, 110, 111, 112, 115, 122, 125, 129, 130, 131, 138, 139, 140, 145, 148, 149, 150, 155, 157.

chosen course. Not, however, by Lord Carrington, who as early as October 12 1979, following Nicholas Ridley's visit to the islands, expressed the view in a memorandum to Margaret Thatcher and the Cabinet Defence Committee 'that the "Fortress Falklands" option and the option of continuing talks but without making any concessions on sovereignty *both carried a serious threat of invasion.*' (Franks, paragraph 75, page 21; this was the fifth of the ninety paragraphs covering 'the period of the present Government.)

By the beginning of October 1981 it was absolutely clear that concessions by the Falkland islanders on the key question of sovereignty were out of the question. Reporting this, the British Ambassador in Buenos Aires protested at the Foreign Secretary's decision not to pursue a policy of changing island opinion by public education or persuasion, in favour of the only realistic option which did not carry the risk of invasion, and described the decision as one which was 'to have no strategy at all beyond a general Micawberism.'

If words mean anything at all, 'a serious threat of invasion' became a confirmed reality following the elections to the Falkland Islands Legislative Council on October 14 1981, which reflected a hardening of attitude on sovereignty: the Island 'Unionists' would talk 'provided that sovereignty was not on the agenda'. From then on, any moves by the British Government which did not take seriously the risk of invasion were tantamount to being an invitation to Argentina, when it was politically suitable, to take the actions it did take. The withdrawal of *HMS Endurance*, decided after the 1981 Defence Review, and confirmed in Parliament on June 30, was a clear enough signal of this general set of conclusions to which the government seems to have been forced, against the judgments of the Foreign Office, and the Ministry of Defence. Margaret Thatcher herself said that the decision to withdraw HMS *Endurance* 'had been very difficult' (February 9, 1982).

From October 1981, when it could be said that 'a serious threat of invasion' was an inevitable consequence of the abandoning of the realistic option of a transfer of sovereignty in exchange for leaseback, until the beginning of March 1982, the need became increasingly clear for military defence to be increased. This was recognised by the British Ambassador in Buenos Aires, had long been recognised by the Foreign Secretary, who had put it many times before the Defence Committee, and should have been clear to the Prime Minister. It certainly became clear to her after the joint British-Argentine communiqué of March 1, 1982, following the New York talks, and then the unilateral Argentine communiqué issued in Buenos Aires on the same day. The ambassador's telegram, which, curiously, is not included in the Franks Report, and is summarised very inadequately, was seen by Margaret Thatcher on March 3, and she wrote on it 'we must make contingency plans'. At that stage it would have been possible to re-deploy naval vessels which were then in the West Indies, the Gulf of Mexico, and off the United States' eastern seaboard. Yet Margaret Thatcher's private secretary did not write to the Foreign Office or the Ministry of Defence until March 8, and the Ministry for Defence did not reply until March 12, pointing out that 20 days' passage was needed (from Britain, of course, not from other sea stations). *Even then,* no defensive action was initiated, beyond a Foreign Office recommendation that Lord Carrington 'should seek Mr Nott's agreement, on a contingency basis, to maintain HMS *Endurance* on station in the area for the time being'.

The Franks Committee indulged in semantics. It was not asked to frame questions, certainly not the 'crucial' questions it did frame, and to which the answers were largely governed by their specific wording. Its conclusions are carefully related to that wording, and naturally exonerate the Government.

The Government was exonerated anyway. A just war had become a successful war, leading to victory. It was impossible, after the decision by the Government at 7.30 p.m. on April 2, the day before the first emergency debate in the Commons, to go back, behind the initiation of war. The key question then, and later, was *necessity*. From the sending of the task force on April 2, to the sinking of the *Belgrano* on May 2, necessity was the overriding political burden, requiring the fullest justification and argument.

Such argument was pre-empted from the start. On the morning of the invasion, at 9.45 London time, before Argentine troops had landed, the Defence Secretary, John Nott, was able to tell the Government 'that a large amphibious task force had been put on immediate alert', and the Cabinet *'agreed* that a *decision* to instruct the task force to sail should be considered later'. In the words of the Franks Committee, 'the Cabinet met and agreed'; in

Margaret Thatcher's words, in the debate on April 3, the Government 'decided'.

The cycle of events undermined more and more deeply the political objectivity with which judgments could be examined and challenged. The carrier group which sailed from Portsmouth on April 5, the departure of three Commando Brigades on board the Canberra on April 9, the introduction of the maritime exclusion zone around the Falkland Islands on April 12, the rendezvous of naval commanders in mid-Atlantic, and finally the successful first operation, between April 21-25, leading to the recapture of South Georgia, all made increasingly inevitable, politically, the decision to sink the *Belgrano* which precipitated the real, or killing, war.

Power politics was played out in the Atlantic, and in the tense and instinctive judgments being made by two tiny groups of people, in Buenos Aires and London. And the shuttle diplomacy carried on by Alexander Haig, in the relentless glare of world publicity, was analogous to the dramatic role played by Chorus in Henry V, a commentary, and a setting of the scene. The mood engendered from April 2 1982 was to make *unthinkable* anything other than victory; to condition, in other words, the British public to the desirability of not compromising; to lay the firm foundation, only of course if it should be necessary, for a naval and military invasion in which the risks would be inescapably enormous. 'Now all the youth of England are on fire . . . . and honour's thought Reigns solely in the breast of every man . . . . For now sits Expectation in the air . . . (the Argentines) advis'd by good intelligence of this most dreadful preparation, Shake in their fear; and with pale policy Seek to direct the English purposes.' It may not have been *quite* all the youth of England; it may have been more difficult, with *Panorama* and *Nationwide,* with Tony Benn and Tam Dalyell, to ensure the absolute unanimity of will; but it was a good effort none-the-less. And, brutal as the reality may often be, the idea of the return of the task force without it having led to the humiliation of the Argentine junta which had shown itself only partially respectful of human life, was quite unthinkable. Two forces were therefore set in motion against each other, each of which had profound reasons for victory.

Any attempt to summarise events or motives opens up fresh arguments, and they are generally vast and inconclusive because information is incomplete. It will remain so, in Margaret Thatcher's own words, for thirty years or so. The following points can be made, however. Firstly, any consideration of the Falklands War has to deal with two critical turning points, April 2 1982 when the islands were invaded, and May 2 when the *Belgrano* was sunk. The first precipitated immediate and serious preparation for war, the second precipitated and made inevitable substantial bloodshed, maiming and loss of life in pursuit of victory.

In the run-up to the first of these watersheds it is clearly on the record that there were grave errors of judgment about warnings of invasion coming from several sources over a long period of time. Secondly, there was either a serious failure of military intelligence, or some truly appalling misreadings or misinterpretations of the knowledge of inescapably substantial preparations which went on in Argentina and at sea off the east coast of South America before April 2. Thirdly, there is clear evidence of an inadequate response by Margaret Thatcher to such intelligence as there was, combined with the weight of advice which had come consistently from the Foreign Office over a number of years; this was particularly the case in respect of the movement of Royal Navy ships following the Buenos Aires telegram of March 3. Fourthly, there is the substantial conflict between Margaret Thatcher's private reactions, and those of several of her ministers, and the public stance she adopted. It is as if she disembarrassed herself, on April 2, of the past, and disembarrassed herself also of its principal and persistent harbinger, Lord Carrington, who is repeatedly on record with a sequence of memoranda which clearly established the options which would have produced a peaceful solution, and those which produced war. Margaret Thatcher subsequently reinforced this process of disembarrassment by deciding on the terminal *event* of the *invasion* of the Falklands Islands, on April 2, for the Franks Committee's investigations, thus precluding any consideration of the substantial change of heart, of mind, and of interpretation of events, which took place during the course of that day, and particularly between 9.45 on that morning and 7.30 p.m., when the Cabinet *agreed*, in effect, to war.

The equation with which she was faced was an ideal one for the circumstances which surrounded her. She had before her, at all times from the autumn of 1979, a chronology of events pointing towards limited options, some of which offered peace, others of which invited either conflict or invasion. In the absence of deliberate choice, either to resolve the Falklands crisis peacefully, by a transfer of sovereignty or a deal on sovereignty, or to defend it even adequately, by the movement of ships or men, she *invited* invasion. Furthermore, she had, as potential invader, an unstable, oligarchic regime whose political ends could be expected to be served, at one time or another, by just such an invasion as took place.

The exact timing, on which the Franks Committee placed so much emphasis, was unimportant, except as a device, whether deliberate or not is one of many matters for conjecture, by which exoneration could be assured. What was important was the ever-present likelihood of invasion, warnings about which were on the record throughout the period of the Government, and which Margaret Thatcher, even as the likelihood grew, chose to ignore. There is little doubt that the events between 1979 and early 1982 reveal consistent Cabinet failure to treat seriously enough what was happening in the South Atlantic. And an additional error was made in the moving of Nicholas Ridley from the Foreign Office to the Treasury at a time (that of Galtieri becoming President) when his detailed experience would have been better used by keeping him in charge of the Falklands. To the equation must also be added the presence of one of the finest and best-equipped fighting machines in the world, sadly in need of exercise and moral revitalising, but ready with equipment and men to be deployed at will. The imbalance between this force, and any like Argentine opposition, even with the handicap of great distance, was massive anyway, and further augmented by civilian and domestic differences between the two countries. A free democracy, grappling to some purpose with inflation and other economic problems, is more likely to respond in a balanced and united way, tempering emotion with realism and confidence based on ancient traditions of military and naval success, than a badly led oligarchy in which the economy, civil liberties and the constitutional rule of law all seemed to have run substantially out of alignment.

Ultimately, the personal judgments and decisions can never be known. Here was an embattled leader, at bay on her economic policies, with unprecedented high unemployment, and low popularity, with no short-term prospect of an upturn, with a hostile caucus at the top of the Conservative Party, ready to deny her the continued leadership should she fail electorally, and the prospect of such failure staring her in the face. It would have been no less than the wisdom of Juvenal, when either bread or circuses ran out, to prescribe war. The burden of evidence suggests that that is what she did.

CHAPTER TWENTY-ONE

'A Nation of Shopkeepers'

Britain, which seemed to have lost its way by the Spring of 1979 – or so it was alleged in the Conservative Party manifesto for the April election campaign – had in reality been reduced to a temporary and very short-term state of demoralisation by 'the winter of discontent', a by-product of the poor judgment of James Callaghan, and the essential Achilles' heel of that Labour administration, which was a belief in an incomes policy as the main weapon with which to fight inflation. Callaghan's misjudgment of this cost him the election and his party power. He had surrendered hostages to fortune, apparently in the belief that his own term in office was secured anyway, that he could go or stay at will, and that Margaret Thatcher, in the end, was not of sufficient mettle to win the hearts and minds of a majority of the British people.

Beneath the state of demoralisation the essential economic situation was stable; indeed, to a degree, Denis Healey had already taken a number of corrective measures which were working. By subsequent standards, the level of unemployment was tolerable, at 5.6 percent in 1978 (or 1.4m.); even the rate of inflation was firmly back in single figures for each of the quarters of the year, having been cut by half in comparison with 1977. Indeed, to an extent that reflects closely the politics of U-turns and the post-electoral honouring of pledges, the inflation rate over the past decade is a curiously accurate thermometer.*

More generally, less politically, the economic situation was responding well to growing realism. Though outstripped by imports, exports were growing at a rate of 3.5 percent with a strong emphasis on exports within the EEC. Britain's balance of payments was in better shape in 1978 than at any time since 1971.

'A Nation of Shopkeepers' 221

Even the mood which prevailed within British agriculture was optimistic, based on the phenomenon of a small but essentially efficient industry benefitting from EEC membership, and continuing to dominate the essential food requirements of the country. Sections of nationalised industry were performing profitably, with overseas earnings up fourfold in the six years to 1978.

The prospects from North Sea oil were improving in absolute terms: a steeper rise in income, from a lower base, was estimated in October 1978, than had been thought likely previously. The actual figures then presented suggested that income would rise from £1.7 billion in 1977 to £2.2 billion (1978), £3.5 billion (1979), £4.4 billion (1980) and a projected £6.6 billion in 1985.

Least one runs the risk of presenting a picture of apparently golden prospects, let it be said that a very real area of failure existed in the management of people, notably organised labour through the trade union movement, and of the unorganised and potentially vociferous unemployed through the mechanism of a permanently expanding social welfare system in which both numbers and amounts paid out continued to rise. So too did costs of health and of other benefits.

Essentially, however, the chosen option of the Labour Party, which was to curb inflation by an incomes policy, was coming unstuck. Following the 1975 incomes peak of 29.5 percent, the three-year incomes policy (1976-78) had brought down the rate, and should have led to a further pay agreement. It was the failure of this to come about which not only led to the 'winter of discontent', but suddenly made the alternative Conservative option of controlling the growth of money and credit seem fresh and attractive, with the apparently very wholesome prospect of cutting Government borrowing and spending. It was not to work out; at least, not as planned. But then that is normal in politics. What mattered was how it looked.

---

* Annual figures: 1973, 9.2 percent (oil crisis, and initial impact of Edward Heath's change of policy); 1974, 16.1 percent (fuller impact of changed policy, and then of Labour's return to power); 1975, 24.2 percent (record level for decade, Labour's answer to getting the economy 'moving'); 1976, 16.5 percent (the austerity measures imposed by the IMF after the fall in sterling); 1977, 15.8 percent (the price, also, in this and previous year, of keeping unemployment at 5.2 percent and 5.7 percent respectively); 1978, 8.3 percent (Healey's major contribution, prodigally wasted in the decision not to go to the country that autumn).

Margaret Thatcher, in keeping with her politically combative and aggressive style, and her perception that power derived from taking a stance which relied on urgency in a given direction which was clearly defined, adopted a position which favoured a set of options from which she could not easily retreat should they turn out to be wrong.

The options were given certain priorities, the first being an attack on inflation 'through the pursuit of firm monetary and fiscal policies'. The underlying principle was that of sound money; implicit in it was either state control or self-control in the realm of wage and salary increases. The principle of competition would then take care of price inflation. As Geoffrey Howe said in his first Budget speech, June 12 1979, the basic problem causing Britain's poor economic performance was not shortage of demand, but failure of supply. It was not the absence of a market, either domestically or internationally, but an inability to lead competitively within the market which had persistently undermined Britain's performance. If this could be got right then the state's response would be to encourage the incentive, initiative and hard work by reducing taxation. This, in turn, would be made possible by cutting public expenditure and passing over to the private sector greater responsibility for large areas of commerce and production which had drifted in under the expanding umbrella of state control during the previous thirty-odd years. Prosperity through efficiency would become the key to survival.

*

Great stress was laid on this set of central objectives throughout 1979 and the early part of 1980, with Margaret Thatcher herself defending strongly the Government's policies in the pre-Budget economic debate of February 28 1980, on a Labour Party no-confidence motion, and with James Callaghan, who was still Labour leader, suggesting that the policies which were being pursued were 'recklessly widening the divisions in our society'. Who was believed? At that stage, Margaret Thatcher's claim that the Government was 'facing Britain's long-standing and deep-rooted problems with firmness and realism', had the greater credibility. 'Attitudes are changing,' she claimed, 'and the mood of realism is spreading fast.'

Her Chancellor was more cautious; though the inevitability of the policies was inescapable, time was needed both for their effectiveness and for public acceptability. And in his Budget speech of March 26 1980, he introduced for the first time a medium-term financial strategy dealing with monetary policy and the rate of growth in money supply for a four-year period. In the realm of overall fiscal and monetary strategy the perspective was an inescapably lengthening one: the Government needed more time, the miracle of recovery was becoming stretched beyond the natural life of the parliament, the addiction to deficit spending in the seventies had become a habit not easily shaken off, and the realisation that the abnormal but accepted policy of the country spending its way out of inflation simply could not go on, would still take time to filter through the system. Politically, consent had to be worked for. As an expression of the balance of judgments implicit in this, Geoffrey Howe's Budget speech of 1980 is a model, just as his early performance as Chancellor represents his best, because most independent, period in that responsibility.

One may argue with the fundamentals of Conservative policy for the economy, and blame the strategy for the unforeseen and dreadful consequences in unemployment which were to follow, but as an expression in practical terms of what the electorate had chosen the previous year, the 1980 Budget was basically right.

However, the underlying money supply theories were coming unstuck in a major departure from the plans and targets. Reality was proving a painful, if not easily grasped, handicap to the fundamentals on which the options had been constructed. Iran, Afghanistan, Poland, all seriously shook the basic sense of security, undermined confidence over oil, and contributed to fairly substantial adjustments in the key element of Margaret Thatcher's economic policy. The gap between the money stock target at the beginning of her term and the actual figures widened. Even with the reclassification which makes direct comparison difficult, the money stock which showed a 12.7 percent increase in 1979, and was targeted in 1980 to be in the 6-10 percent bracket for 1981-82, in fact went up to 24 percent in 1981. And in that year unemployment, at 10.6 percent, was almost double the 5.6 percent figure which had been Denis Healey's 1979 legacy.

*

Side by side with the presentation of Howe's 1980 budget there was published the Government Whie Paper on public expenditure plans for the same period as that of the medium-term monetary and fiscal policy up to 1984. It showed a fairly drastic revision of what the Labour Government had previously intended, the reduction being a progressive one over the four-year period, to a volume level in 1983-84 4 percent lower than in 1979-80. By comparison with Labour, the Conservatives were planning to cut some £10,000 million a year in public expenditure by the latter end of their four-year planning period. Moreover, since expenditure was to *increase* on defence, law and order, health and social security, the real damage in those areas which were to bear the brunt of the cuts – education, housing, industry, trade and employment – was to be commensurately greater. The earliest casualty was housing, the programme for which was cut by £300m within six months of the Conservatives coming to power.

This lack of balance between what were, in effect, interest groups, prejudiced the necessary 'grip' on the economy in the first year to eighteen months of Conservative rule. It was not until the late autumn of 1980, backed up by the depressing fact of unemployment having passed the two million mark, that the problem of public sector pay was seriously addressed. Too many unnecessary concessions made to Conservative interest groups, such as the armed forces and the police, had pushed up public sector pay by levels approaching 20 percent in 1980, with a generally demoralising effect on all other restraints. And it was to counter this that Margaret Thatcher belatedly fixed a six percent ceiling for public service employees. They had, she claimed in a speech at the Lord Mayor's Banquet on November 10, received substantially more in the previous eighteen months than private sector employees, and it was now time to impose restraint. Not all, however, had received the level of increase given to the armed forces and the police, and the gap between the favoured and the disfavoured was manifesting itself in confrontation with weaker groups such as nurses and local authority workers.

Nevertheless, with the background of high unemployment and the determination bred out of the 1978-79 'winter of discontent', the restraint imposed on local authority employees eventually worked. The job of government, 'to decide how much those outside the public service can afford to pay for those in the public service', was being pursued on the basis of the cash limit being the main determinant of pay settlements for the Civil Service. At least, this was the theory. And when in practice it was applied to a category over which some muscle could be exercised with relative immunity from serious challenge, then the practice followed in the steps of the theory. This happened with local authority employees who took grave exception to the six percent ceiling, but then, after a long strike, accepted a settlement only marginally above what they had rejected.

*

The divergence between theory and practice, however, the widening gap between targets on a host of different economic fronts, and the actual out-turns, was causing growing alarm, not least within the Conservative Party itself. Moreover, doubt and hesitation were felt strongly by former high officers of state. And it led to a period for Margaret Thatcher of curiously poignant loneliness. Her own private winter of discontent came at the end of 1980, with the realisation that her economic policies had been reduced considerably in scope, that their prospects, within a single parliamentary term, were very limited, and that within both party and government she was faced with disaffection, loss of confidence, loss of popularity, serious and growing doubts about future electoral prospects, and a rising tide of criticism as to the justice and indeed logic of what was being attempted.

That winter was vitally important in one respect: it marked the transition from the selective prodigalities which had prejudiced the full implementation of the promised economic rectitude, to its more comprehensive spread, at least in terms of pay. That most political of equations, which relates pay and inflation with unemployment, and the Government's courage and capacity in taking on organised labour, began to work out in real successes over modest settlements and also over the record on industrial disputes. Figures for these in 1980 were the lowest in forty years, with the number of days lost, at 11.9 million, below the average for the previous ten years.*

In a highly visible way, therefore, the end of 1980 and the

---

*Three quarters of these were confined to a single strike, in the steel industry.

beginning of 1981 marked a shift. At one level at least, confrontation designed to tackle a major contributing factor to inflation was being undertaken by Margaret Thatcher with a commendable disdain for both the unpopularity involved, and the aggravated element of risk. But, as she emphasised in a speech in the House of Commons on February 5 1981, the task was fourfold, with realistic wages being only one part of the problem. The others, which included monetary control, tax incentives, and the cutting of government spending, remained substantially unresolved, particularly the last. She claimed that the rate of monetary growth in the second half of 1980, which people had judged to be too rapid, had in fact contributed to the low rate of retail price rise of 3.7 percent. And she referred back to adjustments in income tax levels made in 1979.

But the real headache facing her was Government spending, and it was here that a number of adverse factors helped to undermine the necessary progress towards real cuts. Firstly, there was her own lack of experience. There is an irony in her declared taste for the television comedy series, *Yes, Minister*, since she became a victim of its most obvious and most entertaining dramatic device, that of the multiple conspiracies about the saving and spending of public money. Encouraged by the short-term prodigality which had followed the formation of her Conservative Government, and which among other things had led to high initial levels in public sector pay settlements, a wide range of faceless and unidentifiable politicians and public servants made Margaret Thatcher the victim of a succession of what can only be described as polite, well-organised and entirely legitimate conspiracies to resist and defeat cuts. A principle to which she was an alien force, politically, that of the 'old boy' network which is central both to the permanent British administrative system and to the operation of a male-dominated party system, worked against her. It took advantage of her inexperience; it also took advantage of the traditional imbalance between Downing Street and Whitehall; and it fed upon the growing unpopularity which her policies were bringing down upon the Conservative Party.

Conspiracy, disloyalty, disaffection, were all rife. The idea of a change of leadership was gaining ground; the prospect of the Conservatives being led into the next general election by Margaret Thatcher became less and less palatable as the months of 1981 went by. And all of this was being achieved with policies which were the opposite, in certain key areas, from those which she had declared to be her own. In spite of what she was saying in her speeches, backed up by a dwindling group of Cabinet colleagues on whom she pinned more and more hope, public spending was increasing when it should have been declining, public borrowing was also going up, the money supply was more or less out of control, and there seemed always to be a persuasive, and often a convincing argument for another Government subsidy to keep an imperfect economic show on the road. The most controversial, in early 1981, was BL, for which £990m was made available to cover the 1981-83 period. A second was the finding of substantial sums in early 1981 to keep pits open in South Wales.

Was ever political leader beset by such a paradox? Unpopular for policies which she was failing, substantially, to implement; surrounded by colleagues seeking to bring her down; watching her popularity dwindle for all the wrong reasons; what was she to do? It is a measure of her mettle, that blind courage in adversity towards which her political character and her past political acts drove her, that she stuck resolutely with her options, keeping thereby the support of bedrock and backbone Conservatives. Within the party and within the country she was tested by, and in her turn tested out herself, primitive loyalties which had nothing whatsoever to do with sterling M3 or the rising tide of the public sector borrowing requirement of £13,000 or £14,000 million – six percent of the gross domestic product. No, she was going back behind, or forward beyond, reality into a realm of political myth and instinct which cried out to her to hold on.

Her political marriage partner was consistency. Her morality demanded faithfulness. Her repudiation of her predecessor's policies, and her defeat of him for leadership of the party, had been a repudiation and dismissal of weakness and capitulation on the economy. She had blocked off, several times over, the prospect of retreat down the road which the 'wets' invited her to take. And though in several respects she was skidding down it anyway, she demonstrated a coolness and a determination which were truly breathtaking. However inescapable or otherwise had been all the economic recklessness between May 1979 and November 1980, however adverse had been the further developments in the world economy with their substantial impact on domestic economic affairs, including lamentable divergences between white paper and budget planning on public sector borrowing, money supply, public spending, and government subsidies to nationalised industry, and the actual outturn, she resolved during that winter of 1980-81 to tighten the screws and abandon the 'wets'.

*

She learned a lesson in power during 1980. It was that, contrary to the perceptions which prevailed in Britain about what mattered most with the electorate – the pound in their pocket – there is a superior impact made by those politicians who resolve historic conflicts over the leaders who bring down the inflation rate or reduce public spending. It was a lesson which came at a peculiarly appropriate time.

It was reinforced from various quarters. On the international stage during 1979-80, a number of events already mentioned had stirred her leadership ambitions, just as the resolving of the Rhodesia crisis – almost entirely the work of others – had greatly increased her confidence. The American hostages crisis, President Carter's mishandling of the Entebbe-style 'raid', and the subsequent resolution of the matter, had in turn been swept aside by Ronald Reagan's victory, and the arrival in the White House of a leader closer to her own nature, and one likely to endorse, in general terms, the process of learning through which she was going. As in other things, the world has its 'club' of leaders, and they are, in their inescapable isolation, not averse to giving and receiving advice, spreading a message the main focus of which is the retention of power.

*

At the end of July 1981, before the adjournment of Parliament, she spoke in defence of her economic policies, and claimed their success. The only real concession was towards youth unemployment, on which schemes related to the new technology were ostensibly working, providing Britain with a trained manpower reserve in areas where she believed the new jobs would originate. But at the time of the debate unemployment had reached 2.5 million, and all she could say about that was that the *rate of increase* was declining!

In economic terms she took a monumental gamble in 1981, and it failed. She disposed of all the 'wets', and allied herself with a team of her own, all of them committed to the policies which had been maintained in theory since the Conservatives had come to power. But the policies were not there in practice. If things were to come right, it would be by accident rather than design, since the Government was spending more in the public sector, borrowing more, failing massively to keep money supply under the stringent controls which had been promised, and continuing to underwrite the losses of failures in nationalised industries.

If the economic gamble, measured by the usual indicators, failed, so too did the political gamble as measured by the more obvious indicator of public opinion. Doing the wrong things, for the wrong reasons, against the weight of experience and supposed authority within the Conservative Party, Margaret Thatcher played a solitary power game in the autumn of 1981 which nevertheless transformed British politics. It did so less at the time than later. At the time it seemed only that she was on a suicide mission for herself and her party, only marginally countered by the policy modifications which formed part of Geoffrey Howe's economic promises on December 2 1981, to increase spending on employment and to raise national insurance contributions, followed by the Budget provisions. On top of every other economic misdemeanour, the best that could be reported, on the Government's behalf, in the main area of countering inflation, for which all the multiple sacrifices had been made, all the jobs lost, all the punishment sustained, was a rise and fall which did not, at the end of 1981, represent any improvement on the situation over which Denis Healey had presided three years earlier. In mid-1980 the annual inflation rate was 22 percent. By the end of 1980 it had been wrestled down to 15 percent. By the end of 1981 it stood at 12 percent. Geoffrey Howe referred to a Government expectation of bringing it down to 10 percent during 1982. Yet this, precisely, was what it had been when Margaret Thatcher came to power in 1979. 'The outlook, in short, is for gradual recovery,' Howe told the Commons, but, in contrast with previous statements, changed conditions now encouraged increased rather than decreased expenditure.

*

The Budget which followed on March 9 1982 was a 'recovery' Budget, designed 'for industry, for jobs, for people'. £2,5000 million was earmarked for employment schemes. A further £3,000m was allocated to the social services, which were to be raised to compensate for the continuing inflation, a move that went substantially beyond Government undertakings. There were more unemployed, even than predicted; more of them were claiming unemployment benefit; and inadequate budgetary provisions had been made for these eventualities.

In terms of power, however, the Budget became largely academic in April 1982 with the invasion of the Falkland Islands. 'The resolving of historic conflict', which had been Charles Haughey's prescription in preference to bringing down inflation,* became the dominant, indeed overriding political obligation for the British Prime Minister from then on, and the tinkerings with M3, with the public sector borrowing requirement which was by then coming down as a percentage of GDP, and with inflation, were marginal factors in the market place of power from then on.

The Versailles economic summit in June pledged itself to growth, employment, and the continued fight against inflation. By the autumn, inflation was down to seven percent, and falling; the recorded average for 1982 pay settlements was 7 percent also, and predicted to fall further in 1983; and even public expenditure, for the first time since 1977, was not in need of upward revision on the March Budget forecast, in spite of an additional defence bill from the Falklands of £620 million. The lack of world buoyancy could be more fairly blamed for the continued rise in unemployment than at any stage since the Conservatives had taken over, and Geoffrey Howe made it one of a series of points, designed to dispel pessimism, in his autumn speech to bankers at the Guildhall, and in his subsequent statement to the House of Commons on November 8 1982.

A week later, a confident Prime Minister spoke, at the Lord Mayor's Banquet, of Britain's 'healthy new realism', by which she meant that shift in responsibility from Government to people which had been the central purpose of policy all along. 'Material progress depends on the genius, flair and application of our people in industry, trade and commerce. How products

---

* Offered to Margaret Thatcher when they first met in May, 1980.

are designed and how their production is organised is a matter for management. It cannot be done by governments. The task of government is to provide the right framework in which industry and commerce can operate. Then, and only then, will enterprise be able to flourish.'

CHAPTER TWENTY-TWO

Cadenza

Margaret Thatcher went to the Falkland Islands on a surprise visit in early January 1983. She delighted the islanders, who gave her a spontaneous and warm welcome. She dismayed her adversaries, both at home and abroad, by the politically astute and diplomatically aggressive nature of the decision to see for herself, for the first time, the cockpit in which her triumphant war had been fought. It was nevertheless a modest piece of triumphalism, abrupt, unsubtle, an exercise in populism at its brass-band, British best. Its purpose? A summation of achievement and of victory, a demonstration of what was real in the most simple terms: the islands were British once again. The visit followed immediately after the Cabinet reshuffle of Thursday January 6 1983, in which Michael Heseltine was moved to Defence in place of John Nott, and which also saw the arrival in the Cabinet of Tom King. It was the fourth and last of the series of Cabinet reshuffles which had taken place since May 1979, and it followed the others in being as economical as possible. The basic team remained undisturbed. The Falklands visit preceded, by just one week, the publication of the Franks Report, clearing Margaret Thatcher of blame. The visit was an emotional one. She 'blinked back tears', according to Press Association reporter Chris Moncrieff, as she became the first person to receive the freedom of the Falklands. She laid a wreath at the war cemetery with her own message: 'They died in battle that others might live in freedom', and described herself as both 'deeply grateful' and 'deeply stirred' by the occasion. She spoke to Goose Green residents of 'our history and your history' being intertwined. She signed for a pair of army earmuffs in order to deaden the sound of a Royal Artillery 105mm gun which she fired, and was told by the quartermaster concerned she would have to pay for them if she lost them. And, if this piece of predictable humour fell a bit heavily, her husband Denis, a former gunner, was at her elbow to add his usual laconic brand of aside; when the gun failed to respond he pointed out that it was on 'safe', adding, 'Nothing much changes.'

Politically, the purpose of the visit was a form of 'signing off'. With the Franks Report coming up, safely packaging the whole venture away, the primary need was to get the Falklands War into exactly the right perspective for an election. Contrary to the generous advice coming to her, among others from Enoch Powell, that she should 'major' in it in electoral terms, she was shrewd enough herself to see that, although it represented an enormous plus, it could easily be mishandled and overstressed. A more balanced perspective was needed on her performance, covering a wider range of achievements. At the same time, the impetus of 'the Falklands spirit' was not to be lost. Timing was of the essence. It was also, peculiarly, a matter for her. If committees are at best unwieldy mechanisms for decision-making, they are particularly so in crucial moments of judgment; and, in politics, no such moment is more critical for the leader in power in a democratic state than the decision about when to dissolve.

This was the main decision now facing Margaret Thatcher. In the political arena it was really the only one. No new initiatives, and no major changes of direction were possible. They would undermine credibility as this parliament moved towards the end of its fourth year. Even the Budget, the single most important event outstanding, needed to be handled with caution and restraint if it was not to upset that delicate apple cart, constructed like a pyramid of delectable, rosy fruits, during the miraculous year which now divided the Prime Minister from the unhappy memory of being the least popular occupant of the office in recorded memory.

She was the orchestrator of her own cadenza, which the Oxford English Dictionary defines, not inappropriately, as 'a flourish given to a solo voice at the close of a movement; a brilliant solo passage towards the end of the first or last movement of a concerto, in which the main themes are further developed'. To state firmly the theme motif of the Falklands at the outset was politically, as it would have been musically, correct; to overplay it would have been disastrous. More important was to bring in the other key issues, in as vigorous and original way as possible.

Luck plays a part in politics, and Margaret Thatcher had laboriously 'made her own luck', notably over the Falklands, but now in other respects as well. Hard slogging on the economy, over Europe, in industrial relations and combativeness towards the more militant factions of the trade union movement, brought some justified rewards.

A major 'gift' was there in the person of Arthur Scargill, President of the National Union of Mineworkers and Britain's most outspoken trade union militant. The Government's record with mineworkers was not good. Two years previously, in 1981, in a confrontation over pit closures in South Wales, the Government made one of the most ignominious retreats of its period in office when it reversed decisions about closing unprofitable pits – decisions which were central to its economic policy on subsidising loss-making nationalised industry, and cutting out the irretrievable and permanent drain which such subsidy represented in the area of public spending – and made available large subsidies to reprieve the jobs of mineworkers in South Wales. More ominously, it was remembered all too vividly by the Conservative Party that it had been the mineworkers, back in 1974, who had played a critical role in bringing down Edward Heath's Government.

What Britain witnessed in early March of 1983 was a different story, however, for several reasons. Firstly, the 'flying picket', which had previously been an effective weapon in the management of union stoppages and the movement of coal at the pitgate, was now illegal. Secondly, there were abundant supplies of coal, there was cheaper oil, and it was the end of the winter. Most important of all, the leadership of the mineworkers, with Arthur Scargill himself colourfully prominent, seemed increasingly to be engaged in efforts to raise workforce indignation at a process of rationalisation the reversal of which represented a form of blackmail against the public as a whole. Public funds endlessly draining down the mineshafts of pits which could not be made profitable, in order to keep well-paid miners in employment at a time of high unemployment and widespread economic hardship, represented a form of lunacy to the majority.

At the beginning of March an all-out national strike seemed likely. In calling for it, Scargill asked 'every miner to demonstrate solidarity with his union'. And he invited the suggestion that such a strike might well escalate within the trade union movement, and force a general election. Initially, it was to be strike without ballot. But, at rank-and-file insistence, a ballot was held. Scargill hoped for an 'overwhelming vote of confidence' from more than 200,000 mineworkers. The miners voted against a strike by a substantial majority; the Government had won a moral and psychological victory without even having to fight. 'The ballot is good news for the coal industry,' Margaret Thatcher told the Commons, pointing out that her Government had invested more than £3,000 million in the mines, 'twice as much as in the lifetime of the last Government'.

It was an encouraging start to a critical month. More directly amenable to her own control was the Budget of Tuesday March 15. And it needed to be, since in terms of her political judgment it was of crucial importance. Leaving aside the popularity bonus of the Falklands was a difficult but necessary part of the strategy, since only by doing that, and still assuring herself that what she was doing was right, could the budgetary process be carried to a proper political conclusion. And central to that conclusion, in the spring of 1983, were not now so much the lessons learned in the early seventies as a member of the Heath administration which had faltered and turned in the face of economic adversity, but the lessons learnt more recently across the House, from Denis Healey. They were the most obvious of political lessons; that the giveaway, pre-election budget, on the generous pegs of which a campaign could be hung, belonged firmly to the past. The approach had failed with Denis Healey, though not without additional fumblings by James Callaghan to frustrate the archaic process. It had also failed in a number of other economies, including Ireland in 1981. More significantly, it ran in the teeth of Margaret Thatcher's overall strategy, which, for all its failures, did have a shape and purpose; and it transgressed her deepest instincts as well as her well-flexed responses to the mood of the British people as that curious mechanism which sets an election in motion moved slowly up through the gears in the bitter and prolonged spring of 1983.

Nobody wanted a vigorous, dynamic set of new economic departures. They would have been totally out of character with what had gone before, and would therefore have lacked credibility. The electorate were conditioned to small mercies, like inflation coming down, taxes being cut if possible, and most importantly of all their jobs surviving. The economic weapon of unemployment worked just as well for the employed as it did for those dependent on benefit, and it worked best of all with militancy in the trade unions. The Budget coming a week after the very graphic demonstration of this, over the collapsed miners' strike, reinforced, by its neutral, muted tones the belief on which Margaret Thatcher was fashioning out her own more aggressive cadenza; that a broad performance across much more than the economy was required to win an election. This ran completely counter to the general anticipation of commentators, which could be summarised in Adam Raphael's wail of disappointment in the *Observer* on March 20. It was his view (a distinctly old-fashioned one) that 'Budgets should be the peak of the political year', and Howe's, which should have been the object of acclaim after the years of economic slog, and 'the launching pad for a Tory election victory' had gone wrong. Yet the Labour Party, which had come out in advance of the Budget with a massive and pre-emptive reflation package, which promised the injection of some £11,000 million into the British economy, designed to create 500,000 jobs in twelve months, additional borrowing, and some fairly dramatic tax adjustments, had been greeted with considerable scepticism, and a week later this was reflected in the opinion polls. Though they revealed a generally volatile situation, with Alliance support relatively strong, they did not give much cause for hope to Labour.

The word sent out from Conservative sources was in favour of an October rather than a June election, and Geoffrey Howe's Budget was carefully structured to leave open the two options. It was entirely in keeping with that round, owl-like face, since the bland and undramatic limitations of Margaret Thatcher's closest lieutenant are writ clear there for all to see.

The worry, then and later, concerned the unfortunate Michael Foot. His survival as leader of the Labour Party was a critical element. He was judged, with good reason, to be a potential loser anyway, and eminently beatable into the bargain. (The two qualifications are distinctly different.) To what extent the Conservatives could do anything about it was a complex question, but it was resolved for them by a middle-aged, middle-of-the-road socialist of moderate views and in command of hard facts. His name was Ossie O'Brien. He was the Labour Party candidate in the Darlington by-election, and his victory there, on Thursday March 24, achieved several things. It ensured Michael Foot's survival as leader. It produced a setback for the Alliance, pushing them into third place. It represented a setback also for the idea of tactical voting, which Conservatives feared and which simply did not feature as an electoral weapon or strategy of any importance.

For the Conservatives, the opinion poll predictions had been that they would finish a poor third. And this would have confirmed a by-election pattern, since they had finished third in five of the previous six by-elections and had increased their vote in only one of the nineteen by-elections of the Parliament. It was therefore a mark of some confidence in the Government, in the wake of the Budget, and in the obvious run-up to a general election which was at most within a time-span of less than a year, to have done so well in Darlington. If anything, for the Labour Party the solid performance of Ossie O'Brien emphasised the very different situations which had prevailed in Bermondsey in February. There Labour lost for the first time against the Alliance, not because of its militant left-wing candidate, Peter Tatchell, so much as because of Michael Foot's own dreadful procrastinations, first declaring in the Commons the candidate's unsuitability and then supporting him. The Party was undoubtedly deeply divided, its disciplinary structure uncertain and awkward, its attitudes often extreme and at times undemocratic, and its leader out of touch with what was happening in British grassroots politics. In a more benign way than Harold Wilson, he lived in the rarefied atmosphere of Parliament's debating chamber; and even there, in spite of the historic difficulties, he seemed to belong to the past.

Immediately after the Budget, Margaret Thatcher had emphasised clearly the central message of Howe's package, that it did not contain sudden promises aimed at popularity; and she dismissed Labour's package of alternative proposals with a disdainful phrase about 'bubble and bust and boom jobs'. With echoing confidence, a fortnight later, the Confederation of British Industry announced that the recession was coming to an end; or seemed to be. Output was stronger than at any time since the summer of 1979.

It was all a bit like the completion of a large and complicated jigsaw puzzle. There comes a moment, well before the pieces themselves fall into place, when the inevitability of where everything goes becomes clear, and it is then that hand and eye engage in a race to complete what is already a clear picture within the mind. So it was, as Margaret Thatcher foresaw, a series of shapes and patterns rapidly making up a broad and triumphant canvas: undertakings about an EEC rebate for Britain; inflation down to its lowest point in May; confidence emanating from industry; admiration flowing in a spring tide from Fleet Street; positive predictions coming from the market research organisations as they sold their services to political parties, newspapers, radio and television channels in the biggest and most prodigal dispersal of superfluous and repetitive knowledge in British electoral history. Certain final pieces, most predictable of all in the way they would shape and colour the complete puzzle, yet remained: they were the local elections, and the completion of the boundary revisions.

*

It was time to make speeches, give interviews, become available; but it was time for something far deeper than that. If Margaret Thatcher's fundamental image of consistency was to bear fruit in terms of power for a second time, all the strands of her complex political character needed to be brought together in a forceful solo performance which would fuse that character with Britain's. She had been alone in adversity; she had been a solitary political force throughout most of her political career; and she was aggressively so in what only she knew was the closing phase of her first term as Prime Minister. Increasingly under pressure to indicate what no prime minister in the circumstances ever indicates, the date on which Parliament would dissolve, she nevertheless did indicate, and more within Parliament than outside it, a change in tempo, emphasis, even language. Leading up to Easter her twice-weekly 'Prime Minister's Questions' began to have a pedantic air about them.

There was a laboured sense of orchestration about the rolling forth of issues in which not only docile Conservative backbenchers, but Opposition politicians as well, seemed to be feeding her, as the pitiful supporting cast on stage in a music hall supply leads for a comic star turn, dutifully becoming the butt for witticisms and innuendoes which were of their own initiating. Geneva talks on disarmament; the provision of computers for schools; the question of Anglo-American consultations on laser-beam defences in space against inter-continental ballistic missiles; Greenham women, and the advice to them about holding hands along the Berlin wall; Grenada, no less, with Margaret Thatcher defending the right of independent Commonwealth countries, even those 'within the hard-core of the Communist system', to make their own choices; these and other matters were deployed, often laboriously, and with obvious foreknowledge, to make pre-election points.

One occasion coincided with Ossie O'Brien's arrival to take the oath, and in those awkward minutes, as he stood waiting with his sponsors at the bar of the House, he heard Margaret Thatcher telling James Hamilton, 'I am grateful to the honourable member for allowing me to get that quotation out', the quotation in question being a philosophic observation made by Denis Healey, years before, to the effect that the time lag between a rise in output and its beneficial impact on employment could be 'up to a year'.

The pace changed after the short Easter break; it quickened. Greater precision, simpler words and phrases, the shuffling-off of orchestrated quotation and reference to the past. The questions were similar. All of them could be related to the forthcoming election, and most of them were. But the operation was cleaner and sharper. The complicated Berlin Wall advice to the Greenham women was replaced: 'We are the true peace movement,' she told what should have been an astonished House, for she was the first British Prime Minister since Lord Salisbury defeated the Boers to have been responsible for a successful, and purely British, war. 'When the election comes,' she told the House, 'we shall fight it on the Tory record and on Tory policies, and I believe that we shall win.' By Tuesday April 19 she had built the tension within herself to the point when it unleashed itself in the hyena-like confrontation with Michael Foot, when she accused him of being 'frit', and seemed for moments on end to have lost control of herself; a primal atavism surged to the surface; the pent-up purposes and ambitions of her whole career, not for the first time, but in a rare moment of exposure, burst forth in a strange and forbidding jumble of words which the sober record of Hansard reduces almost to a nonsense which fails hopelessly to convey the over-charged atmosphere of the occasion.

Here was power, the exercise of it, the lusting after it, personified within the cradle of the world's democracies. It had nothing whatever to do with right or wrong, with having governed well or badly, with correct or incorrect policies, with consent or consensus, with anybody else except herself. It was about one thing, and one thing only: it was about winning.

PART FOUR

'The New, Happy Life'

CHAPTER TWENTY-THREE

'A Source of Great Strength'

The Conservative Party held its centenary conference of 1983 at Blackpool from Tuesday October 11 to the following Saturday. It should have been an occasion for unprecedented self-congratulation for a party that had won a second term in power in the teeth of a major economic recession and with record levels of unemployment. Instead, it was a disaster. Overshadowed, and then dominated throughout, by the Parkinson affair, it cruelly exposed the Prime Minister's limitations when faced with adversity. But it did far more than that: it exposed the party to acute embarrassment at the precise time in its annual calendar of activities when it is least able to do anything about such embarrassment. If politics have more than their fair share of orchestration and management, the concentration is at its highest in elections and at party 'hostings'. And if this was generally true of the Conservative Party above other political parties — in the case of Labour this is so because Labour shares public interest with the TUC conference — it has been particularly the case since Margaret Thatcher became party leader on account of her liking for such occasions and her ability to use them to the full for the extension of her control and her popularity with both the party faithful and the public at large.

She not only recognises the value, but manipulates it to her advantage, and to the disadvantage of her critics and opponents. Sufficient of the detail of this manipulation has been examined above * to show the circumstances in which she regarded the event, and how well she handled it. From her first conference in 1956, Conservative Party conferences have always been impor-

* See Chapter 16: *The Grassroots*.

tant, playing a direct part in getting her her first nomination, in leading to her meeting her husband, in making her early impact on the Conservative Party, in establishing her ministerial stature, in allowing her to assert herself as new Conservative Party leader in October 1975, in the triumphant victory conference of October 1979, and in the difficult series of party 'hostings' between then and the general election of 1983. Of all of these, however, the October 1983 conference brought together the fact of it being the 100th such event with the triumph it represented personally to her of having brought the party through to victory just four months earlier.

There were shadows. A sense of heightened expectation since June that a vigorous programme for the Government would emerge out of the somewhat bland manifesto and the convincing mandate it had earned was still unrewarded. A belief that Margaret Thatcher's eye operation had in some way impaired her health, and that possibly she was tired, had led to speculation about her sticking power. And she was faced with problems of adjustment to a new Labour leader, different in style and tactic from his three predecessors. In addition, it could not be overlooked that the SDP had also acquired a new leader, Dr David Owen.

The necessary adjustments invoked the broader question of political 'direction'. Margaret Thatcher is a barometer politician if ever there was one. She invites questions in the course of interviews about the direction in which people, party, and country are going, and if they are not asked will ask them rhetorically herself. And she addresses the answers with relish. A number of such questions had been building up, since the election, on specific issues such as the National Health Service, further trade union reforms, and disarmament; but they raised a more fundamental question about movement Left or Right. In circumstances where the remaining balance of British politics consisted of three ideologies to the Left of her own, her instinct would tell her, once the simplicities of the public relations exercise which had won in June were safely behind her, and she had her majority, to move in *towards* her political opponents, taking over the centre which she claims she represents anyway.

The presentation of Conservative 'thrust', both on issues and in principle, is grist to the mill which grinds so publicly each October. The tensions form the material out of which the complicated musical score for a party conference speech, and all that leads up to it, are fashioned. All would be put right by the beating of the big drum, the thumping of the empty tub, the rhetoric which in the past had been so carefully organised and orchestrated by her party chairmen, to one of whom, the most recent, she owed a considerable debt of gratitude, part of which had been paid by her promotion of him to the Cabinet, as Secretary of State for Trade and Industry; part of it, apparently, was still outstanding — at least, in her eyes. Thus, when the Parkinson affair became public, she responded uncharacteristically, with premeditation rather than intuition.

Cecil Parkinson, the cool, clean hero of the general election, made a statement to the press on Wednesday October 5 1983, less than a week before the opening of this centenary Conservative Party Conference. Through his solicitors he acknowledged a 'relationship' with his former secretary, Miss Sara Keays, who was expecting his child. Parkinson said he would be 'making financial provision for both mother and child'. He acknowledged that it had been his intention to marry Miss Keays, that he had told her of this 'wish to marry her', but that he had then changed his mind; 'my wife, who has been a source of great strength, and I decided to stay together and to keep our family together'. The contents of the statement were confirmed by Miss Keays' London solicitor. And a spokesman from Number Ten confirmed that Margaret Thatcher knew of the statement, but that the question of Cecil Parkinson's resignation 'does not and will not arise'.

It emerged the following day that Margaret Thatcher had known about the 'relationship' and about Sara Keays' pregnancy at least three months before. Because of it, the Prime Minister had moved Parkinson out of the Chairmanship of the Conservative Party. Later speculation suggested that she had known for far longer, probably being informed by either the Home Secretary or by the Director General of the Security Service at the time of Parkinson's inclusion in the Falklands war cabinet in April 1982. This would have been in accordance with Margaret Thatcher's own instructions about security, following the Blunt affair. But confirmation, which either way would have been embarrassing, was not forthcoming. What did emerge, in off-the-record press briefings by Parkinson, which were apparently contrary to the private agreement with his mistress, was the claim that 'the full facts' were told to Margaret Thatcher on June 9, after the polls in the general election had closed.

The Conservative Party conference opened in Blackpool on Tuesday October 11, with one backbench member, Ivor Stanbrook, coming out publicly with a statement to the effect that Parkinson, 'a self-confessed adulterer and a damned fool', should have insisted on resigning. Stanbrook repudiated the party establishment's 'evident determination to pretend that nothing is wrong'. From then on, to an absurd degree, every general conference debate or argument was accompanied by a subliminal, but totally unrelated, question, which flashed across the screen of public perception: but what about Parkinson? Tuesday's debate on law and order coincided with details of how Sara Keays was almost selected as the Conservative Party candidate in the Bermondsey by-election in February. Wednesday's discussions about disarmament and the continuing commitment to tax cuts were accompanied by reassuring press comments and articles to the effect that what was feared was an 'over-reaction' on Parkinson's behalf; the demonstration of party support could become excessive.

It was a real fear about which nothing could be done beyond informing the press of the 'leadership' being 'worried', a detail which rated three paragraphs on page one of the *Daily Telegraph*, but which produced material enough for thirteen paragraphs, a full column, from Geoffrey Smith in *The Times*, on the politics and morals of the Parkinson affair. It would be doubly damaging, he claimed, if Parkinson did go at this stage. 'Not only would the party be marked by scandal, but the Prime Minister's bluff would have been called. For just about the first time on a major political issue, as this has become, she would have been forced to surrender an unequivocal position.' But he was able to reassure readers that the mood at Blackpool was to close ranks, and not be programmed by the press.

The careful orchestration reached a double climax on the Thursday. It was Cecil Parkinson's own day. He arrived at the conference, which he should have been attending from the start, in order to make a concluding speech to the debate on free enterprise and industry. He mounted the platform with Margaret Thatcher, sharing in her applause, or she in his, and he was accompanied by his wife Ann. The only reference he made to his own adultery was an oblique one, when he thanked the first of the two women he had confessed to betraying, making no mention of the second. He was warmly applauded for this: 'deft and graceful', said the *Guardian*, 'a poignant moment,' said the *Daily Telegraph*, 'the chivalry of the reception,' said *The Times*, was 'touching.'

'Now I am determined to stay on,' was Parkinson's relieved response to the panting cohorts of Fleet Street, eager to be reassured that their predictions had been right. In conference terms Cecil Parkinson's personal triumph, combined with an ordinary, run-of-the-mill speech, overshadowed a traditional highlight of the past, the debate on immigration and race, as well as extinguishing interest in Norman Tebbit's remarks on the trade unions, and Norman Fowler's on the future of the NHS. How they must have loved their colleague for whom all the orchestrating techniques of the party, many of them perfected by Parkinson himself, were mustered and rolled into action!

But orchestration of a more sombre kind was at work. Late on the Thursday night, with a majority of commentators and politicians of the view that Parkinson and the Conservative Party had weathered the storm, the *Guardian* already telling its Friday morning readers, in the page one lead story, that Parkinson had 'demonstrated he is home and dry', Miss Sara Keays summoned journalists from *The Times* and issued a lengthy statement 'as a public duty and a duty to my family', setting the record straight.

She revealed that a 'long-standing, loving relationship' with Cecil Parkinson had existed since 1979, in which year he had first proposed marriage. She had always believed in that marriage taking place. She became pregnant in May, and Parkinson decided he did not want to marry her, and told her. She replied by saying she would not conceal the paternity of the child, but she did 'implore' him to tell Margaret Thatcher, on account of the implications for the party, and in the formation of a new Government. On polling day Parkinson sought a reconciliation, and proposed marriage again. Sara Keays 'gladly accepted'. He saw the Prime Minister and told her. Before going on holiday with his wife and daughters, Parkinson reassured Miss Keays of his intentions. On September 1 he changed his mind again, and said he would not go ahead with the marriage. This led to negotiations between their respective solicitors, the issuing of the joint statement, and the agreement that nothing further would be said, an agreement which Parkinson broke almost immediately.

It was this which provoked the statement, reinforced by a deep sense of outrage at an editorial comment in the *Daily Telegraph* to the effect that 'the moral (sic) logic is that a quiet abortion is greatly to be preferred to a scandal'.

Cecil Parkinson saw Margaret Thatcher at two in the morning, his view being that the statement made it impossible for him to go on, and that the situation, if not resolved, threatened the Government and the Prime Minister as well as his family. After six sleepless hours he went to see Margaret Thatcher again, and his offer of resignation was accepted. 'Their brief talk', according to *The Times*, 'was said to have been distressing for both', and a friend of Parkinson's said he was 'quite broken'. He and his wife left Blackpool immediately.

The Conservative Party, which had applauded his survival on Thursday, applauded his departure on Friday, and then applauded Margaret Thatcher's praise of him as the organiser of the election victory. The debate began on how much damage the affair had done the Prime Minister, and, with predictable efficiency, opinion poll research commenced the process of informing the country about the shape and texture of its collective mind. The basic message was of immutability. The measurable impact was slight.

Yet Margaret Thatcher was damaged by the affair, even if the degrees measured on the scale were few. The Conservative Party was rather less damaged. The country enjoyed the whole epidode. The press wallowed in it. If the facts recorded in Miss Keays' statement were true in all detail, then Margaret Thatcher knew of the love affair at a time when there was no intention of marriage; knew of the pregnancy and of the decision by Parkinson to leave his wife, divorce her, and then marry Sara Keays; knew of the change in this intention some time in the late summer, and probably before the precipitate appointment of John Selwyn Gummer to replace Parkinson as Party chairman on September 14; and was then faced with publication of the first facts on October 5, in *Private Eye*.

Throughout this period Margaret Thatcher's judgment, normally based on good instinct, was heavily distorted by loyalty. Morality, as she insisted throughout, was not a public but a private issue, at least, as far as the politicians were concerned. What the British people might think was another matter. But if, through loyalty, other weaponry is to be jettisoned, there should be no prevarication. This lady, who was not, and is not, for turning, had once said, 'I believe you should be loyal to the things which put you in power — *totally loyal*! — I couldn't bear disloyalty to those things at all because that would be tantamount to getting in on a false prospectus.' Yet one of 'those things' deserving loyalty from her just happened to be a person, Parkinson, and not an idea, and true to her dictum she extended the loyalty, making it a substitute, as political leaders so often do to their own disadvantage, for the harder values which should have taken precedence. Those values include morality, not because the public say so, but because Margaret Thatcher said so.

Increasingly, as her first term drew to a close, she raised Victorian moral standards as an emblem of general virtue. Only rarely, in the history of mankind, have moral standards been more obviously double ones than those which prevailed in Victorian England. Yet no one anticipated that the double nature would eventually be echoed in Margaret Thatcher's handling of the Parkinson affair, and become a fashionable joke. More serious still, however, was the affair's exposure of her limited judgment of talent. Nothing that Cecil Parkinson has said or done, in his political career, raised him above average. His capabilities were primarily in public relations. He managed well a professional election campaign with very substantial additional talent behind him, and a great deal of money. He made a couple of clever remarks during election press conferences, and he gave a number of off-the-record background briefings to journalists who were critical enough to affect events. He was otherwise expendable, if the heavy principle of rewarding loyalty had not hung so largely round his leader's neck. Had she been the ruthlessly consistent politician whose image she likes to project, she would certainly have dispensed with his future services on polling day, when, allegedly, he told her the facts about Sara Keays, and his marital intentions. She listened, we must presume, and then retained him for the time being as party chairman and raised him to high office within her Cabinet.

None of this has anything whatsoever to do with objective moral judgment. It is a misunderstanding to perceive it as an issue of morality involving the British public, and standards in public life. If those arise at all, they do so marginally. What is central is confined to Margaret Thatcher's stated beliefs and attitudes and her decisions based on them. She has aborted any serious concept of morality, private and public, and placed it well below loyalty as a basis for judgement. This is an irreversible narrowing of her options in the territory of belief and vision. She has demonstrated indecision and inconsistency in the handling of a relatively minor problem, as it emerged to her privately on June 9, and by such demonstration was responsible for letting it become a major problem by October, humiliating to herself, and mildly damaging to the Conservative Party. Her misjudgment of the problem was compounded by a misjudgment of her man.

It is a point of view with which the *Economist* disagrees profoundly. In that curiously attractive way in which it distances itself from, and then shows up, the frequent lapses into sheepishness of the Fourth Estate, it criticised Margaret Thatcher for giving in: 'A prime minister more resolute and convinced of Mr Parkinson's value might have brazened it out and challenged Miss Keays and Fleet Street to do their work.' And it went on to pinpoint accurately the real dilemma: 'this summer's question mark over Mrs Thatcher's resolution and self-confidence must remain'.*

In practical terms, the Parkinson affair undermined the party conference and blighted any intended launch of a new ideological initiative. And this was an inevitable price of loyalty, whether he ultimately survived or not. Knowingly, she paid that considerable price in advance.

An essential element to the politician interested in power is the expendability of everything, even loyalty, for self-interest. Principles, politics, objectives are always on the casualty list; morality is as well; even truth, when the pressure is great, must be sacrificed in the interest of winning and of keeping what is won. On this occasion, deep loyalty produced a sequence of errors. Enoch Powell, in another context, had said of Margaret Thatcher, 'There are some moments when you really have to hand it to the Prime Minister. It must be the triumph of instinct over expediency; but she has a knack of doing things that nobody thought were still possible.'**

This was not such a moment. Expediency, bolstered by over-

---

* *Economist*, October 22 1983.
** 'Nothing succeeds like succession'; article in *The Times*, June 22 1983.

much loyalty, played her false and the clockwork mechanisms which lay behind the careful attempts at conference orchestration fell apart, revealing a fairly rudimentary piece of machinery behind her own image, which should have dominated and triumphed. This famous image has always suggested a woman of firm moral principle who believed in marriage, repudiated divorce, indiscretion and domestic instability in those in public life, and chose members of her team with these standards clearly in mind. Yet she abandoned them in the case of Parkinson.

The image suggested, furthermore, that she believed in resolution, firmness and consistency. Yet she supported a man who could not make up his mind, and repeatedly betrayed, first his wife, then his mistress and his wife, finally dragging in his party and his leader. She is on record in her dislike of double standards: 'I don't like it if people say one thing in private and another in public. They must say the same thing on both occasions.'*

And those around her are conscious of this: 'She would forgive error and misjudgment, particularly if you were candid in discussing it with her. I think the only thing that would lead her to being less than forgiving of an error or misjudgment is if she thought your errors had become chronic, as she has little respect for a weathervane approach to issues . . . she is a politician of commitment for whom most views are very firmly and consistently held.'** Yet in mid-October 1983, Margaret Thatcher sacrificed consistency, judgment and belief on the altar of loyalty. And she cannot get them back.

---

* Patricia Murray, op. cit.
** Sir Geoffrey Howe, in conversation with Patricia Murray, op. cit.

CHAPTER TWENTY-FOUR

Murdering Prime Ministers

It was a black October. In the week following Cecil Parkinson's resignation the Grenada crisis came to a head with the killing of Maurice Bishop of Wednesday, October 19. A week later the American marines invaded the island, and, after initial stiff resistance, gained control and restored the Governor General, Sir Paul Scoon, who set about the formation of an interim administration.

Britain's role was marginal throughout. The Foreign Secretary, Sir Geoffrey Howe, did not know what was going on. He told Parliament on the eve of the invasion that 'the American presence off the island in no way foreshadowed possible intervention by the United States in the island's affairs'. These words were followed, later that (Tuesday) evening, by information from the British Embassy in Washington that US Chiefs of Staff had been summoned to the White House on Monday, preparatory to an invasion; and late that night Margaret Thatcher talked with President Reagan. She 'communicated to the United States our very considerable doubts which the Government has about initiating action, and asked them to weigh carefully several points before taking any irrecoverable decision to act'.*

It was made clear to her, in that conversation, as it had been made clear in independent Foreign Office information, that the invasion would go ahead. In later exchanges in the Commons on Tuesday she said: 'We understand that what weighed heavily and conclusively with the US was the view taken by a number of Caribbean States who see things in a very different perspective from that which we do. They are very much closer. They have

* *Hansard*, Tuesday October 25 1983.

been prepared and have contributed forces to the Grenada invasion.'

She did not take part in the more substantive debate on Grenada, the following day, Wednesday October 26. Not until Sunday, in a BBC World Service broadcast, did she explain more fully her attitude, which was that 'if you are going to pronounce a new law that wherever Communism reigns against the will of the people . . . the United States shall enter, then we are going to have really terrible wars in the world.' It was an unconvincing, *post hoc* explanation, which failed to reassure those who had witnessed Britain being ignored and the Commonwealth superseded.

Her own position on Grenada had been made frostily clear on an earlier occasion, long before the murder of Maurice Bishop. As far back as March, before the general election, she had regretted the fact that Grenada was 'within the hardcore of the Communist system', but had gone on to assert that 'once countries are independent they are free to pursue their own systems. The Commonwealth sets its own standards, and I am afraid there is no exclusion of those who operate as one-party states.' There is no escaping, however, the implicit wish so to exclude, and, in default of being able to do that, a certain indifference which manifested itself six months later.

It was apparent in her Foreign Secretary's faint hint of disdain as he was giving his ill-judged assurances to Parliament, on Tuesday October 25, that there was 'no question' of American military intervention: 'It must be remembered,' he lectured the House unnecessarily, 'that the Prime Minister, Mr Maurice Bishop, who lost his life in the coup, was a friend and associate of Castro, and the Cuban Government lamented the death of Mr Bishop and deplored the events taking place, so it is difficult to conclude in what respect the matter has changed significantly.' It was a remark which put a low value on killing prime ministers.

Britain had missed the point of much that had been happening in Grenada during the previous fortnight, and responsibility was equally shared between the Prime Minister and the Foreign Secretary. It was a form of public relations cover-up for Margaret Thatcher to claim that she was 'delighted' that the people of Grenada were free and that those of the Eastern Caribbean could sleep more soundly in their beds, while at the same time condemning United States action. She seemed to have overlooked the fact that a widely supported and recognised regime, even if it had come to power by means of a coup, and was unattractive to those who dislike one-party states and Communism, had been overthrown violently, and its leader murdered. She expressed reserve at the fact that the United States had not given Britain 'an opportunity of consultation'.

Yet the bewildering reality, underlined clearly by the expressed attitude of Sir Geoffrey Howe, was that little, if anything, was done to initiate action, mobilise either Commonwealth or NATO personnel, gather reliable intelligence, and work out a basic position. A regime, distasteful anyway before the murder of Bishop, was spiralling downwards into worse chaos, under the muddled and conflicting influences both of the Soviet Union and Cuba, and was to be left to that fate, as far as the British Government was concerned. Neither the neighbouring Caribbean states nor the United States were content to let that proceed. But they saw little purpose in involving Britain in any counter-offensive, and for good reason: Britain was not interested.

In its encapsulated form, the Grenada coup, followed by the joint invasion by America and other neighbouring states, cruelly exposed Margaret Thatcher on a number of different points. The central one was very general: that in which principle and self-interest collide. Margaret Thatcher's judgment is at its most cool and calculating where her own self-interest is concerned. This governed her behaviour over the Falklands crisis, and paid off. And to all appearances, there was common ground between her political self-interest then, and Britain's interests. This was not the case with Grenada. No initial self-interest was served by adopting any profile at all and Britain's interests, of a limited kind, were only perceived when it was too late for Britain to play a part. Even if limited, Britain's potential role was important, and the failure to exercise it has resulted in permanent if circumscribed loss. It involved the possible deployment of the Commonwealth, and it involved our position as a major NATO power. In either of these two quite distinct respects there was justification for greater British involvement in this particular Caribbean crisis. The Caribbean, whether we like it or not, is a cockpit for East-West confronation, and every allegedly 'free' and 'independent' state there is prone to the kind of ideological power struggle which brought Bishop to power and ousted Geary, in May 1979, and then resulted in Bishop's murder. For a

British Prime Minister who is seemingly tireless in her defence of freedom and democracy, her attitude towards the events in Grenada during the fortnight prior to the American invasion seem to have been governed by the earlier judgment, of March, about Grenada being 'within the hardcore of the Communist system', and somehow irredeemable because of that. Countries which are serious about their foreign policies, like the United States, regard no situation as irredeemable. They also tend to run such policies on the basis of national, rather than personal, self-interest.

As far as Britain is concerned, there are 'two views', as Sir Geoffrey Howe repeatedly claimed during the Grenada crisis. One is against any continued role in the Caribbean, either for Britain or for the Commonwealth, and for a commensurate limitation in interpreting the extent of NATO's role on the Western side of the Atlantic. The other is a belief in a positive and active foreign policy, which sees the British Commonwealth, Anglo-American relations and NATO as part of a wider power balance in a world where freedom and democracy are permanently at risk, and must be defended from quite different, totalitarian regimes. In such a simplified division one thing is patently clear: the position occupied in theory by Margaret Thatcher. In terms of principle, in terms of making Britain great, in terms of defending, and where possible restoring, democracy, in terms of her stated dedication to NATO and Western defences, and finally in terms of her dedication to the principles on which the British Commonwealth worked, she had duties towards Grenada which she abandoned. She clutched instead for a frail kind of consistency: that aggression was wrong, and should not be allowed to succeed. This had been her public argument on the Falklands. It had been her justification for fighting a war in which many died. And she could not lightly drop it. So she switched into the subjunctive mood and, like a headmistress on the touchline, watching a hockey match drawing to a close, with her own side victorious, though guilty of having bent the rules more than somewhat, she admonished them with generalisations. It was wrong for the West 'to walk into other people's countries. You have to be absolutely certain if you do, that there is no choice, no other way.'

If she had been less concerned, as a politician, with the moral questions of 'right' and 'wrong' and more concerned with pragmatic issues and national self-interest and how best to pursue it, she could have acted differently. But her 'performance' on the stage of power was paramount; and the country suffered as a result. The same obligation, of being 'absolutely certain', does not apply if the aggression is the other way round, as it was in the case of the sinking of the *Belgrano*. And it was clear that both this, and the heavily stated principles behind the Falklands war, were uppermost in Margaret Thatcher's mind during the week between the Grenada invasion and her considered statements the following Sunday, when according to *The Times* of Monday October 31, 'Thatcher comes off the fence'. As the *Spectator* put it: 'During the Falklands War, Mrs Thatcher very unwisely chose to generalise her justification for recapturing the islands as a vindication of the principle that aggression should not pay, whereas the sensible argument was simply that Britain would not allow British land and people to be taken over by a foreign power. Now the United States has been thoroughly aggressive, and of course there is nothing that Mrs Thatcher can do and very little that she can say about it. It serves her right for always being high-falutin about the cause of liberty, instead of practical about the defence of Britain.'*

It serves her right for creating circumstances which then imprison her in her own obligation to be consistent. At the best of times inflexible, she had effectively queered her own pitch as far as freedom and defence of the West were concerned, not by actions taken eighteen months before, but by the elaborate verbal gloss she had put on those actions.

She demonstrated many of her own most telling limitations during the Grenada crisis, not least of which was that her perceptions are unsubtle and narrow. For Paul Johnson it was 'this huge failure of judgment, by far her worst since she took office'.

Margaret Thatcher's most considered input during the Grenada crisis would seem to have been a repeat of her tediously familiar lecture on how to run the world. And running the world is something which, in her view, does not require the British Commonwealth or any of its subsidiary groupings. Only 'when the United States has cleared the island of its present resistance' would either Britain or the Commonwealth be 'sympathetic to calls for help'.

* *Spectator*, October 29 1983.

Most seriously of all, Margaret Thatcher's ideas on how to run the world do not appear to require the British Foreign Office. What was significant and striking about the Grenada crisis, as it developed, was the extent to which *it did not seem to matter* in its own right. It mattered as a domestic and parliamentary issue, and then as one which was affecting adversely close Anglo-American accord. For one who is now famous for the amount of time she is supposed to spend reading the contents of the red boxes in Downing Street late at night, the boxes coming from the Foreign Office seem to have been woefully neglected.

Her problem was not simply one of arrogance about the complicated and subtle machinery of diplomacy, though she does have this arrogance; nor was it simply a brittleness in her overall perception of world politics, which too often construes major issues in terms of East-West tensions and fails to give sufficient time and energy to a whole range of alternative world perceptions such as the North-South dialogue, the views of non-aligned countries, the differing attitudes of black, Islamic, island and oriental peoples, though she does suffer persistently from this brittle simplification process; the problem spills over, increasingly as her power is extended, into the far more fundamental and deep-seated area of judgment about people.

That hint of a desire, on Margaret Thatcher's part, months before, to exclude one-party states from the Commonwealth, were it possible, and her admission that 'I am afraid there is no exclusion', is part of an attitude which must feel increasingly chilly to the leaders of such one-party states, as they struggle to remain in operation as part of the world's independent polity without succumbing to the even more dangerous forces of unconstitutional dictatorship. Why, then, should dependence be placed on a British connection within the Commonwealth when an American connection outside it promises either a better structure of support, or a more serious threat, depending on the view adopted? Whichever the perception, the Caribbean, as an area of Commonwealth influence, as a strategic resource, as a modest pawn in world power balance, had slipped from the British grasp to such an extent that Britain's input under Margaret Thatcher's leadership at the time of the crisis was negligible. For a woman of such determined views and with so ready a disposition to enter the fray on behalf of the allies and against enemies of the ideological battle, her acceptance of things as they were is astonishing. It did not really matter which approach she adopted subsequent to her own Foreign Minister's extraordinary statement to Parliament that 'it is difficult to conclude in what respect the matter has changed significantly'. After that, her own 'very considerable doubts' expressed to the United States could safely be ignored.

CHAPTER TWENTY-FIVE

Pavlov's Dogs

Geoffrey Howe as Chancellor was pavlovian in his responses to the established principles of Margaret Thatcher's economic and fiscal policies, deploying his energies and talent, as is appropriate when the question of principles has been already decided, in the realm of management and adjustment to events. Allowing for the upheavals and setbacks which derived from domestic and international forces during the period of the first Conservative administration, he did well.

Temperamentally, he was well-suited to an order of priorities by which performance had to be fitted to a set of firm and principled objectives. The same rules apply to a Foreign Secretary only occasionally, and generally in circumstances of crisis, when clear principle has to be pursued in the teeth of pressures, international and domestic, which are often severe. Much of the rest of the time an effective Foreign Secretary is weighing a broad range of diverse interests against each other, and pursuing that delicate and complex target of overall national interest by means of a whole range of mechanisms involving Europe, NATO, the UN, the British Commonwealth, the OAU, and the established diplomatic network.

On his performance over Grenada, Geoffrey Howe would seem to be psychologically ill-suited to the job. Quite abruptly, from being a Chancellor of apparent firmness tempered with a moderate and selective flexibility, making him a fairly central figure in the 1983 general election victory, he was brought down in size to schoolboy proportions, fumbling in the House over a relatively straightforward issue with which he had failed to come to grips. Quite suddenly and specifically, Howe's performance over the Grenada crisis raised serious and fundamental questions about the Prime Minister's discretion and judgment. Had she made a serious error in appointing him? Did he have the stature and breadth for the job, or was the primary motive that of having a loyal and biddable subordinate in the Foreign Office? What were these high offices of state for? Was the whole business a political game of musical chairs played to the tune of 'The Vicars of Bray' ('When loyalty no harm meant')?*

From the perspective of the late autumn of 1983, the principled attitudes of the politicians who had been in the Foreign Office at the beginning of her first terms in power under Lord Carrington, and with Sir Ian Gilmour as principal spokesman in the House of Commons, took on a different colouring and political independence. Personal stature and determined clear views based on belief, facts, logic and experience, were suddenly notable for their absence. And, in human terms, the simple reality that in a period of just over four years she had managed to dispose of two able Foreign Secretaries, Lord Carrington and Francis Pym, as well as at least two more junior figures experienced in diplomacy and with the necessary international range of judgments, Lord Soames and Sir Ian Gilmour, as well as other even more junior men, and all leading to a situation where the Foreign Office was presided over by Geoffrey Howe, gave a chilly perspective to the processes by which this had been achieved, and invited a consideration in broader terms of her management of talent.

Not two weeks before the Grenada crisis broke she had been faced with a need for Cabinet change, consequent on Cecil Parkinson's resignation, and had moved Norman Tebbit from Employment into Industry and Trade, replacing him with Tom King, and putting Timothy Raison into Transport as the new addition to the Cabinet. If politics at the top is viewed as a game involving punishments and rewards, then the upward movement of all three men is 'consistent' with a sense of purpose on Margaret Thatcher's part which also accounts for the departure from her cabinet of Carrington, Pym, Soames, Gilmour, Carlisle, Howell. And the result of that process by which talent has been thinned out, demonstrated in the Grenada crisis in a raw fashion, raises questions about the seriousness with which Margaret Thatcher regards the job to which she appoints those men in whom she believes most strongly. She put before the

---

* Leon Brittan and Nigel Lawson are known, incidentally, as 'the Rabbis of Bray'.

public, at the time of the general election, and as a prominent protagonist of central Conservative policies on further trade union reforms, a man who himself indicated a readiness to complete unfinished business in that area, only to move him out of it on the first occasion which presented itself.

Taken in the context of the apparent absence of any bulging package of policies for the current term, this approach had a trivialising impact which might just have been excusable under a Prime Minister like Harold Wilson. But Margaret Thatcher had presented herself in a very different light. She meant business. She was there for the real process of government. She had been elected, twice over, to change the economic and social face of the country, revive hope, stimulate endeavour, make Britain 'great' again internationally. She brought to the task enormous stamina, determination and vigour in addition to her apparent domination in the realm of policies and ideas. As she had so convincingly demonstrated, in the succession of daily press conferences during the general election, she could answer questions on virtually every topic, ignoring the relevant ministerial colleague at her side, and often did just that. But the idea that she might *have* to operate such a system, on a regular basis, was a bleakly different prospect altogether.

Though it is an exaggerated perception, Margaret Thatcher's own words about choosing her cabinet are curiously revealing of a certain superficiality. In the late summer of 1983, before the Parkinson affair forced upon her the untimely first reshuffle of the present administration, she was asked about the individual and collective strengths of a cabinet chosen in June 'with great care'.

She replied: 'We are now, I think, profiting from having had one period in government. You now start to move some people around and about. This adds to the wisdom and efficiency of your whole Government. A number of Ministers have come to know the inner workings of more than one department. You have to remember that the cabinet is not merely a collection of departments, it is a Government. Collectively it is important that you have a number of Ministers who have experience of several departments. On individual moves, well, bluntly, it has been done in the past to put your Chancellor of the Exchequer to Foreign Affairs. Geoffrey has in fact gained quite a lot in this context from being Chancellor of the Exchequer and travelling on

Treasury matters. Nigel, as you know, has total command in everything financial. Leon was a very, very good Minister of State at the Home Office, quite outstanding; and now has his chance as Home Secretary. It is really very exciting, that we have those three in these positions. Michael Heseltine has not been long in the Defence Service, so he knew that if he went there he would have to stay there. It is a very important job. So you do a few each time. You don't have enormous re-shuffles.'*

This lengthy and considered answer, to one of a series of questions the broad content of which she knew in advance, is faintly alarming. The tone and language is wrong: 'You do a few each time', 'You now start to move some people around and about', 'Leon . . . now has his chance', and 'if he went there he would have to stay there'. Further, there is something odd in the reasoning used to justify appointments: Is 'travelling on Treasury matters' really a qualification for the high office of Foreign Secretary? It may have looked so in September; it was a very different perception at the end of October. And if Nigel Lawson 'has total command in everything financial' why was he in her previous Cabinet for less than two years, and in Energy rather than closer to the economic responsibilities?

These may seem like quibbles, deriving from Margaret Thatcher's rather limited use of language, her somewhat cavalier approach to interviewers when she feels safe with them or their publications, and her desire to give them what they want in non-controversial territory. Certainly, at the time, back from her holiday in Switzerland, and with the as yet unclouded prospect of a centenary conference in Blackpool, the encounter did not threaten. With the benefit of hindsight, and in the context of other changes, the alarm bells begin to ring. *Doing* a few each time has been a process since May 1979 by which several able doers have been shuffled out the door altogether, and by which potential opponents who can't be shuffled out have been isolated. In the first category belong Francis Pym, Ian Gilmour, Mark Carlisle, Norman St John Stevas, William Whitelaw, arguably Lord Carrington as well, though this was a special case. In the second category belong James Prior, Peter Walker, Michael Heseltine.

But doing a few each time has also been applied to those

---

* Margaret Thatcher interviewed by George Bull, *The Director*, September 1983.

closest and most loyal to the Prime Minister, and this in turn can have a destabilising impact. Moving people 'around and about', far from adding to 'the wisdom and efficiency of your whole Government', can have a quite opposite effect. It weakens the politician in relation to his own senior civil servants, and also in relation to his Prime Minister. The constants are Margaret Thatcher and the two dozen or so permanent secretaries. The variables are the team, having their 'chance', gaining 'quite a lot', having 'to stay there'; 'it is really very exciting'.

It runs, however, in precisely the opposite direction from that in which Margaret Thatcher had indicated she would move. Her deepest and most permanent objectives, which included the reversing of that trend in British life by which the role of the state and the sheer size of the state machine had been enlarged or extended to the disadvantage of the individual, depended upon the politicians dominating the permanent civil service. She has consistently created a movement in the opposite direction. She has weakened the most senior elected 'guardians of freedom' – her own cabinet ministers – and in the process strengthened the permanent civil service and, of course, herself. This last is the most serious objective of all. Prime ministerial government has been superseding cabinet government inexorably. While it is possible to present an almost light-hearted view of Margaret Thatcher moving her ministers 'around and about' on a trial and error basis, there are also more sombre interpretations. She does not, for example, move her mentor, Keith Joseph, 'around and about'. He occupies a serious responsibility concerned with minds, attitudes and perceptions among tomorrow's voters; he has taken serious and far-reaching policy decisions about education; he is not a candidate in the merry-go-round since he has work to do. And the contrast underlines the belittling process which is going on with many of the others. 'One of the more eccentric quangos' is how one senior cabinet minister describes the cabinet, and he emphasises the seriousness with which concentration of power in the Prime Minister's hands has been pursued.

John Hoskyns, who was head of Margaret Thatcher's policy unit at Number Ten for virtually the whole of her first term in power, is on record* with the expressed belief that *since the war*

---

*'Strip down the state machine and start again'; *The Times*, February 16, 1983.

'successive governments began to create an unstable economy, which in turn helped to destabilise society'. And he goes on to present, for the first time since leaving his Downing Street job at the end of 1982, a comprehensive view of successive government policy failures. As one of many accurate and detailed assessments of what had been going wrong, and how it should be put right, his analysis was unexceptional. The only problem: it represented vast hostages to fortune. Not only was most of what he claimed to be wrong in early 1982 *more wrong* than it had been when Margaret Thatcher became Prime Minister in 1979, and he took over as her head of the policy unit, it was almost certain that it would get worse after a general election, and possibly much worse.

Substantially, the argument advanced was one of confusion and chaos by successive governments, leading to a surreal world in which cause and effect had no relevance for the majority of people. It was 'paternalism gone mad', in which paying for those employed in the public service, and paying for the social welfare system, and paying for the protections which trade union law and practice gave to the individual at work, went hugely beyond what the country could afford. In turn, this led to a tax burden which generally exceeded the benefits received by those paying it, acted as a disincentive to extra effort, was unfairly distributed, compared unfavourably with other Western countries, and had a stifling effect on business and industry. 'It must be doubtful whether the British economy can make a genuine and lasting recovery while it carries the double burden of the welfare state and the unions in their present form.'

Margaret Thatcher knew all this better, in 1975, than did the leaders of the other political parties, and came to power in 1979 committed to rectifying what Hoskyns, *in 1983,* was to describe as 'this tottering Babel of fiscal sticks and carrots, special favours and foolish commitments'. Dismantling it, and putting 'something sensible' there instead, was the prerequisite for economic recovery and political health.

One year later, it is worse, not better. A year ago, when Margaret Thatcher returned to power, one waited in vain for any programme of action to emerge. That second term, so necessary and so universally predicted, had no blueprint at the outset, and has none now which measures up to the magnitude of a set of problems her clear knowledge of which can be dated back a full decade. If she has been consistent her consistency has been that of rhetoric, not action; it is the semblance rather than the reality with which we deal.

The reality is of continued and continuing reliance on tax in default either of cutting public expenditure through the only really effective method which is Hoskyns's reform and replacement theory. The dismantling process has not been envisaged, still less attempted. There was no plan for it. If anything, it has been strengthened, and the politicians, who should be reformers, by being moved 'around and about', have been weakened in their relationship to the establishment and to Margaret Thatcher herself.

More fundamental, more far-reaching and far more critical, in terms of judging her, than her performance on the economy, must be her attack on the processes of government itself. Without that being a proven achievement, even in part, her approach to fiscal and economic management must ultimately be judged as tinkering in a hopeful, if muddled way. Promising to bring down public spending she has in fact put it up; promising to bring down inflation, she sent it soaring higher than it had done under Labour before she brought it back down to around 5 percent. She achieved this at the huge human cost in unemployment at more than 3 million. She achieved it at the expense of oil resources, and through the sleight-of-hand of apparently reducing some areas of public expenditure by selling off assets, a course which in fact was motivated by concealment and camouflage, and which, in the light of the overall public spending account, means that things are even worse than represented.

Oil has been handled in an irresponsible way, if one treats seriously the basic moral and principled political character of the Prime Minister. She has used it up to reduce current deficits, knowing it to be an exhaustible asset anyway and one which should have been reserved for more fundamental and more lasting achievement. In addition, very much against her frequently paraded instincts about saving and hoarding, she has failed to reverse the Labour government's prodigality over North Sea gas, preferring to see it burnt off and British technology deployed in the teeth of United States opposition to aid the Russians in bringing *their* gas across thousands of miles into Europe to be sold in place of Britain's own.

Rectitude, change, reform; 'stripping down the state machine and starting again'; making Britain great again by the proper deployment of human and natural resources; restoring economic health through action on inflation, trade unions, taxation: Margaret Thatcher, like some of her predecessors, has been a not unmixed blessing as Britain's leader, and has had a measure of success in certain areas. She has not been particularly consistent in any broad policy areas; rather, she has identified and singled out for her own particular brand of rhetorical consistency comparatively small issues or narrow, self-imposed tasks in order to assert the characteristic without invoking the more profound and underlying implications which are raised.

For example, and demonstrative of the characteristic as it applies to her management and control of power by the concentration of her undoubted determination on a small issue, take the following: within the complex tragedy of Northern Ireland, the hunger strike and her approach to it; within Europe, the singling out of Britain's payments to the EEC; internationally, the global East-West tensions and where Britain stands on them; within the British Commonwealth, an assumption of Britain's traditional authority; domestically, a belief in 'values' as a solution to human problems. Morally, a reliance on atavistic assumptions; in conflict, by choosing an island in the South Atlantic, wrongly invaded by foolish and desperate men, and fighting there a hugely expensive and high-risk war which could have gone catastrophically wrong, and has only so far gone marginally right, save in one important respect: its impact on the hearts and minds of a demoralised electorate.

It is entirely consistent with Margaret Thatcher's view of power that she should single out points of dramatic, tense focus, and *be consistent* about them. In this narrow respect she has been consistent, dangerously so. But, in these and other examples, the broader context is one of inaction, limited understanding, inflexibility, absence of vision.

Correct though her specific and detailed response to the H-Block hunger strike was, it was unsupported by any real grasp of the Northern Ireland question. She has been the easy victim of the intellectual authority of Enoch Powell, the pressures of right-wing Conservatives, the instinctive Unionism she feels herself, and the even more deeply instinctive 'Little Englander' approach which falls back on constitutionalism as a locking mechanism. Within the EEC she is far less consistent than her Conservative predecessor, Edward Heath, and in a sense less consistent than socialist opponents of Britain's membership. The intellectual vigour which Enoch Powell has displayed in arguing against Britain being a member has been a powerfully persuasive one with Margaret Thatcher, not in terms of her convictions about Europe, which are generally expressed in emotive and vague terms, but as an option, to be deployed in negotiating table conflicts about Britain's contribution.

Both in international and Commonwealth terms she has tended to single out a very simple set of broad perceptions, not unlike those by which, in childhood, we separate the 'good' from the 'bad'. Starting with the simple, and wrong, assumptions on these lines, as between Muzorewa, who was 'good' because he worked within the constitution agreed with Ian Smith, and was a bishop as well, and Nkomo and Mugabe, who were 'bad', because they were engaged in armed rebellion, Margaret Thatcher has trod a dangerously combative path in world affairs. She was lucky, electorally, to be handed the timely invasion of the Falkland Islands at the beginning of April 1982, an invasion which should have been foreseen and prevented. And she was lucky to have on hand a still great fighting force to fulfil her decisions. But she has left many people anxious about those other British outposts round the world, like Hong Kong and Gibraltar. They could represent a different story.

The anxiety is related to the core of her political character, which she has sought to represent, in a profusion of carefully orchestrated interviews, press conferences, encounter sessions, speeches and responses to question in Parliament, as a firm, resolute and convinced defendant of values and intentions the examination of which has been an essential part of this book. Because the consistency has been of a narrow, rhetorical, even questionable kind, defence of it has induced a combative and confrontational approach. Choosing carefully her ground, as she did with Robin Day in that famous interview in which he undoubtedly failed to subject her to that proper interrogation which would have informed viewers of her shortcomings, she accomplished a 'victory' over him which left many people conscious that it had been a hectoring form of counter-attack, a well chosen set of confrontational arguments, which had dismissed him, and that somehow logic and reason had slipped sideways out of the picture and off the screen.

With reason and logic goes truth. A truthful picture of Britain in the mid-1980s has been invoked by the failure of greatness as it was offered five years ago, and by the illusory substitution of a narrow set of achievements which by no means fill up the sums of human happiness on which most people spend their lives working. Margaret Thatcher has had the salutary impact on her country of shattering one set of illusions, only to substitute another set. She has shifted perceptions irreversibly. She has shaken down certain pillars in the temple of power, those representing trade union domination. But she has used for this purpose economic weapons which have created another set of pillars, built out of the rising numbers of unemployed, the rising tide of disaffection, the growing disharmony which results from the forces of law and order emulating that same combative confrontation which she has taught.

CHAPTER TWENTY-SIX

The Consistency of Rhetoric

It seems she has been consistent; that is the overriding quality around which Margaret Thatcher's character has been built. It is also how she described, on the eve of 1984, her own Government, as one with 'a reputation for consistency'.* But it is the consistency of rhetoric, and the building of the character a shrewd and calculated process the primary concern of which has always been power. In the course of that process much good has been achieved. The coincidence of interests has revitalised many areas of political life, and produced a new sense of direction and purpose. But the distinction must be made beween such benefits as by-products, and as central to that political life.

They are not necessarily the same. And the examination of Margaret Thatcher's handling of power must be seen, if possible, as a separate entity from her achievement of certain goals for the economy, for social balance in Britain, and for any of the grander objectives about defending the realm and 'our way of life'.

In this process the criteria for judging her are different in kind from the criteria which one might have applied to any of her immediate six predecessors, and to the majority of prime ministers in Britain during the past two centuries.

The largeness of this claim is not, of necessity, a measure of her greatness so much as of her approach. In seeking to make Britain great she has concealed deliberately a collateral purpose, which is the extension of her power and of the period of her performance on the political stage. It is an entirely legitimate and natural purpose, the very stuff of politics, and her skill in fulfilling it is wholly admirable. It has nothing to do with morality, or

* 'New Year Message', *The Times*, December 31 1983.

with being right on policies. It has to do with winning and then staying in front.

One's admiration should not be confused. Margaret Thatcher deserves to be greatly admired for her acquisition of power, for her ability to retain power, and for her general handling of power. She understands it as a resource and as a weapon. She values it far above people, who are its casualties if they do not have a comparable understanding. And few do. Until a politician with comparable grasp can challenge her for the centre of the British political stage, not just in terms of beliefs and actions but in terms of her manipulative skills in the power game as well, she will remain an extremely difficult leader to dislodge. In this she undoubtedly possesses the raw material of greatness. In this her determination and combativeness are admirable and formidable forces, not necessarily for good, nor for bad, but for the pursuit of power.

She has made her own beliefs and actions into the raw material of her management of power. She has combined and deliberately confused belief with personal self-interest, morality with Britain's greatness, policy with vision, social change with standards of behaviour, economic stringency with ambition, achievement with the common good. Within the confusion her own singleness of purpose, the semblance of consistency, the repeated declaration of her remarkable determination, have shone like beacons. She has become the focus of all political interest, whether the motivation is hope or despair. And this is the first essential of power. Some political systems encourage it. Some ideological, national and racial tendencies can not do without it. It is the marrow of the political bone-structure, from which the blood is recycled, strengthened and purified.

But this has not been the case in British democracy's evolution. Neither the system nor the temperament responds to a confusion of objectives, beliefs and standards through which drive the hammer-blows of a single person's interpretation. This could change. But, if it does, it will come about through the confrontation between the individual in question, and democracy. Margaret Thatcher, in the end, will be driven into conflict with the very system she most emphatically declares herself to be defending.

The source of the conflict will be the increasing likelihood of the democratic system attempting to disembarrass itself of her. It will not be automatic. She will do everything in her power to prevent it, and has already done a great deal to change perceptions about the nature and permanence of the safeguards of political freedom which, for generations, indifferent Britons have taken for granted. And she has achieved this change through the mechanism of identifying herself with the country and its values. By so doing she camouflages the implicit confrontation. It remains, however, always a possibility where power is deployed within such a parliamentary democracy.

If the first essential of Margaret Thatcher's power has been to make herself the focus of all political interest, the antidote must begin with the dismemberment of that focus, its nature, its beliefs, its attitudes, its achievements. She has manufactured her own beliefs, making them simple, direct, wholesome, appealing. Yet are they real? Take, for example, her Christianity. Paul Johnson called her 'the first proper Christian as a political leader that we've had for a very long time'! And he said, moreover, that she is 'an orthodox Christian . . . . She *does* believe in the ten commandments.' Margaret Thatcher is happy to allow such speculation about her relationship with her God, and to extend it by judicious extrapolations on these strangely intrusive comments by outsiders on the nature of her faith, and, by implication, on the faith of other politicians. She is 'on record' about her beliefs. What she says does not always make sense. Nor is it necessarily proof that she is a more *proper* Christian than, say, James Callaghan, Edward Heath, Denis Healey or David Owen.

Is it *relevant*? It is, because she has made it so. With Margaret Thatcher the question of politicians being Christians as well, and being *proper* Christians into the bargain, has been pushed onstage as an element of political character likely to appeal to ordinary people, a majority of whom still imagine that they are either Christian, or adhere to certain 'Christian' values.

The relevance is extended, by a process of spiritual osmosis, into the realm of morality. 'She says and fervently believes that the Conservative Party is there to uphold certain absolute moral standards such as it's wrong to steal; it's wrong to kill; ordinary ten commandment stuff. She says this with complete passionate intensity and conviction and I think it evokes a very definite response among ordinary people — not the sort you meet at West End dinner parties — but ordinary people throughout the country. They like to hear someone at the top of public life speak out for these ordinary things.'* Yet does Margaret Thatcher genuinely repudiate adultery? Does she totally eschew the telling of lies? Does she, as an active politician, adhere to the first, second, fourth and ninth commandments? The idea is preposterous. What is in no sense preposterous is the fact that saying these things 'with complete passionate intensity' certainly 'evokes a very definite response'. And a great part of her command in the political arena, resulting in her being so powerful a politician, derives from being able to identify those things which evoke definite and clear-cut responses in large numbers of men and women.

This does not mean that the beliefs are not there. It simply means that they have been turned into political ammunition. She has manufactured a new version of her own beliefs, making them simple, direct and strong. She has done the same with other things. She has manufactured the homespun quality of her childhood upbringing, the simplicity and austerity of the early years, the struggle and challenge of educational advancement, the logic of evolving political thought. And she has given it all shape and detail, defining the edges of the picture, its colour, its tone, its composition, its content. Nothing is left to the imagination. The picture of consistent certainty is a complete one. The fact that it is free of doubt is unnerving. The fact that it is so well remembered is puzzling. The fact that it is so freely given, and yet in so limited and circumscribed a form, is faintly frightening. The fact that it is so moral and so virtuous is the planting of an acorn of doubt. The self-assurance, the assured recollection and presentation of self, in one who keeps no diary, retains no personal papers, deals always and emphatically in the present, is itself a kind of consistency. And it emerges all the time from the personal life into the professional life of the politician.

We are meant to see all as one: sober, dutiful child into careful, hard-working girl; diligent and ambitious student at Oxford into dedicated and clear-sighted political novice; youthful member of parliament, defined by speeches and statements into a convincing representation of Toryism of the Right; consistency of performance giving depth and purpose to consistency of ideas. Thus she sprang, fully armed, and yet from nowhere, into

---

* Paul Johnson, quoted in Patricia Murray, op. cit.

the leadership contest, victory, winning the election, becoming Prime Minister, winning a second term.

Was the semblance reality, or was it rhetoric? Was the consistency real, or has it been manufactured? And what are the degrees? And how do we judge? Once one enters the realm of the manufacturing of image, of belief, of faith, of diligence, of determination, the disintegration of credibility begins to take place. If Margaret Thatcher is a proper Christian, how did she tolerate for so long Cecil Parkinson's adultery? If she spends so long, late at night, poring over the red boxes, how did she get Grenada so wrong? If she believes in Britain's greatness and leadership in the Western world, how has she developed so introverted, so short-sighted and so selfish a set of perceptions about Europe and its future unity? If she believes in peace, why did she not try much, much harder to avoid war, even if avoiding it would probably have cost her the 1983 general election?

At the beginning of 1984 she took upon herself an interpretative view of George Orwell. It was very simple and very direct: 'George Orwell was wrong, 1984 will be year of hope and a year of liberty.' It was a very silly interpretation, not just misunderstanding and misrepresenting a massively wronged writer, but indulging in the very techniques and political devices which he spent a lifetime attacking. She invoked Orwell as a climax to her new year message. That message twice invoked consistency: she wrote of the need for 'a government which follows a consistent and coherent policy, and sticks to it'; and she wrote: 'This government already has a reputation for consistency . . . . This is only the beginning of the revival of Britain.' And she said, 'No one can accuse this government of complacency.' She told people to 'set their hopes high and carry them through into reality'. And she claimed 'we have kept in tune with the people of this country'. She invited one judgment of Conservative policies: 'Do they make life better for individuals and their families?' And she concluded that 'we are just getting into our stride'. The Government had stayed 'right on course'; it had remained 'true to our ideals'; 'we believe what we say, we say what we believe, and have the courage to see it through'.

If one turns to any page in *Nineteen-Eighty Four* in which an announcement is being made over the telescreen, the language is not dissimilar, and the sentiment and tone of forward movement into a 'new' era is reminiscent of Margaret Thatcher's political revivalism: ' "Comrades!" cried an eager youthful voice. "Attention, comrades! We have glorious news for you. We have won the battle for production! Returns now completed of the output of all classes of consumption goods show that the standard of living has risen by no less than 20 percent in the past year. All over Oceania this morning there were irrepressible spontaneous demonstrations when workers marched out of factories and offices and paraded through the streets with banners voicing their gratitude to Big Brother for the new, happy life which his wise leadership has bestowed upon us. Here are some of the completed figures . . . ." '

The satire was a warning, not a prophecy; it dealt with the present and the immediate past, as Orwell saw them, and it identified dangers of attitude rather than of creed. 'Danger,' he wrote, 'lies also in the acceptance of a totalitarian outlook by intellectuals of all colours. The moral to be drawn is a simple one: don't let it happen. It depends on you.'*

To call Margaret Thatcher totalitarian, even in outlook, may seem shocking. Yet if we interpret the meaning of the word in its simple, defined sense as 'of or pertaining to a policy which permits no rival loyalties or parties' this is precisely the basis on which she has constructed her own political creed. Since the early days of her leadership of the Conservative Party, when she went to the United States and so openly attacked socialism, the very consistency which is at the heart of her political character has been sustained by the simple political equation of Conservative philosophies with Britain, the real Britain, and the identification of socialism with the ills of the past and the threats of the future. And this belief is what is so outrageous in her handling of the GCHQ controversy. The whole of Margaret Thatcher's new year message was cast in this politically narrow and slanted mould: a Conservative Party had won a Conservative victory and had shaped a Conservative future out of Conservative ideals. 'The British people once again rejected State socialism . . . And we must all work hard to ensure that Conservative policies for Europe bring a Conservative triumph in the European elections in June.'

Margaret Thatcher is not only the leader of the Conservative

---

* From Orwell's own press release, written at the time of the publication of 'Nineteen Eighty-Four'.

Party. She is, for the time being, leader of Britain as well. Yet it is clear from her words quoted above, as it is clear in so many of her speeches quoted in the preceding pages, that, if she were able, she would permit 'no rival loyalties or parties'. That is her outlook, the same outlook against which Orwell warned us. The safeguard is democracy. And democracy is people. It is only as strong as the ability of a small minority of those people — perhaps 'intellectuals of all colours' — to change their mind and outlook every so often, not out of fear, as happened in the general election of 1983, but out of belief in an older and wiser and more subtle set of political circumstances than have dominated the scene during the past five years. Margaret Thatcher believes that she and the party she leads have all the answers for 'the revival of Britain'. British democracy is based on the belief that there are always equal and opposite answers. Power derives from resolving the conflict one way or the other. The ultimate exercising of that power remains in the hands of the British people. 'It depends on you'.

APPENDIX

Margaret Thatcher's Cabinet Changes 1979-1984

THE CABINET: May 1979

Prime Minister, First Lord of the Treasury and Minister for the Civil Service	Margaret Thatcher
Secretary of State for the Home Department	William Whitelaw
Lord Chancellor	Lord Hailsham
Secretary of State for Foreign and Commonwealth Affairs and Minister of Overseas Development	Lord Carrington
Chancellor of the Exchequer	Geoffrey Howe
Secretary of State for Industry	Keith Joseph
Secretary of State for Defence	Francis Pym
Lord President of the Council and Leader of the House of Lords	Lord Soames
Secretary of State for Employment	James Prior
Lord Privy Seal	Ian Gilmour
Minister of Agriculture, Fisheries and Food	Peter Walker
Secretary of State for the Environment	Michael Heseltine
Secretary of State for Scotland	George Younger
Secretary of State for Wales	Nicholas Edwards
Secretary of State for Northern Ireland	Humphrey Atkins
Secretary for State for Social Services	Patrick Jenkin
Chancellor of the Duchy of Lancaster and Leader of the House of Commons	Norman St. John-Stevas
Secretary of State for Trade	John Nott
Secretary of State for Energy	David Howell
Secretary of State for Education and Science	Mark Carlisle
Chief Secretary to the Treasury	John Biffen
Paymaster General	Angus Maude

This was Margaret Thatcher's first Cabinet. In addition to its 22 members, Mr Norman Fowler, Minister of Transport, though not a member, attended Cabinet meetings. No further changes were made in 1979; none in 1980.

On January 5 and 9, 1981, she carried out a reshuffle. It was consequent on two departures from the Cabinet: Angus Maude resigned, Norman St. John-Stevas was dropped. John Nott replaced Francis Pym as Secretary for Defence. Francis Pym was given three jobs: Paymaster General, Chancellor of the Duchy of Lancaster and leader of the House of Commons. John Biffen, became Secretary of State for Trade, and was replaced at the Treasury by Leon Brittan who was the only newcomer to the Cabinet's deliberations, though Norman Fowler was made a full Cabinet member.

THE CABINET: January 1981

Prime Minister, First Lord of the Treasury and Minister for the Civil Service	Margaret Thatcher
Secretary of State for the Home Department	William Whitelaw
Lord Chancellor	Lord Hailsham
Secretary of State for Foreign and Commonwealth Affairs and Minister of Overseas Development	Lord Carrington
Chancellor of the Exchequer	Geoffrey Howe
Secretary of State for Industry	Keith Joseph
Secretary of State for Defence	John Nott
Lord President of the Council and Leader of the House of Lords	Lord Soames
Secretary of State for Employment	James Prior
Lord Privy Seal	Ian Gilmour
Minister of Agriculture, Fisheries and Food	Peter Walker
Secretary of State for the Environment	Michael Heseltine
Secretary of State for Scotland	George Younger
Secretary of State for Wales	Nicholas Edwards
Secretary of State for Northern Ireland	Humphrey Atkins
Secretary of State for Social Services	Patrick Jenkin
Chancellor of the Duchy of Lancaster, Leader of the House of Commons and Paymaster General	Francis Pym
Secretary of State for Trade	John Biffen
Secretary of State for Energy	David Howell
Secretary of State for Education and Science	Mark Carlisle
Chief Secretary to the Treasury	Leon Brittan
Secretary of State for Transport	Norman Fowler

On September 14 and 15, 1981, Margaret Thatcher dropped from the Cabinet Sir Ian Gilmour, Lord Soames and Mark Carlisle. She moved James Prior from Employment to become Secretary of State for Northern Ireland, replacing him by Norman Tebbit, a newcomer to the Cabinet, and she moved Keith Joseph to Education and Science, replacing him by Patrick Jenkin, whose job as Secretary of State for Social Services was given to Norman Fowler. Other newcomers were Nigel Lawson as Secretary of State for Energy, and Baroness Young who took over part of Francis Pym's responsibility as Chancellor of the Duchy of Lancaster. David Howell was moved to Transport, Humphrey Atkins became Lord Privy Seal. The job of Paymaster General was given to Cecil Parkinson, who was not a member, but attended Cabinet meetings.

THE CABINET: September 1981

Prime Minister, First Lord of the Treasury and Minister for the Civil Service	Margaret Thatcher
Secretary of State for the Home Department	William Whitelaw
Lord Chancellor	Lord Hailsham
Secretary of State for Foreign and Commonwealth Affairs and Minister of Overseas Development	Lord Carrington

Chancellor of the Exchequer	Geoffrey Howe
Secretary of State for Industry	Patrick Jenkin
Secretary of State for Defence	John Nott
Lord President of the Council and Leader of the House of Commons	Francis Pym
Secretary of State for Employment	Norman Tebbit
Lord Privy Seal	Humphrey Atkins
Minister of Agriculture, Fisheries and Food	Peter Walker
Secretary of State for the Environment	Michael Heseltine
Secretary of State for Scotland	George Younger
Secretary of State for Wales	Nicholas Edwards
Secretary of State for Northern Ireland	James Prior
Secretary of State for Social Services	Norman Fowler
Chancellor of the Duchy of Lancaster and Leader of the House of Lords	Baroness Young
Secretary of State for Trade	John Biffen
Secretary of State for Energy	Nigel Lawson
Secretary of State for Education and Science	Keith Joseph
Chief Secretary to the Treasury	Leon Brittan
Secretary of State for Transport	David Howell

On April 5, 1982, following the invasion of the Falklands, Lord Carrington and Humphrey Atkins resigned from the Cabinet. In the reshuffle Francis Pym was moved to the Foreign Office, and Baroness Young became Lord Privy Seal as well as remaining leader of House of Lords. John Biffen became Lord President of the Council and also leader of the House of Commons. New Cabinet appointments were Cecil Parkinson as Chancellor of the Duchy of Lancaster, remaining also Paymaster General and Lord Cockfield as Secretary of State for Trade.

THE CABINET: April 1982

Prime Minister, First Lord of the Treasury and Minister for the Civil Service.	Margaret Thatcher
Secretary of State for the Home Department	William Whitelaw
Lord Chancellor	Lord Hailsham
Secretary of State for Foreign and Commonwealth Affairs and Minister of Overseas Development	Francis Pym
Chancellor of the Exchequer	Geoffrey Howe
Secretary of State for Industry	Patrick Jenkin
Secretary of State for Defence	John Nott
Lord President of the Council and Leader of the House of Commons	John Biffen
Secretary of State for Employment	Norman Tebbit
Lord Privy Seal and Leader of the House of Lords	Baroness Young
Minister of Agriculture, Fisheries and Food	Peter Walker
Secretary of State for the Environment	Michael Heseltine
Secretary of State for Scotland	George Younger
Secretary of State for Wales	Nicholas Edwards
Secretary of State for Northern Ireland	James Prior
Secretary of State for Social Services	Norman Fowler
Chancellor of the Duchy of Lancaster and Paymaster for the Civil Service.	Cecil Parkinson
Secretary of State for Trade	Lord Cockfield

Secretary of State for Energy — Nigel Lawson
Secretary of State for Education and Science — Keith Joseph
Chief Secretary to the Treasury — Leon Brittan
Secretary of State for Transport — David Howell

On January 7, 1983, as a result of John Nott's decision to leave politics, Margaret Thatcher carried out a modest reshuffle of her Cabinet, bringing in only one new member, Tom King, to take the job which Michael Heseltine had held since 1979, as Secretary of State for the Environment. Heseltine replaced Nott as Secretary of State for Defence.

THE CABINET: January 1983

Prime Minister, First Lord of the Treasury and Minister for the Civil Service — Margaret Thatcher
Secretary of State for the Home Department — William Whitelaw
Lord Chancellor — Lord Hailsham
Secretary of State for Foreign and Commonwealth Affairs and Minister of Overseas Development — Francis Pym
Chancellor of the Exchequer — Geoffrey Howe
Secretary of State for Industry — Patrick Jenkin
Secretary of State for Defence — Michael Heseltine
Lord President of the Council and Leader of the House of Commons — John Biffen
Secretary of State for Employment — Norman Tebbit
Lord Privy Seal and Leader of the House of Lords — Baroness Young
Minister of Agriculture, Fisheries and Food — Peter Walker
Secretary of State for the Environment — Tom King
Secretary of State for Scotland — George Younger
Secretary of State for Wales — Nicholas Edwards
Secretary of State for Northern Ireland — James Prior
Secretary of State for Social Services — Norman Fowler
Chancellor of the Duchy of Lancaster and Paymaster General — Cecil Parkinson
Secretary of State for Trade — Lord Cockfield
Secretary of State for Energy — Nigel Lawson
Secretary of State for Education and Science — Keith Joseph
Chief Secretary to the Treasury — Leon Brittan
Secretary of State for Transport — David Howell

After the 1983 general election, Margaret Thatcher formed a Cabinet of 22.

THE CABINET: June 1983

Prime Minister, First Lord of the Treasury and Minister for the Civil Service — Margaret Thatcher
Secretary of State for the Home Department — Leon Brittan
Lord Chancellor — Lord Hailsham
Secretary of State for Foreign and Commonwealth Affairs and Minister of Overseas Development — Geoffrey Howe
Chancellor of the Exchequer — Nigel Lawson
Secretary of State for Trade and Industry — Cecil Parkinson

Appendix

Secretary of State for Defence	Michael Heseltine
Lord President of the Council and Leader of the House of Lords	William Whitelaw
Secretary of State for Employment	Norman Tebbit
Lord Privy Seal	John Biffen
Minister of Agriculture, Fisheries and Food	Michael Jopling
Secretary of State for the Environment	Patrick Jenkin
Secretary of State for Scotland	George Younger
Secretary of State for Wales	Nicholas Edwards
Secretary of State for Northern Ireland	James Prior
Secretary of State for Social Services	Norman Fowler
Chancellor of the Duchy of Lancaster and Leader of the House of Commons	Lord Cockfield
Secretary of State for Trade	Cecil Parkinson
Secretary of State for Energy	Peter Walker
Secretary of State for Education and Science	Keith Joseph
Chief Secretary to the Treasury	Peter Rees
Secretary of State for Transport	Tom King

In October, Cecil Parkinson resigned and was replaced by Norman Tebbit as Secretary of State for Trade. Tom King was moved to Employment and Nicholas Ridley became Secretary of State for Transport.

THE CABINET: October 1983

Prime Minister, First Lord of the Treasury and Minister for the Civil Service	Margaret Thatcher
Secretary of State for the Home Department	Leon Brittan
Lord Chancellor	Lord Hailsham
Secretary of State for Foreign and Commonwealth Affairs	Geoffrey Howe
Chancellor of the Exchequer	Nigel Lawson
Secretary of State for Trade and Industry	Norman Tebbit
Secretary of State for Defence	Michael Heseltine
Lord President of the Council and Leader of the House of Lords	William Whitelaw
Secretary of State for Employment	Tom King
Lord Privy Seal and Leader of the House of Commons	John Biffen
Minister of Agriculture, Fisheries and Food	Michael Jopling
Secretary of State for the Environment	Patrick Jenkin
Secretary of State for Scotland	George Younger
Secretary of State for Wales	Nicholas Edwards
Secretary of State for Northern Ireland	James Prior
Secretary of State for Social Services	Norman Fowler
Chancellor of the Duchy of Lancaster	Lord Cockfield
Secretary of State for Energy	Peter Walker
Secretary of State for Education and Science	Keith Joseph
Chief Secretary to the Treasury	Peter Rees
Secretary of State for Transport	Nicholas Ridley

INDEX

Afghanistan, 199, 223
Alliance, *see* SDP-Liberal Alliance
Amery, Julian, 130
Anglo-American relations, 81, 136, 138, 140, 195, 200, 239; Grenada, 251-7
Anglo-Irish relations, 82, 202-6
Arif, Ali, 57
Atkins, Humphrey, 177, 203-4
Attlee, Clement, 24, 89

Baldwin, Stanley, 24, 25
Banana, Canaan, 194
Barber, Anthony, 111, 121
BBC, 67; World Service, 252
  See also under individual programmes
Belaúnde, President Fernando, 78, 79
Belgrano, sinking of, 71-83, 95, 215-17, 255
Bermondsey by-election (1983), 237, 245
Biffen, John, 176
Bishop, Maurice, Prime Minister of Grenada, killed, 251-3
Brittan Leon, 176, 259n.; Home Secretary, 98, 261
Brooke, Henry, 119, 121
Brussels EEC meetings (1981, 1982), 199, 200
Budgets: 1961, 121-2; 1977, 150, 151; 1978, 152; 1979, 196, 222; 1980, 223, 224; 1982, 230; 1983, 235-7
Bull, George, 261n.

Callaghan, James, 125, 151, 155, 157, 161, 220-2, 235, 270; Chancellor of the Exchequer, 123; Foreign Secretary 139; Prime Minister, 135, 137-8, 149, 164, 220; and Rhodesia, 188; and EEC, 195; and MT, 137-8; underestimates her, 137, 220; marginal majority, 149, 151, 156; agreement with Liberals, 150-2; postpones general election, 152-4, 160; attempted wage restraint, 154, 220, 221; 'winter of discontent', 154-5, 160-1, 224; defeated in Commons, 25, 155; 1979 election, 25
Carey, John, and Conservative manifesto (1983), 50, 52
Caribbean Times, 57
Carlisle, Mark, dropped from Cabinet, 176, 179, 259, 261
Carr, Robert, 105, 111, 128
Carrington, Lord, 53; Foreign Secretary, 177, 185, 190, 199, 209, 212, 259; and Rhodesia, 191-3; and the Falklands, 214, 215, 217; resignation, 177, 212, 259, 261
Carter, President James E., and US hostages, 228
Castle, Barbara, 123, 127
Central Policy Review Staff, and unemployment forecasts, 60-2, 64
Chamberlain, Neville, 145
Chapple, Frank, 94
Chataway, Christopher, 85
Cheysson, Claude, 29
Chicago, Roosevelt University lecture by MT (1975), 140
Christianity, MT's, 16, 270-2
Churchill, Sir Winston, 14, 80, 89, 198
Cockfield, Lord, 177
Commission for Racial Equality, 158

Conquest, Robert and MT, 144, 145
Conservative Party: MT's membership of, 11-12, 17, 117, 130-3; Centre for Policy Studies, 107, 110, 131; 1970 election, 126; 1974 elections, 100, 102; and leadership election rules, 128-9, 132; advertising campaign (1978), 152, 159, 160; 1979 election manifesto, 51, 161, 165, 167 and n., 175, 179, 220
    1983 election: manifesto, 25, 45, 47-59, 243; advertising campaign, 26, 47, 48, 56-7, 85, 88; Campaign Guide, 26, 36-8
Conservative Party Conferences, 181-2; 1968, 123; 1975, 141-3, 243; 1979, 84, 170, 182-5, 243; 1980, 182, 185, 186; 1981, 178, 182, 185-6; 1982, 182; 1983 (Centenary Conference), 242-7, 261
Confederation of British Industry, 237
Cook, Stephen, 57
Cosgrave, Patrick, 106, 134 and n., 145
Crossbow, Bow Group magazine, 129

Daily Express, 43, 45, 76
Daily Mail, 43, 76, 94, 95n.
Daily Star, 45, 75
Daily Telegraph, 75, 120, 245, 246; and 1963 election, 18, 23-5, 28, 57-8, 88
Dalyell, Tam, 81, 211, 216
Darlington by-election (1983), 237
Day, Sir Robin, 48, 49, 82, 96; interviews MT, 39, 53, 68, 85-7, 93, 266
Deedes, William, 18, 120, 122
Defence, MT and, 39, 53, 81, 87, 139, 144, 146, 147, 149, 185, 195, 197, 205
Defence Review (1981), 214
Détente, MT and, 138, 139, 144, 146
Devolution, 149, 154-7
Diary of an Election (Carol Thatcher), 26-7, 90
Douglas-Home, Sir Alec, 14, 123, 128, 134; resigns from leadership, 123
Dublin, EEC summit (1979), 197-8, 200
Du Cann, Edward, 130
Duffy, Terry, 95

East-West relations, MT and, 138, 144, 146, 191, 195, 200, 253
Economist, The, 180, 249 and n.; and 1983 election, 46, 67-9

Eden, Anthony, 14
EEC, 129, 139, 172, 195-201, 220, 265-6; Britain and EEC budget, 29, 98, 185, 195-201, 238, 265; Dublin summit, 197-8, 200
Eliot, T.S., 11
Endurance, HMS, proposed withdrawal from South Atlantic, 214, 215
English, Sir David, 43
European Economic Community, *see* EEC
Everett, Kenny, 53, 54, 92

Falklands Islands and Falklands War, 16, 34, 36, 37, 40, 53, 54, 65, 66, 135, 169, 170, 172, 176, 177, 200, 209-19, 234, 235, 253-5, 266; Argentine invasion, 210, 212, 217; sending of task force, 211, 215, 216; *Belgrano* sinking, 71-83, 215-17, 255; Franks Committee, 81, 212-15, 217, 218, 232, 233; MT's visit (Jan. 1983), 38, 232-3
    See also South Georgia
Family Allowance Bill (1961), 123
Financial Times, 94; Share Index, 21
Finchley, MT's constituency, 14, 26, 70, 118, 184
First Circle, The (Solzhenitsyn), 145
Foot, Michael, 30, 53, 64, 92, 168, 169, 236, 237, 239; Labour Party leader (1980), 173; and Rhodesia, 188; 1983 election, 22, 27, 28, 33, 42, 43, 46, 76, 80 and n., 82, 84; replacement inevitable, 98
Fowler, Norman, 176, 177, 246
Franks, Lord and Franks Committee on the Falklands, 81, 212-15, 217, 218, 232, 233; on British foresight and possible prevention, 212-13; British Government's options, 213-14; and threat of invasion, 214
Fraser, Hugh, and 1975 leadership election, 129, 130
Fraser, Malcolm, 190

Gairy, Sir Eric, 253
Galbraith, J.K., 165n.
Gale, George, 211
Galtieri, President, 218
General elections: 1964, 14; 1966, 123, 131; 1970, 21, 107, 126; February 1974, 15, 24, 100, 101, 103, 107-8,

Index

136, 146; October 1974, 15, 100, 101, 108, 131, 146
1979, 17, 25, 148, 182; Conservative manifesto, 51, 161, 165, 167 and n., 175, 179, 220; election figures, 183
1983, 10, 17, 21-98, 169, 243, 258; dissolution of Parliament, 21, 31; opinion polls, 21, 35-6, 60, 88; Alliance manifesto, 31-3, 45; Labour Party manifesto, 31, 33-4, 45, 69; Conservative advertising campaign, 26, 47, 48, 56-7, 85, 87-8; Conservative manifesto, 25, 45, 47-59, 243; MT's press conferences, 25, 61-7, 91-6; Fleet Street support for Conservatives, 43
Gibraltar, 266
Gilmour, Sir Ian, 166, 173, 259; dropped from Cabinet, 176, 179, 259, 261
Giscard d'Estaing, Valéry, 200
Goodhart, Philip, 118
Gould, Mrs Diana and the *Belgrano* sinking, 71-6, 79, 80, 82, 83
Gow, Ian, 69
Grenada, 172, 193, 251-9; Communism in, 239, 252; killing of Maurice Bishop, 251-3; US invasion, 251; Britain's marginal role, 251; MT and, 251-7
Guardian, The, 45, 246; and 1983 election, 22-3, 57, 68, 69, 88
Gummer, John, Selwyn, Conservative Party Chairman, 247
Gymnich, foreign ministers' conference (May 1983), 29

Haig, Alexander, 78, 79, 216
Hamilton, James, 239
Hanover, speech by MT (1976), 146
Harris, Kenneth, interviews MT (May 1983), 38-9, 174
Hattersley, Roy, 33, 150
Haughey, Charles, 202-6, 254; and MT, 205-6, 230 and n.
Healey, Denis, 30, 42, 132, 152, 153, 235, 239, 270; and IMF loan (1976), 150; 1977 Budget, 151; successful handling of economy, 156, 160, 220, 223, 229; and 1983 election, 33, 75-7, 83, 91; and leaked report on unemployment forecasts, 60-2, 64
Heath, Edward, 67, 100, 106, 111, 124-5, 134, 136, 143, 173, 178, 234, 270;

Prime Minister (1970), 14, 21-2; his Government (1970-4), 100-3, 107, 125-7, 131, 144; U-turns, 14-15, 101, 103, 104; underestimates MT, 102, 105, 126, 128; loses two general elections (1974), 15, 100, 101, 104, 146; question of his continued leadership, 108, 109, 127, 128; and new leadership election rules, 128-9; defeated by MT, 112, 130; Blackpool Conference (1975), 141-2; does not join MT's Cabinet, 174-5; attacks her, 186
Helsinki agreement, 147
Henderson, Sir Nicholas, 79
Heseltine, Michael, 48; Defence Secretary, 232, 261
Hong Kong, 266
Hoskyns, John, 64, 262-4
Howard, Anthony, 42
Howe, Sir Geoffrey, 48, 49, 60, 64-6, 150-2, 156, 250 n.; Chancellor of the Exchequer, 95-6, 199, 229, 230, 258, 260; Budgets, 196, 222-4, 236, 237; Foreign Secretary, 98, 258-60; and Grenada, 251-5, 257, 258
Howell, David, 98, 259

Ilford, North, by-election (1978), 158
IMF (International Monetary Fund), 139, 140; loan to Britain (1976), 150
Inflation, MT and, 124, 222, 226, 264
Iran, 199, 225
Ireland, Republic of, 82, 202-6

Jenkin, Patrick, Industry Secretary, 65, 66, 177
Jenkins, Roy, 27, 32, 43, 46, 98, 169
Jenkins, Simon, 77, 180
Johnson, Frank, 49, 58, 68, 69, 97
Johnson, Paul, 77, 78, 255, 270-1; on MT's Christianity, 16, 270
Jones, George, 84
Joseph, Sir Keith, 12, 14, 101, 125, 129, 142; and the Conservative Party leadership, 106-9; and MT, 106, 109-10, 113, 119-20, 262; Conservative Centre for Policy Studies, 107, 110; Birmingham speech (Oct. 1974), 108-9, 111, 113, 127; decides not to stand for leadership, 109-10, 128; Secretary for Education and Science, 177
Junor, Sir John, 43

Kaunda, Kenneth, 190, 193
Keays, Sara, 244, 246-7, 249
Kellner, Peter, 48-9
Kennedy, Ludovic, 85
King Tom, 232, 259
Kinnock, Neil, 35, 75-7, 83, 98
Kohl, Dr. Helmut, 30

Labour Party, 220-1, 237; and Marxism, 141; and race relations and immigration, 157-9; and trade unions, 166-7; and the Falklands, 210; and 1983 election, 33-4, 75-7, 97-8; manifesto, 31, 33-4, 45, 69; press conferences, 66
Laird, Gavin, 94
Lamb, Sir Larry, 43
Lancaster House Conference (1979), 193
Langdon, Julia, 69
Lawley, Sue, 72, 74
Lawson, Nigel, 177, 259n.; Chancellor of the Exchequer, 96, 252
Let Our Children Grow Tall (collection of MT's speeches), 139
Liberal Party, 154, 155; agreement with Callaghan Government, 150-1
See also SDP-Liberal Alliance
Liverpool Daily Post, 106
Lusaka, Commonwealth Conference (1979), 189-92
Luxembourg: MT delivers Winston Churchill Memorial Lecture, 197; EEC summit (1981), 200
Lynch, Jack, 197, 203-5; and MT, 202-3, 205

MacDonald, Ramsay, 25n.
Macleod, Iain, 123, 124, 128
Macmillan, Harold, 14, 117, 119, 134, 198
Macmillan, Maurice, 130
Madam Prime Minister (Mayer), 134n.
Manley, Michael, 190
Margaret Thatcher, Prime Minister (Cosgrave), 134n.
Margaret Thatcher, A Profile (Murray), 9n.
Marxism and Marxists, 141, 144, 147, 194
Maude, Angus, 176
Mayer, Allan J., 97, 134 and n., 142n., 153 and n.
Maze H-Block hunger strike, 205, 206, 265

Millar, Ronald, 160
Mrs Thatcher's First Years (Stephenson), 174
Moncrieff, Chris, 232
Monetarism, 103, 164-5
Money stock (1979-82), 223
Morning Call, BBC programme, 96
Morning Star, 23
Mugabe, Robert, 189, 193, 194, 266; Marxism, 194
Murray, Patricia, 9n., 97, 175n., 250n.n., 271n.
Muzorewa, Bishop Abel, 189, 191-3, 266

National Front, 158
National Health Service, 243, 246
National Union of Mineworkers, 234
Nationwide, BBC programme, 45, 71, 72, 75, 80, 82, 216
NATO, 32, 37, 87, 139, 185, 195, 197, 200, 205, 253, 254, 258
Neave, Airey: support for MT, 134, 202; murdered, 25, 202
New Statesman, 48, 78, 79
Newsnight programme, 79
Nigeria, nationalises British Petroleum, 190
Nineteen Eighty-Four (Orwell), 272-3
Nkomo, Joshua, 189, 193, 266
North Sea oil, 10, 221, 264
Northern Ireland, 177; MT and, 48, 53, 149, 185, 202-6, 265; Unionist MPs, 154, 155; Constitutional Conference (1980), 203-4; Provisional IRA, 205-6; Maze H-Block hunger strike, 205, 206, 265
Nott, John, Defence Secretary, 176, 215, 232
Nyerere, Julius, 190, 193

Oakley, Robin, 76
O'Brien, Ossie, 236-7, 239
Observer, The, 38, 174, 236; and 1983 election, 42-3
Opinion polls, significance of, 22
Orwell, George, 272-3
Owen, David, 169, 270; SDP leader, 98, 243

Paisley, Ian, 205
Panorama programme (BBC), 53, 85, 216

Parkinson, Cecil, 48, 50, 98, 177, 244; Conservative Party Chairman, 32, 57, 65, 94, 96, 244; the Parkinson affair, 172, 242, 244-9, 251, 272; resignation, 247, 259
Patten, Christopher, 166
Pen and the Sword, The (Foot), 76
Perth, MT's speech at (May 1983), 36
Peyton, John, 130
Poland, 199, 223
Powell, Enoch, 117, 249, 265; and the EEC, 266
Pre-Retirement Choice magazine, 129
Prior, James, 111, 261; and 1975 leadership election, 129, 130; moved from Employment to Northern Ireland, 177
Private Eye, 80n., 247
Public Expenditure, MT and, 165, 224, 226-7, 263; White Paper (1980), 224
Pym, Francis, 48, 49, 66-7, 111; and devolution, 157; moved from Defence, 176; Foreign Secretary, 29, 78, 79, 177, 212; deprecates 'landslide' majority, 56, 63, 66; dropped from Cabinet, 98, 259, 261

Queen's Speech: 1978, 154; May 1979, 170, 183; June 1983, 98

Race Relations Act (1976), 157-8
Race relations and immigration, MT and, 136, 149, 157-60, 191
Raison, Timothy, 128, 259
Ramphal, Sonny, 190
Raphael, Adam, 236
Reagan, President Ronald, 28, 38, 54, 228; and MT, 228; and Grenada, 251
Redmayne, Martin, 120
Reece, Gordon, 72, 152, 160
Rees, Merlyn, 158
Rhodesia, 53, 172, 185, 188-94, 271; 'Six Principles', 188
See also Zimbabwe
Ridley, Nicholas, and the Falklands, 214, 218
Rippon, Geoffrey, 128, 179
Rodgers, William, 169

Saatchi and Saatchi, 48, 85, 88, 160
Scargill, Arthur, fails to obtain pit strike (1983), 234-5
Schmidt, Helmut, 197 and n., 198, 200
Scoon, Sir Paul, 251

Scotland and devolution, 157
Scott, Nicholas, 128
Scottish Nationalist Party (SNP), 154, 155, 157
SDP, 44, 98, 243
SDP-Liberal Alliance, 174, 236, 237; and the Falklands, 210; and 1983 election, 28, 31-3, 45, 85, 88, 97-8; manifesto, 31-3, 35
Selsdon Park Hotel Conservative conference (1969) and 'Selsdon Man', 107, 108, 125, 126, 146
Sherrett, Steven, 71
Shore, Peter, 33
Smith, Geoffrey, 58, 245
Smith, Ian, 189, 266
Soames, Lord, 193; dropped from Cabinet, 176, 177, 179, 259
Solzhenitsyn, Alexander, 11, 145
South Georgia: Argentine invasion and British recapture, 210, 211, 216
Soviet Union: MT and, 136, 144-7, 185, 198; Anglo-Soviet trade, 138, 144; the 'Iron Lady', 144
Spectator, The, 77, 106, 110, 255 and n.
Stanbrook, Ivor, 246
Steel, David, 27, 32, 46, 88, 98, 168, 169; agreement with Callaghan, 150, 152
Stephenson, Hugh, 174-5, 190n., 191n.
Stevas, Norman St. John, 173; dropped from Cabinet, 176, 179, 261
Strasbourg, European Council meeting (1979), 197
Stuttgart European Council meeting: planned for June 1983, 28; held after election, 30, 98
Sunday Express, 43
Sunday Telegraph, 84, 165n.
Sunday Times, 95; and Hitler diaries, 42-3; and 1983 election, 43-4, 50, 85, 88
Swift, Jonathan, 76, 80

Tatchell, Peter, 237
Tebbit, Norman, 48, 177, 246, 259; and 1983 election, 48, 50, 60, 93-6; and trade union reform, 93-6
Thames Television, 45
Thatcher (Wapshott and Brock), 68n., 116n.
Thatcher, Carol, 26-7, 70, 73, 90, 96, 97, 118
Thatcher, Denis, 69, 233

Thatcher, Margaret: upbringing in Grantham, 115-17; education, 117; and the Bar, 117, 118; marriage and birth of children, 117-18; candidatures at Dartford, 117, 118; enters Parliament for Finchley (1959), 14, 118; maiden speech, 119; private member's Bill, 119-20; speech on 1961 Budget, 121-2; junior Minister, 14, 119, 122-3; Shadow Treasury team, 123-5; Shadow Cabinet, 125, 128; Secretary of State for Education and Science, 14, 101, 105, 125, 126; and the Heath Cabinet, 14-15, 101-5, 126-7

1974 elections, 101, 105; Shadow Cabinet posts, 105; and Sir Keith Joseph, 106, 109-10, 119-20, 128; candidate for the leadership, 128; defeats Heath in first ballot, 112, 130; wins second ballot, 130; Conservative Party Leader, 11-12, 17, 112, 130-3

Leader of the Opposition, 134-61; and Wilson and Callaghan, 137-8, 144; visit to USA, 138-41, 144, 147; Party Conference (1975), 141-4, 243; and the Soviet Union, 144-7; the 'Iron Lady', 144; press lobby and media management, 148; and Conservative advertising campaign (1978), 152, 159, 160,; carries 'no confidence' motion, 155; General Election (1979), 17, 75, 148, 182, 183; Conservative manifesto, 51, 161, 165, 167, 175, 179, 220

Prime Minister, 1979-83: formation of Government, 174-6; wish to include Heath, 174-5; Party conference (1979), 84, 170, 182-5, 243; Cabinet management, 171, 173-80; Cabinet changes, 176-9, 232; 1980 conference, 182, 185, 186; disloyalty in Cabinet, 176, 179, 180, 226, 227; timing of reshuffle (1981), 178, 198; 1981 conference, 178, 182, 185-6; management of Conservative Party, 171, 181-7 and Rhodesia, 53, 172, 188-94; EEC, 195-201, 265-6; Dublin summit, 197-200; Ireland, 202-6, 265; and Haughey, 205-6, 230n.; and the economy, 220-9; and timing of dissolution, 233, 236, 238-40; and Scargill, 235; 1983 Budget, 235-7; the Falklands, 34, 36, 40, 54, 65, 66, 135, 169, 172, 176-8, 200, 209-19, 234, 235, 253-5, 266; Commons debate (April 3, 1982), 210-12, 216; sending of task force, 211, 215, 216; Carrington's resignation, 212; sinking of *Belgrano*, 71-83, 215-17, 255; Franks Committee, 81, 212-15, 217, 218, 232, 233; British options, 213-14, 217-18; proposed withdrawal of *Endurance*, 214, 215; threat of Argentine invasion, 214, 217, 218; visit to Falklands (Jan. 1983), 38, 232-3

General Election (1983), 10, 17, 22-98, 243; leaves start of campaign to Opposition parties, 25-6, 58; attends Williamsburg summit, 28; and Labour manifesto, 31; Perth speech, 36; Sir Robin Day interview, 39, 53, 68, 85-7, 93, 266; Conservative manifesto, 45, 47-55, 86; Healey's accusations, 60-2, 64; press conferences, 61-7, 91-6; 'headmistress' approach, 66-7; campaign tours, 67-9, 96-7; the *Belgrano* sinking, 71-83; election results, 97-8; Government changes, 98

since 1983 election: Party conference, 242-7, 261; Parkinson affair, 172, 242, 244-9, 251, 272; Grenada, 172, 193, 239, 251-7, 259; Cabinet changes, 258-62; New Year message for 1984, 268 and n.; and George Orwell, 272-3

Thatcher, Mark, 118
Thatcher's Torpedo (Dalyell), 211
Thomas, George, Speaker, 30-1
Thorneycroft, Lord, 179
Time Out, 61, 63
Times, The, 47, 85n., 245, 246, 249n., 262n., 268n.; and 1983 election, 33, 49, 57, 58, 68, 97
Today (BBC programme), 56
Tokyo economic summit (1979), 197
Trade unions and trade union reform, 93-6, 155, 156, 165-8, 183, 243
Trident missile, 48
TUC, 95; and Callaghan Government, 151, 152, 154, 155

Index

TV Eye, 88

Unemployment, MT and, 61-3, 86-7, 228-9

Van der Post, Laurens, 118n.
Venice, EEC summit (1980), 199
Versailles economic summit (1982), 230
Victorian values, 10, 11, 23, 248

Walden, Brian, 16
Wales and devolution, 157
Walker, Peter, 111, 127-8, 199, 261
Walls, General G.P., 189
Wapshott, Nicholas, and George Brock, 68n., 97, 116 and n., 118, 122, 127, 134 and n.
Warden, John, 76
Warne, Peter, 69
Wedgwood Benn, Anthony, 216
Weighell, Sid, 94
White, Michael, 68
Whitelaw, William, 48, 49, 98, 111, 131, 158-9, 261; and 1975 leadership election, 129, 130
Williams, Shirley, 32, 169
Williamsburg economic summit (May 1983), 28-9, 53, 65, 66, 87
Wilson, Harold, 24, 124-5, 135, 136, 237; 1966 election, 124, 131; 1970 election, 21-2, 126; 1974 elections, 102, 108, 127, 131; and EEC, 129, 195-6; and MT, 137-8; underestimates her, 137; resignation (1976), 137, 138, 149, 159-60
Winchester, Simon, 85
Wintour, Charles, 43
Wolverhampton, racial tension (1978), 158
World at One, radio programme, 87

Young, Lady, 177

Zimbabwe, 172, 193
  See also Rhodesia